KING ARTHUR BAKING COMPANY'S
THE BOOK OF PIZZA

THE BOOK OF PIZZA

RECIPES FOR EVERY PIZZA MAKER

MARTIN PHILIP AND DAVID TAMARKIN

WITH JESSICA BATTILANA, YEKATERINA BOYTSOVA, AND RYAN SALERNO

SIMON ELEMENT
NEW YORK AMSTERDAM/ANTWERP LONDON
TORONTO SYDNEY/MELBOURNE NEW DELHI

Contents

- 9 Introduction
- 13 Tools

- 19 The Elements of Great Pizza
- 21 *The Dough*
- 33 *The Sauce*
- 39 *The Cheese*
- 43 *The Toppings*
- 47 *The Bake*
- 52 *The Finishing Touch*

- 61 Pizza Tonda/Roman-Style Dough
- 62 Squash, Fontina, and Bacon
- 67 Zucchini, Ricotta Salata, and Pistachio Salsa Verde
- 68 Pizza Rossa
- 71 Soppressata and Salad

- 75 Chicago Tavern-Style Dough
- 76 Spinach and Artichoke
- 79 Cheeseburger
- 80 Sausage and Giardiniera
- 85 Calabrian Chile and Cheese

- 89 New Haven–Style Dough
- 90 Cheese
- 93 Brussels Sprouts and Smoked Mozzarella
- 94 Amatriciana
- 99 Puttanesca
- 100 Clam

NEW YORK STYLE

- **105** New York–Style Dough
- **106** Cheese
- **109** Pepperoni and Jalapeño
- **112** Caprese
- **117** Cheesy Greens Calzone

PIZZA ALLA PALA

- **121** Pizza Bianca Dough
- **122** Prosciutto and Arugula
- **125** Ricotta and Pistachio Salsa Verde
- **126** Tonnato and Tomato
- **129** Potato

WEEKNIGHT

- **132** Weeknight White Dough
- **133** Weeknight Wheat Dough
- **135** Broccoli and Cheese
- **136** Sausage and Peppers
- **139** Quattro Formaggi
- **140** Magic Mushroom

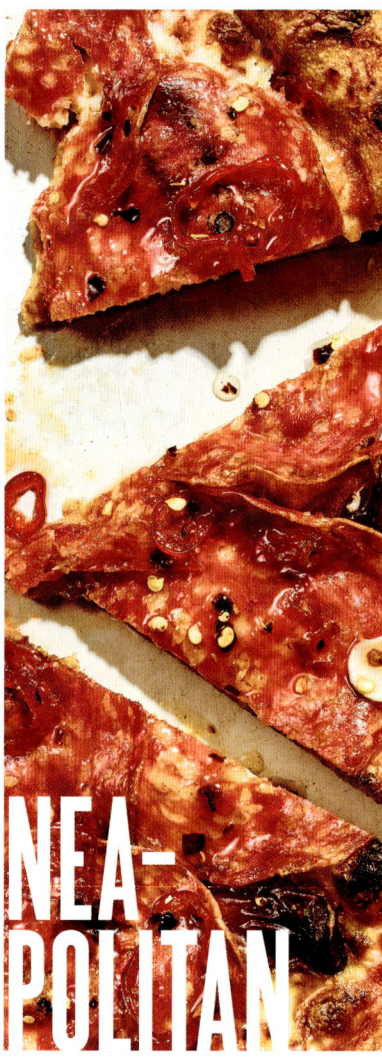

WEEK-NIGHT (CONT'D)

- 145 Popeye
- 147 BBQ Chicken
- 151 Soppressata and Date
- 153 Smoked Salmon
- 157 Grilled Pizza

NEAPOLITAN

- 161 Neapolitan Dough
- 162 Margherita
- 167 Prosciutto and Hot Honey
- 168 Pesto, Asparagus, and Fried Egg
- 171 Mortazza

NEW AMERICAN

- 177 New American Dough
- 178 Corn, Cheese, and Chiles
- 183 Rossa with Kale Salad
- 187 French Onion
- 190 Triple Fennel

PIZZA NIGHT SALADS 231

- 233 Butter Lettuce Salad with Herby Buttermilk-Avocado Dressing
- 234 Farm Stand Salad
- 237 Deep Green Salad with Cheesy No-Cheese Dressing
- 238 Chicory Caesar with Parmesan Frico

PIZZA NIGHT DESSERTS 241

- 243 Italian Rainbow Cookies
- 247 Glazed Ricotta Cookies
- 248 Pizzicati
- 253 Piped Shortbread Cookies
- 254 Biscotti

GRANDMA

- 195 Grandma Dough
- 196 Buffalo Chicken
- 199 Tricolore
- 200 Roasted Cherry Tomato and Garlic Confit
- 203 Eggplant Parm

WEEKNIGHT DETROIT

- 207 Weeknight Detroit Dough
- 208 Garlicky Broccoli Rabe and Black Olive
- 211 Loaded Baked Potato
- 212 Roasted Pineapple, Ham, and Jalapeño
- 215 Meatball Sub

SOURDOUGH DETROIT

- 219 Sourdough Detroit Dough
- 220 Motor City Classic
- 225 Roasted Cauliflower and Gruyère
- 226 Sausage and Vodka Sauce
- 229 Cacio e Pepe

- 257 Pignoli
- 258 Chocolate-Hazelnut Skillet Cookie
- 261 Tiramisu
- 264 Lemon Ricotta Cake
- 267 Chocolate-Glazed Olive Oil Cake
- 268 Mocha Mousse with Espresso Whip
- 271 Spumoni Semifreddo

- 272 Aperol Spritz Granita
- 275 Raspberry-Pistachio Eton Mess
- 276 Salty Maple Pears with Brown Butter Streusel
- 279 Pizza Fritta

- 281 Acknowledgments
- 282 Index

INTRODUCTION

Making a cookbook is a process full of long days, but one day in particular was longer than most. We were in the middle of the photo shoot. We'd started early, when the windows of our photo studio, an old mill building perched above New Hampshire's Mascoma River, were still iced over, and stayed late. As the day progressed we'd covered every surface with pizza: Grandma pies, Detroit pies, thin and crispy slices of Roman tonda style. Each one had been baked, styled, fussed over, photographed, and then, always, eaten. And yet somehow at the end of the day we had a stack of slices left, as well as a few balls of dough.

We looked expectantly at each other—surely *somebody* would polish it off. But one by one the group of us put our hands up in surrender. We couldn't eat any more pizza. We'd hit the wall.

So we wrapped the slices and divided them among us. We'd give them to friends and family, we said. One of us had to drive home that night—a two-hour drive—and she took the three balls of dough with her. For the freezer, she said. For later.

The next morning we admitted to each other the truth: We'd gone home, opened our packets, and inhaled the contents. And we had a text from our coworker who'd taken the dough. It was a photo: three pizzas, fresh out of the oven. She'd baked them the minute she'd gotten home.

"Can't stop, won't stop," her text read.

Pizza has a gravitational pull. It doesn't really matter how much you eat—it always pulls you back for more. Most Americans eat over twenty pounds of pizza a year, and on January 1 they excitedly start all over again.

Luckily, we live in a world where pizza is never in short supply. In this moment—call it Peak Pizza—there are more great options for pickup or delivery, more magnificent pizza joints (high-end, low-end, and in-between), and even more good options in the freezer aisle than ever before. And at home it's even better: New technology and techniques mean you can bake unbelievable pizza as many nights as you want. Every night, if you really want to. Because baking pizza at home is the easiest and most exciting it's ever been. Which is why you probably know somebody who's neck-deep in pizza every weekend, perfecting their doughs and fussing with their high-heat tabletop pizza oven. We know of only one other food that is as thrilling and habit-forming to bake at home, and that's bread.

But then, pizza *is* bread.

Before agriculture, before the pyramids, before Detroit style, before Chuck E. Cheese—before all of this, there was pizza. They were flatbreads made with foraged pulses, grains, and seeds, baked on hot coals or stones. You can see traces of pizza in the names these flatbreads went by: *pita, pide, pinsa*.

For centuries these flatbreads were served more or less unadorned. The tomato sauce, the cheese, the pineapple and pepperoni all came later. Pizza was first and foremost bread, and as far as we're concerned, it still is.

The King Arthur approach to pizza is through the crust. We start with its texture. Does it eat light and fluffy like the best focaccia? Or crisp and oily and salty like a cracker? Does it have the character of a crusty loaf of sourdough, or is it more like a classic baguette? The questions we ask before making pizza are the same ones we ask when we make bread—they are questions of fermentation, shape, form, and flavor. We think about pizza like this, from the dough up, because while toppings and cheese are important, there is no saving a pizza with a bad crust.

And so this book is organized by crust style. We start with thin-crust recipes for crackery tavern-style and tonda doughs; move into classics like Neapolitan, New York, and New Haven styles; and end on thick, focaccia-like square pies, including two styles of Detroit—one for weeknight bakers, the other for sourdough heads. Not that you have to choose one over the other. In fact, you shouldn't. The hope is that the more you dive into this book, the more styles you'll fall in love with. Eventually your repertoire will include pizzas for every mood and situation: A couple of Detroits for a pizza party. A pizza alla pala to share with somebody for lunch. A Neapolitan margherita you bake hot and fast in your tabletop oven. A single tavern pie you make just for yourself. There are salads and desserts in these pages to round out and enhance your pizza meals, but let's be real: We're focused mostly on the pies here. What can we say? We couldn't stop making—or eating—it if we tried.

TOOLS

When you're dealing with something that has as few ingredients as pizza, the details matter. So do the tools. You don't need a lot of gear to make great pizza, but you do need some, and you should aim for the best you can afford. The right tools will get you the right pie.

BAKING STEEL/STONE

If pizza is all about the crust—and it's our position that the quality of the crust is what differentiates a bad pizza from a good one—then getting the crust to the right color and crispness is a pizza baker's highest priority. That's where steels and stones come in.

Steels and stones are slabs of material that have exceptional thermal mass, which is another way of saying they get very hot—and stay that way. These slabs also conduct and transfer heat well, which is the point of using them: When the heat from the steel or stone transfers to the bottom of your pizza, it gives the bottom (or "undercarriage," as the pros say) of the pie great color, gets it maximally crispy, helps the dough rise high, and overall gets it as close to a pizza shop pie as possible. In short, if you want to make great pizza, a steel or stone is key. (Sheet pans are the alternative to pizza steels and stones, but, really, they're a poor substitute—they're too thin to produce a good crust.)

Both stones and steels work well, but if you can choose, go for a steel—they simply get hot faster and transfer heat better. Stones (which are often not actually made of stone, but rather a ceramic called cordierite) don't transfer the heat as well. They also deteriorate and crack, whereas steels (which are literally slabs of steel with sanded edges) are pretty much indestructible. Whichever you choose, get one that is rectangular (not circular) and as big as can fit in your oven—rectangular slabs are more versatile than round ones, and the bigger your stone, the easier it is to slide your pizza onto it.

Some bakers keep their steels or stones in the oven all the time. They're good not just for free-form pizzas but also for pan pizzas (put the pan directly on the stone) and loaves of bread. But they need to be thoroughly preheated, or else they're pretty much useless. We recommend preheating your oven, steel or stone in place, for at least an hour before baking a pizza; if you have an infrared thermometer, look for the steel or stone to be at least 500°F. (For more on baking, see page 47.)

Whenever possible, give the steel or stone at least five minutes to recover in between pizzas. If you don't, you'll notice diminishing returns: Each pizza will be paler and less crisp than the last. Some bakers put two steels or stones in their ovens for specifically this reason; they alternate which steel or stone they use, which gives the empty steel or stone time to thoroughly reheat.

PEEL

You need a way to transfer your pizzas in and out of the oven; for this, peels are the best option. They come in two materials: wood and metal. Pizzas are less likely to stick to a wooden peel, but metal peels are typically thinner, so it's easier to slip them under a pizza to turn it or remove it from the oven. Because of this, very serious pizza people may want to have one of each. The rest of us? We'll be just fine with a wooden peel. (In lieu of a peel, a large cookie sheet or the flat underside of a rimmed baking sheet, coupled with a good pair of tongs, can do the trick.)

A wooden peel should at a minimum accommodate a 12-inch pizza, but it's better to have a little extra room. A 14- or even 16-inch peel can be helpful for loading larger pizzas (or, if you're using it for bread, two loaves at a time). When you're shaping your pizzas, be sure not to make them any larger than your peel and steel or stone can accommodate. This happens more often than you think!

For tabletop pizza ovens, an additional tool called a turning peel, which is a smaller metal peel specifically designed for rotating pies, is especially useful. When you bake at very high temperatures (700°F and up) you need to turn the pizza almost constantly as it bakes to ensure even cooking; a turning peel makes that easy.

ROUND PIZZA PAN

While not strictly necessary to make great pizza at home, these thin metal pans, perfectly shaped for round pies, make it easy to load and remove pies from the oven—they simply slide on and off your baking steel or stone. Some have a corrugated or perforated surface that allows hot air to flow under the pie, getting the bottom crust crispy. Sizes vary, but a bigger one (16 inches or so) gives you the most flexibility and is especially useful if you want to make pizzas that are bigger than your steel or stone would otherwise be able to support.

TONGS

A pair of long tongs is useful for turning pies as they bake and grabbing the finished pizzas to pull them out of the oven. Get an all-metal pair, not one with plastic tips, which could melt if they touch a hot pizza stone.

DIGITAL SCALE

As with all baking, a scale makes pizza making an easier, more accurate, and more tidy operation. After all, pizza dough is bread dough, and as such the hydration of the dough is key—add too much (or too little) water or flour and your dough could be much less lovely to work with (in other words, it will be a sticky mess, or a brick that won't stretch). Even worse, the crumb structure could suffer (no impressive airy interior!).

A basic digital scale with roughly a 5- to 10-pound capacity, an easy-to-read display, and a tare button is all you need. Nobody wants a bulky scale, but you don't want one that's too small, either. Think about the vessels you'll be putting on the scale (dough buckets, metal bowls, etc.) and make sure you'll be able to read the display under them.

As your pizza making gets more serious, you may want to add a micro scale to your toolbox as well. These scales measure small amounts (from 0.1 gram up to 25 grams) that other scales aren't sensitive enough to handle. While buying a micro scale may seem uptight, ingredients that are added in small quantities are often high-impact. In doughs like our Neapolitan (page 161) and New York style (page 105), very small amounts of yeast, combined with long fermentation, ensure that we have just enough dough activity, but not too much. Your doughs will appreciate your attention to detail and accuracy. (But in the meantime, measuring spoons will suffice.)

TABLETOP PIZZA OVEN

They're relatively new in the world of pizza making, but in the short time they've been around, tabletop ovens such as those from Gozney, Breville, and Ooni have revolutionized home pizza making. With their advent, high-heat baking (we're talking 900°F) is now safely possible in backyards, on balconies, and even in indoor kitchens. Models vary in size, design, fuel source, and cost. Consistent among all of them, though, is the fact that every type of pizza that you know and love, from ninety-second Neapolitans to eight-minute New York–

style pies, can be made in them with the same quality as your favorite pizza joint. That is, once you learn how to use it. (The learning curve can be steep; see page 50 to gain an edge.)

Tabletop ovens are not just hotter than regular ovens; they also heat up faster. The intense heat goes from cold to just shy of nuclear in as little as twenty minutes. Compare that with the one-hour preheat a home oven needs and the attraction is apparent before you even taste anything.

But it's not just about speed. These ovens unlock flavor and texture territories normally unreachable for home cooks and bakers. The high, searing heat produces true "leoparding" (the term for those coveted, sporadic spots of char that appear on a pizza's crust) that just isn't possible at normal temperatures. Quicker bakes also support crusts that skate the line between a moist interior and a crispy bottom.

Tabletop ovens can be powered by wood, wood pellets, a gas burner, or electric coils. As great as it is to cook with wood, we like the gas-powered models best—choosing gas eliminates all the hassles of managing a fire and makes it much easier to dial in on a specific temp. Buy the largest model you can afford. The bigger the oven, the more control you'll have over your pizza—and the bigger the pizzas you'll be able to make!

DOUGH BUCKET

Pizza dough can rise in any vessel, but we like using dough buckets for a few reasons. First, they come with a tight-fitting lid, essential for ensuring the dough doesn't dry out during bulk fermentation. Second, they're clear, so it's easy to check the status of our dough and make sure it's fermenting. Finally, they come with markings on the side that can be used to determine how much the pizza dough has risen—much more accurate than relying on our memory or iffy cellphone pics.

DOUGH BOWLS/TAKEOUT CONTAINERS

Almost every pizza goes through a stage of being balled and rested (except for square or rectangular pan pizzas). We store these dough balls individually in round vessels so that what starts round will stay round when it comes time to shape the dough into the final pie. A tightly covered bowl will work, but round plastic takeout containers with snap lids are even better: They're airtight, stack beautifully, and can be used again and again. You can buy these from restaurant supply stores, but we just save the ones we get when we order takeout. In testing, we've found that a lidded storage container with a diameter of roughly 5 inches and a height of about 3 inches is perfect for many doughs that have been divided and rounded. The wide shape allows the dough to expand, giving us a head start on stretching, whereas a narrower shape (like a quart-size yogurt container) is too constrictive and thus not as helpful.

PARCHMENT PAPER

A lifesaver for transferring shaped pies into the oven. Pros dust their pizza peels with flour, semolina, or cornmeal, and you can do that, too, but parchment adds a layer of assurance that your pie won't stick to the peel. To use parchment, place a sheet of it on the peel, transfer the shaped dough on top of it, top your pizza, and slide it, parchment and all, onto your baking steel or stone in the oven. Most parchment paper is only safe to use in ovens up to 450°F; to remedy this, we use kitchen shears to trim the excess parchment from around the pizza's edges, leaving no naked parchment exposed. If there's a downside to parchment, it's that it can slightly (and we stress the word *slightly* here) interfere with crust formation. So some pizza bakers wait for the bottom crust of the pizza to just set, then quickly remove the parchment from under the pie with a set of tongs. If you do this, feel free to reuse the piece of parchment for at least one more pizza.

DARK ANODIZED ALUMINUM PAN

These pans, which pros have been using forever, are the secret behind the world's crispiest and most compelling pan pizzas. In the anodizing process, the outermost layer of the pan is oxidized, which creates a dark, protective, scratch-resistant surface. The color has an important function: Like a black car in the sun, these pans absorb heat quickly. More importantly, they *give* heat easily and quickly right where it matters: to our crust. This is great not just for pizza but for focaccia, cornbread, and even things like blondies (though anything with sugar should be watched carefully so that it doesn't burn). LloydPans is the most famous producer of American-made dark anodized pans, and the one we trust.

INFRARED THERMOMETER

A digital instant-read probe thermometer is an essential tool for pastry and bread baking, but for pizza we also recommend an infrared. It does everything a digital probe thermometer can, plus it measures the temperature of your baking surface, be it a baking steel or stone or the hearth of your tabletop oven. This is useful because internal oven thermometers are famously unreliable: When your oven dings to announce a full preheat, the *air* in the oven may be at temperature, but the baking surfaces could be significantly cooler. (And sometimes the inverse is true: If your oven has been on a while, the baking surface may be hotter than the oven says it is.) Infrared thermometers provide assurance that the oven is really ready for pizza making. They're particularly useful for knowing when a steel or stone has recovered between pizzas.

CHEESE GRATERS

We prefer to buy cheese whole and grate it at home (see page 16), but to do that you of course need a cheese grater. Actually, you need two. A large-gauge grater (such as a box grater) will move quickly through blocks of aged mozzarella, cheddar, and gouda, and a rasp-style grater (such as those made by Microplane) will make quick work of hard cheeses such as pecorino Romano and Parmigiano-Reggiano. (Note that the volumetric measurements of all hard cheeses in this book assume you grated with a rasp-style grater; if you use a box grater or buy preshredded, use only half the amount called for. If you're measuring using a scale, keep the amounts the same.)

TAPE MEASURE/RULER

It may seem fussy, but measuring your pies to ensure you've shaped them to the right size has an impact on the finished pizza. A ruler helps you nail the right thickness of the dough: If you shape your pizzas too large, they will be too thin (and possibly won't fit on your baking surface); roll them too small and the crust might be unpleasantly thick (and possibly won't bake through before the toppings and edge crust are done). Any tape measure or ruler will do, though it's nice to have one that is exclusively used in the kitchen.

SMALLWARES

There are a few other things you probably already have that are crucial for pizza making. A good set of **oven mitts**, which combine dexterity and heat tolerance, is necessary for everything from moving baking stones to grabbing pans of pizza. An **oven brush** for brushing off your pizza steel or stone is helpful between bakes in order to keep errant semolina from burning. **Ladles** with rounded bottoms are great for both applying and spreading sauce. A **squirt bottle**, **cruet**, or **oil can** of olive oil is great for judicious application of good oil both before and after baking. A **pizza wheel** can handle everything from thick Detroit to thin Chicago tavern-style pizzas and is often a better pizza-cutting tool than a chef's knife. For New York–style pies, a pair of **scissors** works wonders; we also like them for Neapolitan pies as they don't compress the cornicione (the pizza's puffy outer ring of crust). A **mandoline** is a lifesaver for prepping thinly sliced toppings such as zucchini and onions. Finally, you need a **wire rack** for maintaining the crisp crust you worked so hard for—slide your finished pizza onto one and let it sit for a few minutes before transferring to a cutting board. (If you go straight to the cutting board, your pizza will steam and soften.)

THE ELEMENTS OF GREAT PIZZA

21 The Dough
33 The Sauce
39 The Cheese
43 The Toppings
47 The Bake
52 The Finishing Touch

THE DOUGH

he foundation of every good pizza is a great crust. The texture has to be right—maybe it's thick and chewy, maybe thin and crispy—but, crucially, so does the flavor. Sometimes pizza makers rely on toppings to provide all the flavor, but if the crust is bland, your pizza will be, too. It's easy to spot a pizza like this—just look for all the uneaten crusts.

There are a few ways to get great flavor into your dough. One, of course, is salt—we're generous, but not overzealous, with it. Your choice of flour makes a big difference, too—a little bit of whole grain flour adds complexity and aroma to your crust, not to mention a gorgeous speckled appearance. And then there's fermentation, which is, hands down, the very best way to give a pizza dough all the yeasty, floral, and sour characteristics of great bread.

The pizzas in this book use a combination of these techniques. The Weeknight Wheat (page 133) is a same-day (also known as a "direct") dough that has a relatively short fermentation period but a healthy dose of whole wheat flour; the Neapolitan (page 161) uses 100 percent white flour but follows a multiday (or "indirect") method, which includes a long room-temperature fermentation followed by an overnight chill. Many of the doughs fall somewhere in the middle, fermenting for several hours but still doable all in one day. Can you find pizza doughs that are quicker to make than the ones in this book? Sure. But pizza dough that's ready in an hour generally doesn't taste like much, and if all you need is a vehicle for cheese and meats, well, may we suggest nachos?

Pizza is, at its core, bread, and the pizza dough process closely mirrors that of making a perfect loaf: the dough is **mixed**, **bulk fermented**, **balled**, then often **rested** before being **shaped**. After that, the toppings come into play—but if you make your dough right, they're just the icing on the cake.

MIX

Mixing dough is the easiest part of the pizza making process. There's really nothing to it: You measure (with a scale, preferably), dump, and stir. (We'd say a five-year-old could do it, and they *could*, except making dough also requires two things most kids lack: patience and foresight. More on that in a second.)

If you've made pizza or bread before, the ingredients in the dough will look familiar. The list almost always looks something like this:

Flour: Wheat flour is the base of all the recipes in this book, though what kind of wheat flour depends on the pizza we're making. Many of our pan pizzas use *bread flour*—the high protein content (King Arthur's is 12.7 percent) means that a dough made with it is stronger and can capture more air, allowing it to rise high and support the weight of, say, a pound of sausage.

We also use bread flour for some of our thinner doughs, such as the New York and New Haven styles. Here again it's bread flour's strength we're after, but for a different reason: it helps the dough stretch very thin without tearing.

Some recipes call for King Arthur's *00 pizza flour*, a finely milled flour made from both hard and soft wheat. For doughs that go from mix to oven quickly, like our weeknight pizzas, 00 flour provides the extensibility that a long rest would typically provide; that slight increase in extensibility makes the dough easier to handle and stretch. And 00 flour makes for a supremely tender crust, thanks to the softer wheat and slightly lower protein (11.5 percent). (See sidebar, page 26.)

When we want a dough that will be both tender and strong, we use *all-purpose flour*. This is particularly true when the dough has a higher percentage of fat, as our Chicago tavern style does. Fat can inhibit gluten formation, so to counteract that—but still end up with a tender crust—we rely on a flour that has just slightly more protein than 00 (King Arthur's all-purpose flour clocks in at 11.7 percent).

None of the recipes in this book uses *whole wheat flour* or *semolina flour* exclusively, but they show up as inclusions in several of the doughs. Whole wheat flour adds flavor, color, and nutrition to doughs, making them overall more interesting and enjoyable. Semolina—coarsely ground durum wheat—provides texture (a little crunch) and color (a sunny yellow). It's also one of the best flours to dust pizza peels with.

Mix

In a medium bowl, combine all the dry ingredients (flour, yeast, salt, sugar, etc.).

Add the wet ingredients, such as water and oil.

Use your hand to combine the ingredients into a cohesive, homogeneous dough.

Water: No water, no dough. Water is critical to fermentation and gluten development, and the amount of water in a dough (aka the dough's "hydration") is a key indicator of how it will feel to work with. When flour and water are combined, gluten formation is kicked off. The gluten proteins in the flour link together and form a web that will eventually catch the gases expelled by the yeast. Water also plays a big role in the appearance, shape, and texture of your final pizza. Doughs with less water will generally be thinner and crisper; they will also be less sticky, and so may be easier to work with. Doughs with more water will often result in bubbly, taller pizzas with an irregular and more open crumb. That said, even the higher-hydration doughs in this book aren't very wet; most of them hover between 50 and 80 percent hydration.

Yeast: Yeast provides the gases that make doughs rise. In pizza the yeast can come from commercial yeast or sourdough culture. The more yeast (or culture) a recipe has, the faster it will rise, which is why the weeknight pizza doughs in the book have almost triple the amount of yeast of those that rise slowly over a longer period of time. Our choice for commercial yeast is instant—it's shelf stable, easy to find, and it always works.

Fat: The vast majority of the pizzas in this book contain olive oil—and one of them, God bless it, contains butter (see page 75). Fat adds flavor to doughs and also contributes to the texture of the baked pizza crust. When gluten proteins get coated with fat, it makes it hard for them to link together, which results in less gluten development. Put another way, it makes doughs more tender, less chewy, and more likely to crisp up in the oven. Doughs with a lot of fat (like the Roman tonda pizza, which is almost 10 percent olive oil) are fabulously cracker-like. Meanwhile, our Neapolitan pizza, which is distinguished by its puffy, chewy edge crust, has no fat in the dough at all.

Sugar: Like salt, sugar is a seasoning agent, an additive that enhances the flavor of everything around it. But that's only one reason you'll see a little bit of sugar (sometimes in the form of honey) in most of our doughs. The other reason is color: Sugar helps crusts get beautifully browned. As we'll discuss later, browning can be a particular challenge in a home oven. Sugar gives us a leg up.

Salt: Pizza dough is typically well seasoned. Whereas most breads clock in at 2 percent salt, pizza doughs have between 2.5 and 3 percent. Most of the doughs in this book follow a precedent set by pro pizza makers and land on the generous end of that range. We're meticulous about getting flavor into our doughs via fermentation, olive oil, honey, and good flours, and we rely on salt to make sure that flavor actually comes through. Salt also plays an important role in fermentation: It regulates yeast, preventing it from reproducing too quickly. For doughs that ferment for several hours or overnight, salt is a critical control measure. Without it, you'd wake up to overfermented dough spilling out of the bowl and onto your floor.

HOW MUCH DOUGH SHOULD YOU MAKE?

Most of the dough recipes in this book make enough for two pies, but we often double or triple the recipes. (Once we made a 7x batch, but that was a math error. We ate a lot of pizza that week.) Balled dough rounds can be stashed in the freezer for a month (see page 30); thaw them in the fridge for twenty-four hours before using, the same way you would any frozen dough you'd buy at the grocery store.

Baked (and parbaked) pies also freeze well, and, trust us, it will not be long before you find yourself in a situation where you can make use of them.

Here's a literal hot tip: Before freezing fully baked pies, cut them into slices. Take one or two slices out at a time and revive them in a toaster oven set to "toast" or—one of our favorite methods—on a regular toaster, set right on top of the slots. The heat from the toaster will warm it through and really get the bottom crispy. (Whatever you do, do not insert pizza slices *into* a regular toaster, a situation that is guaranteed to end up in one kind of disaster or another.)

Mixing flour, water, yeast, fat, sugar, and salt takes about thirty seconds. But that's just the beginning of a process that, by design, takes time. The most flavorful doughs rest for eight hours or longer, a period during which fermentation takes place. As bakers, we live for fermentation—it's what gives pizza doughs character and nuance—but the long resting period has other benefits as well. One is that a long rest makes dough easier to handle and stretch. Another is that doughs that rest a long time are easier to fit into your day. **A dough that can hang out on the counter or in the fridge for anywhere between eight and forty-eight hours (or longer!) provides a huge window of opportunity—pizza at more or less a moment's notice.** All you need is the foresight to start your pizza a day or two before you want to eat it.

Unfortunately, that means that if you've opened this book at 5 p.m. hoping to eat pizza for dinner tonight, the best advice we have for you is to pick up the phone and order delivery. But don't worry—you'll only make that mistake once. Pizza bakers realize quickly that they need to start their pizzas when they aren't hungry, a day or two before they have a pizza craving. It's not hard to anticipate this: When do you *not* have a pizza craving?

BULK FERMENTATION

Once it's been mixed, a batch of pizza dough sits at room temperature for anywhere between one and ten hours, a process called bulk fermentation. Sometimes the dough gets briefly kneaded, or simply gets a few folds, at the beginning of this period, but otherwise it remains undisturbed. The dough doesn't look like it's doing much during this time, but a lot is happening underneath the surface. As it rests the dough ferments. The yeast eats the available sugars, then expels organic acids, alcohol, and carbon dioxide. The acids and alcohol add flavor and strength to the dough; the carbon dioxide makes the dough rise. In many of our dough recipes the minuscule amount of added yeast means that this process happens slowly. That's purposeful—the longer the dough sits and ferments, the more flavor it develops.

The "bulk" in bulk fermentation refers to the single mass of dough; the term is reserved for dough that hasn't been divided and shaped yet. **But fermentation doesn't stop after a dough is divided—it continues all the way up to the moment the pizza is baked.** Many pizzas, including several in this book, get their longest fermentation period after the dough has been divided, balled, and placed on the counter or, in many cases, in the refrigerator, where the fermentation process slows dramatically but doesn't stop.

A long fermentation period—whether before or after dividing—does not make a dough a "project." Just the opposite. Doughs with long fermentation periods are more convenient and easier to fit into your schedule; most of the fermentation can happen while you sleep or go to work. Doughs made via a multiday method, where the dough is balled and chilled, have even more flexibility—you can make your dough on a Wednesday and not think about it again until you want to bake pizza on Friday night. (See sidebar, page 30.) And when you do finally go to shape it, the benefits of fermentation will be clear: Your dough will be vibrant, a little pillowy, extensible, elastic, and overall just a dream to work with.

ON MALTING

As you ratchet up your pizza game, you may come across discussions around malt, especially in professional pizza-making forums. In those instances, malt most often refers to active, naturally occurring flour enzymes that support fermentation as well as browning during baking. Occasionally, bakers add a very small amount of malt to long-fermented doughs. As doughs ferment, the sugars get consumed by the yeast, and a little added malt ensures there's sugar left in the dough when it hits the oven. So should you add malt to your doughs? Not necessarily. The flours that we prescribe most often (King Arthur bread flour and all-purpose flour) already contain an enzyme that mimics the effects of malt. However, if you find that your long-fermented doughs don't brown as much as you'd like—and you've already used a thermometer to confirm that your oven is hitting the right temps—malting might be in order. In that case, try adding 0.5 percent of diastatic malt (avoid nondiastatic, which does not contain active enzymes) as a percentage of the flour and note if it makes a difference.

DIVIDE AND BALL

After bulk fermentation—but before we shape our pizzas—we often divide our dough and go through the process known as "balling." Experienced bread makers will recognize this step as the pizza equivalent of the preshaping step in bread making. In both cases, **preshaping or balling supports a better final form**.

For our same-day doughs such as Weeknight White or Wheat styles, we are gentle at the balling stage. Same-day doughs go from ball to shaped pizza in a matter of minutes, so we don't want to tighten the dough by treating it aggressively, which would make it more difficult to shape. For multiday doughs such as the New York and New American styles, the opposite is true: They might rest for several days after balling, so we tension them tightly, adding strength and removing gas in the process.

Regardless of which dough you're balling, the method is similar:

Divide the dough into two equal pieces (1). Gently pat the dough to remove any large air bubbles (2). Grab one edge of the dough, stretch it upward, then bring it to the middle of the dough, pressing gently to seal (3, 4). Repeat this folding motion four to six times, working your way clockwise around the dough until you've made roughly one lap around the entire piece. For same-day doughs, you're done—with these doughs, we're only chasing a round form that will become a round pizza. For multi-

Divide and ball

day doughs, continue folding, making another lap or two around the dough, until a smooth, tight ball forms (5, 6).

Balled doughs should be transferred to lightly greased storage containers (see page 15), covered, and rested according to the recipe instructions until it's time to shape. Same-day doughs may rest for only an hour or two; multiday doughs rest overnight or much longer. (Most of the multiday doughs are happy to sit in the fridge for days while you find the perfect time to bake them. They should be brought back up to room temperature, though, before shaping and baking. **A good rule of thumb is to take your dough out of the fridge when you turn on your oven to preheat.** Both the dough tempering and the oven preheating should take about an hour.)

SHAPE

There are many ways to shape a round pizza; the best method depends on how thin a crust—and how puffy an *edge* crust—you're going for.

For cracker-style doughs such as the Chicago tavern style or the Roman tonda, we find that a rolling pin works best for achieving an even dough with no thin spots. For pizzas with a puffier edge crust, including our New York–style and weeknight doughs—and even the heralded Neapolitan, with its signature "cornicione"—hand shaping is best. Both methods start the same way:

Transfer your balled dough from its container to a floured work surface. (If your container was well oiled, you should be able to simply invert it and let the dough drop; this will help retain the dough's round shape, and make it easier to shape into a circle.) Gently flip the dough over to thoroughly coat both sides with flour—any flour works here, including semolina, which is particularly nonstick and will add a little texture to your dough. Gently but authoritatively press on the center—and only the center!—of the dough to de-gas it (that is, get rid of any large air bubbles), then proceed with one of the techniques on the following pages.

WHAT'S THE DEAL WITH 00 FLOUR?

You don't have to dip your toe too deep into pizza culture to find a conversation about 00 flour. Of all the flours, this one has the biggest myth surrounding it. That myth is that it makes good—no, *superior*—pizza (and, for that matter, pasta).

This is true. And it's also a lie.

00 is not a type of wheat, but rather a milling specification. In Italy, flour is not categorized as "whole wheat" or "white"—or even "all-purpose," "bread," or "pastry." Instead, the Italian system grades flour on a range from 100 percent whole grain ("integrale") to 00 ("doppio zero"). 00 is the whitest and finest milled flour on the spectrum, followed by 1 (which has a touch more color and ash content), 2 (even more), and so on, until we reach the other end of the spectrum for integrale, or what we'd call whole wheat.

Why is 00 flour widely touted as a perfect flour for pizza? Because the finely milled grain creates doughs that hydrate well, mix evenly, and ferment beautifully. It can be the perfect flour for Neapolitan pies, contributing to the puffy edge, or cornicione, that is that pizza's trademark. But the idea that 00 is the best flour for *all* pizzas is flawed. Pizza is a big world, and a one-size-fits-all approach doesn't work. Here's why:

00 can be produced from high- or low-protein wheat. King Arthur 00 is milled using a blend of soft wheats for extensibility and hard wheats for elasticity; it is slightly lower in protein than our all-purpose, landing around 11 percent. But other 00 flours have different protein levels and characteristics. With some 00 flours landing on the lower-protein end of the spectrum, we wouldn't reach for it for, say, some of our pan pizzas. For those, we would use higher-protein bread flour, which has the strength and structure that something like a Detroit pizza needs.

So reserve your 00 flour for Neapolitan or similar pies, such as our Weeknight pizzas. And don't worry if you don't have any at all—you can always make a pan pizza instead.

Pressing

Good for Neapolitan (page 161), New American (page 177), New York Style (page 105), Weeknight White (page 132), and Weeknight Wheat (page 133)

Using your hands like paddles, with your fingers pressed together, make a light depression in the center of the dough (1). Continue pushing the dough from the center out, being careful to avoid the outer rim (2, 3). (This is key! Always avoid the outer rim: You want to leave a half inch to an inch of dough all around the perimeter untouched so that it will puff.) As you press, flip the dough over once or twice to ensure it doesn't stick to your work surface. Holes and tears often begin with sticking, so err on the side of a little extra bench flour.

With softer doughs like the Neapolitan and Weeknight, this pressing method can get you most of the way to your desired size. Firmer doughs, such as the New American and New York, will require some stretching to finish them off. When the pizza is almost as big as you want it, with an inch or two in diameter to go (yes, we use a ruler!), begin to stretch the dough gently using the stretching method below.

Stretching

Good for New York Style (page 105), New American (page 177), New Haven Style (page 89), Weeknight White (page 132), and Weeknight Wheat (page 133)

Use the pressing method above to shape the dough a few inches shy of the final pie (or however big you can get it; some doughs will resist more than others) (1). Gently grab the dough on the east and west sides, careful to position your grip *over* the edge crust, so as not to deflate it. Give the dough a solid, confident, but still gentle pull—lifting the dough off the counter for a moment (2)—then release it and let it fall gently back into place. Give the dough a quarter turn and repeat (3). Keep patiently stretching and turning the dough like this. You can use this method exclusively to get the dough to the size you want, or you can finish shaping your pie using one of the gravity methods.

Pinning

Good for Tonda (page 61), Chicago Tavern Style (page 75), and New Haven Style (page 89)

"Pinning" refers to shaping your dough using a rolling pin; this method could just as well be called "rolling." To begin, using the pressing method above, lightly flatten the dough into a roughly 4-inch circle (1), then roll from the center out, once to the north, then to the south. Continue rolling on this axis—up then down, up then down—until you have an oval (2). Flip your dough over (to make sure it isn't sticking) and give it a half turn; your oval should now be stretching east-west. Begin to roll to the north and south again, evening the oval into a circle (3). Depending on the style of pizza you're going for, you may or may not want to try to avoid the outer rim. The tonda and Chicago tavern-style pies are thin end-to-end, so the edges should be the same thickness as the rest of the pie; for the New Haven style, you want to leave a half inch of untouched dough around the rim. A small rolling pin is helpful in the latter case, or you can make do with something from the kitchen (like a clean bottle of hot sauce). You can also use the stretching method above to give the New Haven–style dough its final inch or two.

Gravity

Good for New York Style (page 105), New American (page 177), Weeknight White (page 132), and Weeknight Wheat (page 133)

Earth's gravitational pull is a great tool for shaping pizza. Start by using the pressing method above to shape the dough a few inches shy of the final pie (or however big you can get it; some doughs will resist more than others). Then choose your method: For the tabletop method, grab a section of dough, careful to position your grip *over* the edge crust (so as not to deflate it), and pull, lifting it a few inches above the work surface. Let the dough hang for a second or two; it will naturally stretch away from your hands, toward the counter (1). Repeat with other sections of the dough until you've made your way around the edge of the entire pie. Alternatively, use the knuckling method: Drape the dough over your fists and gently move the dough in a circle (keep your fists just inside the perimeter of the pizza, avoiding the edge crust) (2, 3). As you move the dough, it will naturally stretch downward; just let gravity do the work for you. If the dough resists stretching, return it to your floured work surface and let it rest for five to ten minutes to allow the gluten to relax, then try again.

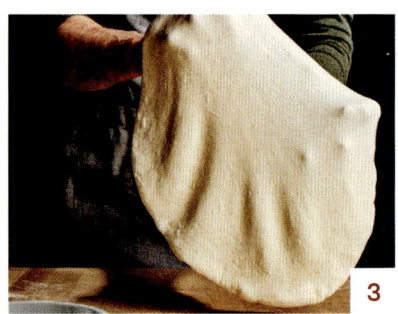

THE BENEFIT OF A LONG REST—OR HOW TO GET PIZZA ON THE TABLE ON A FRIDAY NIGHT

Most of the multiday recipes in this book follow a method that's designed to maximize fermentation and fit into any schedule. A typical process looks more or less like this:

Mix the dough and let it **bulk ferment** on the counter for a bit, usually one hour.

Divide and **ball** the dough into individual rounds and place them in individual containers.

Rest the shaped rounds at room temperature overnight, or for eight to ten hours. The dough can be used immediately after this period, or . . .

Chill the shaped rounds in the fridge until you're ready to bake. This could be anywhere from a few hours to a few days later. (To keep the dough even longer, see Freezing on page 30.) Pull the dough from the fridge an hour or two before baking to let it warm up.

What does that mean in practical terms? It means that if you put in a few minutes of active work earlier in the week, you can eat pizza on a Friday night (or Saturday night, for that matter) with basically no effort whatsoever:

Wednesday, 8 p.m.: Mix, bulk ferment, divide, and ball your dough. Transfer the balled dough to greased containers, cover, and let it rest at room temperature overnight.

Thursday, 8 a.m.: Good morning! Put your containers of dough (the dough should look a little puffy now) into the fridge.

Friday, 5 p.m.: Preheat your oven and take the doughs out of the fridge to come to room temperature on the counter.

Friday, 6 p.m.: Shape your first ball of dough into a pizza. Sauce it. Top it. Bake it. Eat and repeat!

TRANSFERRING TO THE PEEL

Once your dough is fully shaped, it's time to transfer it to the peel. And this is when the clock starts ticking. The longer your dough sits on the work surface, the more likely it is to stick. The dough is also drying out every minute that it's left exposed to the elements. Also, you and your guests are probably hungry by now—what are you waiting for?

You have a choice: Transfer your shaped pizza dough directly to the peel, or use a piece of parchment between dough and peel. Using parchment is much more fail-safe because it eliminates the possibility that your pizza will stick to the peel when you try to load it into the oven. If you're not using parchment, generously dust your peel with cornmeal or semolina flour. If you *are* using parchment, put a piece large enough to hold your pie on the peel, then dust the parchment with semolina or cornmeal.

There's no secret trick to transferring your dough off the counter and onto your peel: You just lift it, gently but confidently, using both hands and always avoiding the edge crust. During the transfer your pie will usually tighten up and shrink a little, and when you set it down on the peel it might look a little wonky—all that hard work shaping it into the perfect round, gone! But don't worry. With a few gentle nudges and tugs, you'll get it back to the right size and shape. If you're using parchment, trim off any excess; the pizza should basically cover all the parchment on the peel. Exposed parchment can burn in the oven.

Have your sauces and toppings ready before you transfer your dough to the peel (or, preferably, even before you shape the dough—you don't want the dough to be hanging out, getting sticky, while you rush to shred your cheese). Sauce and top your pie and load it into the oven immediately.

FREEZING PIZZA DOUGH

Pizza dough can be frozen as rounds of dough or as fully shaped and topped parbaked pies. Will it perform exactly as it would if it had never been frozen? Not really. As pizza doughs nap in the freezer, some of the yeasts die, making for a less lively dough. If you're especially particular about your pizza, you may notice; for the rest of us, the trade-off is worth it. We recommend the techniques below for our Weeknight White (page 132), Weeknight Wheat (page 133), and Neapolitan (page 161) doughs.

To freeze rounds of dough

Mix, divide, and ball your dough into rounds as directed by the recipe, then give them their full period of rest/fermentation. When your dough rounds are ready to be either transferred to the refrigerator or shaped into pizzas, dust them lightly with flour and wrap them tightly with plastic wrap. Put the wrapped dough rounds in a freezer bag, seal it, label it, and store in the freezer for up to one month. When ready to use, thaw overnight in the fridge, then let it warm up on the counter for an hour or two. Your dough is now ready to be shaped into a pizza.

To freeze parbaked pies

Follow the recipe up to the point that you've shaped your dough into a pizza, but stop short of topping it. Bake the naked pizza at 425°F on a preheated steel or stone for five to eight minutes, just until the crust has set but not taken on any color. Feel the dough to gauge its doneness—it should feel airy and dry on the surface, and not at all tacky or doughy. (If, during baking, any big air bubbles form anywhere other than the rim of the pie, open the oven and pop them with a fork.)

Let the parbaked pies cool completely on a wire rack. Assemble the pizzas as you normally would with sauce, cheese, and toppings, then set them on a baking sheet. Place the pizzas in the freezer, covered loosely with parchment or waxed paper, until they feel just frozen, about one hour. Wrap each frozen pie tightly in plastic wrap. Place each wrapped pizza in a plastic bag, seal it, and store the bag in the freezer. Parbaked pizzas will last in the freezer for about a month. Bake them directly from frozen as directed in the recipe, using the same cues to determine when they are ready to eat.

WHY WE MEASURE

We've designed these doughs with the relationships between toppings, bottom crust, and edge crust in mind. Stretching to a specific diameter ensures that those relationships are intact, so the bottom crisps (due to thinness), the edge puffs (because there's enough dough there—but not too much!), and so forth. These details add up, so we implore you: Grab a ruler! It really is harder than you think to eyeball it, and if you shape your pizza too big or too small it can overcook, undercook, or simply look weird.

HOW LONG CAN DOUGH SIT IN THE FRIDGE?

In the course of writing this book we made an ungodly amount of pizza, so much that we occasionally lost track of some of our doughs, only to find them a week later tucked in the back of the fridge in our test kitchen. Every time we found a forgotten dough, we baked it, just to see what would happen. And you know what? They were completely fine, and sometimes better than fine—sometimes the pizza was downright great, "leoparding" (that is, getting colored with spots of char) more than our younger doughs.

There *are* downsides to doughs that have sat around: As the dough sits, the yeast continues to consume the flour's sugars, and less sugar in the dough means less browning in the oven. Older doughs also tend to be weaker, tear more easily when shaped, and puff up less when baked. But none of these things is a big deal, and we'd always rather bake a dough (and eat a pizza) than throw it in the compost. Most of the doughs in this book can be held in a lidded container, refrigerated, for at least one week, but obviously you should discard it if it smells off, feels off (dry and tough), or has any signs of mold.

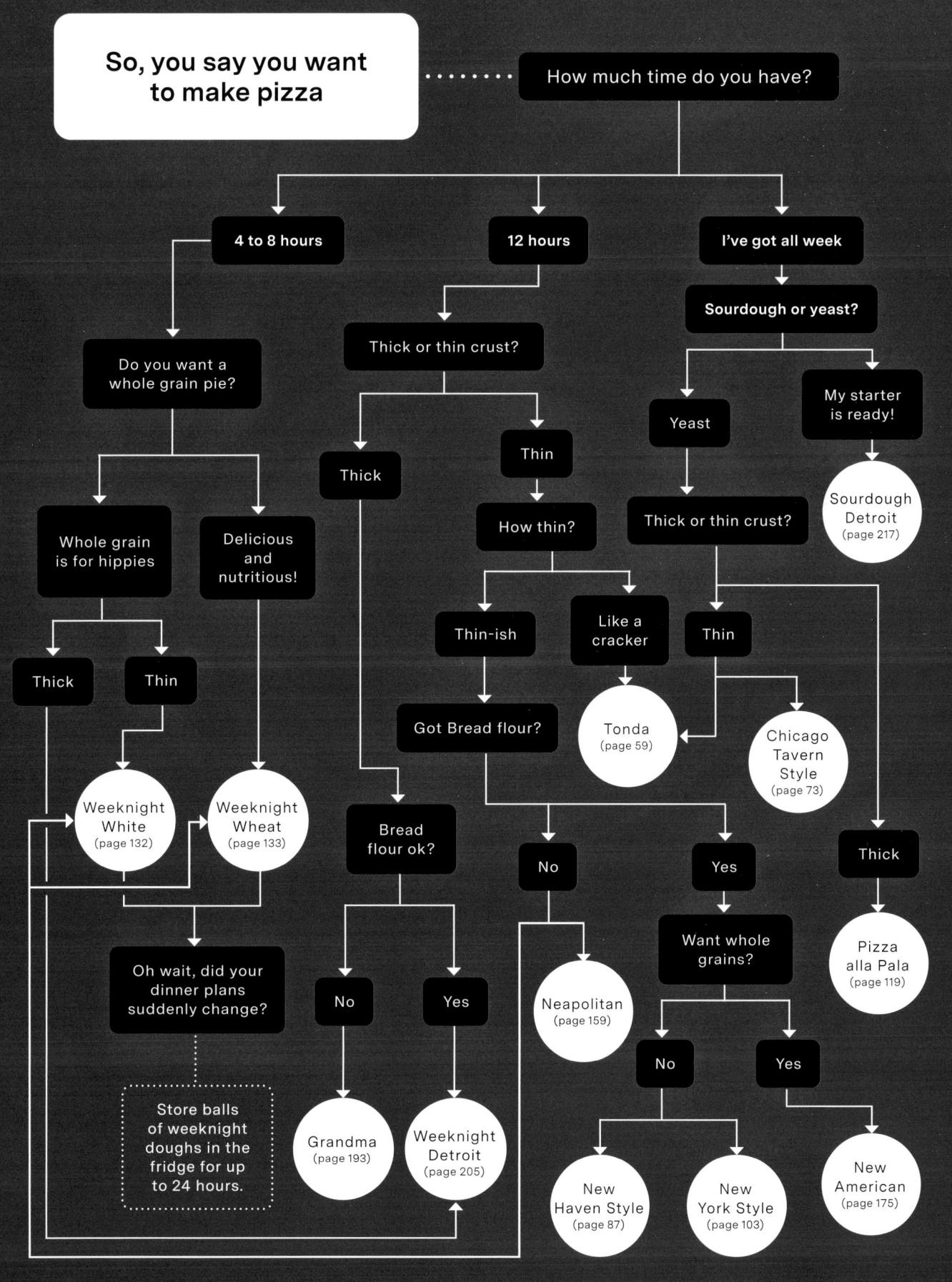

THE SAUCE

A *good pizza sauce is a partner to all of a pie's* other components. And in the case of the most popular pizza sauce, tomato sauce, it is also a counterpoint. Like vinaigrette on lettuce or lemon squeezed over schnitzel, a tomato-based pizza sauce brings the acidity that keeps everything lively and makes a pizza taste complete.

But other pizza sauces serve other functions. On one of the pizza-eating trips we took while writing this book, we grabbed a thick square slice of cacio e pepe pizza from a well-known New York shop. It had a snow pile of Microplaned pecorino about an inch high and a layer of whipped mascarpone beneath it. This thing was all decadence, and the mascarpone, which was essentially the pizza's sauce, was no reprieve—in fact, it doubled down on the richness. You could only really eat a few bites, but those bites were mind-bendingly good. (Find our version of that pizza on page 229.)

So sauces contain multitudes, and play multiple roles. One thing all sauces do is add moisture. Tomato-free white pizzas can of course be great, but even when there's technically no sauce, there's usually something slick, oily, or creamy on every slice—caramelized onions, fresh ricotta. Something to ensure the slice doesn't feel dry when you bite into it.

Some pizza sauces take less than a minute to put together. Others take a while on the stove. But don't let the ubiquity of jarred pizza sauces fool you into thinking that pizza sauce is a burden, something you can't be bothered to do. You can. You should. You shall! And if you occasionally have to rely on a jarred sauce, well, you'll lie! But once you know how easy—and how much *better*—it is to make your own sauce, you won't reach for the jarred stuff very often.

HOW MUCH SAUCE?

A lot or a little, but not *too* little and definitely not too much—got it? Different styles of pizza dictate different styles and amounts of sauce. Pan pizzas can generally take a lot of sauce—their thick crusts can handle the weight, and the long bake times ensure the pizza gets baked all the way through. Thin-crust pies are typically lighter on sauce as they bake for a shorter time, meaning there's less opportunity for the sauce to reduce in the oven. Of course, the dynamics of proportions are also at play here: A thick crust begs for more sauce to keep the flavors and textures in balance.

That said, **too much sauce on any pizza can negatively impact the bake.** An overzealous layer of sauce can prevent the crust from fully baking, leaving a thin layer of raw dough between the crust and the sauce. (The pro term for this phenomenon is "gumline." We know, we know—too real.)

There are ways around getting a gumline. One is to put a layer of cheese directly on the crust and put the sauce on top of that. (This is traditional on Detroit pies, one hallmark of which is those wide, generous stripes of sauce right on top.) Another tactic is to use a sauce that has reduced on the stove for a while, allowing the water in the sauce to evaporate. Of course, that assumes you want a reduced sauce on your pie, which is a key choice every pizza baker has to make.

FRESH VERSUS REDUCED

The absolute easiest sauce—and the one we use the most, no matter the crust—is a raw tomato sauce. Here's how you make it: Pour a can of peeled whole tomatoes into a blender, add salt (and sometimes sugar), blend.

Calling this sauce raw is actually a misnomer: Tomatoes are heated in the canning process, so they have a lightly cooked quality even if you never simmer them. Still, this sauce celebrates the unadulterated flavor of great tomatoes more than any other. It's a side benefit that this sauce is fast, ready at a moment's notice, whereas other sauces require more foresight and planning. If there's a downside to this sauce it's that it is entirely dependent on the quality of the canned tomatoes, and canned tomatoes can be transcendent—or tinny and terrible. The only way to know is to taste the tomatoes right out of the can. (We love the tomatoes from Bianco DiNapoli, the brand owned in part by legendary pizza baker Chris Bianco. We also tend to have luck with Cento brand tomatoes.)

While it goes without saying that good tomatoes are preferable for every sauce, we'll admit that less-than-great canned tomatoes can be saved, to an extent, by using them in a reduced sauce. Cooking tomatoes softens the acids. Also, cooked sauces are easy to infuse with other flavors such as dried herbs, garlic, and even—shhh—a little sugar.

Finally, there are plenty of reasons to use a reduced sauce even if your tomatoes are great. Reduced tomato sauces are richer, rounder, more robust. For those of us who grew up eating globalized corporate-chain pizza, the sweet, tomato paste-like qualities of a reduced sauce can be a nice hit of nostalgia.

SO MANY SAUCES

White pies often use béchamel. Green pies use pesto or other herb-based sauces. One of the authors of this book insisted again and again that we needed a pizza with barbecue sauce (and he got his way—see page 147). Sour cream, mascarpone, and crème fraîche can all be the base of a pizza (see page 153), and you know that there are people out there who have used mayo. Anything saucy—Sriracha! Mustard!—is fair game. Here are the sauces we use most.

NO-COOK PIZZA SAUCE

Great canned tomatoes need almost nothing done to them to become a vibrant (and effortless) pizza sauce. Got less-than-great? Those can work, too, though you may want to add a little sugar, especially if they're tasting too acidic. (If you're going for New York style authenticity, add sugar regardless—see the variation.)

Makes 585 grams (2¼ cups)

794 grams (one 28-ounce can) whole peeled tomatoes

1 teaspoon fine salt, plus more to taste

Open and strain the tomatoes; discard the liquid or save for another use. Using a blender, food processor, or immersion blender, pulse the tomatoes just a few times to a coarse consistency. Stir in the salt. Taste and adjust the seasoning as necessary. Use immediately or transfer to a lidded container and refrigerate for up to 5 days.

Variation: New York–Style Pizza Sauce
Stir in 1 teaspoon sugar when you add the salt.

CHICAGO TAVERN-STYLE PIZZA SAUCE

A no-cook sauce that, thanks to some tomato paste and olive oil, has the robust flavors of one that has simmered all day on the stove.

Makes 992 grams (4 cups)

794 grams (one 28-ounce can) whole peeled tomatoes

170 grams (one 6-ounce can) tomato paste

25 grams (2 tablespoons) extra-virgin olive oil

2 tablespoons Italian seasoning

12 grams (1 tablespoon) sugar, plus more to taste

10 grams (2 teaspoons) red wine vinegar

1 teaspoon garlic powder, plus more to taste

1 teaspoon fine salt, plus more to taste

Combine the tomatoes, tomato paste, oil, Italian seasoning, sugar, vinegar, garlic powder, and salt in a blender, food processor, or with an immersion blender and blend until mostly smooth. Season to taste with additional salt and sugar; the sauce should be tangy and sweet. Use immediately or transfer to a lidded container and refrigerate for up to 5 days.

MARINARA SAUCE

Marinara has more going on than other tomato sauces: It's sweeter, and has more of an umami edge. Use it wherever you want classic Italian American vibes, such as on the Eggplant Parm (page 203) and Tricolore (page 199) Grandma pies.

Makes 725 grams (3 cups)

37.5 grams (3 tablespoons) extra-virgin olive oil

1 small onion, finely chopped (about 170 grams/6 ounces)

5 garlic cloves, thinly sliced

20 grams (1 heaping tablespoon) tomato paste

794 grams (one 28-ounce can) whole peeled tomatoes, crushed by hand

1 teaspoon sugar

1 teaspoon fine salt, plus more to taste

1 teaspoon dried oregano

2 sprigs fresh basil

In a large saucepan over medium heat, heat the oil until shimmering. Add the onion and cook, stirring, until translucent and just starting to brown, 5 minutes. Add the garlic and cook until fragrant, about 30 seconds. Add the tomato paste and cook, stirring constantly, until slightly darkened in color and beginning to stick to the bottom of the pot, 2 minutes. Add the tomatoes, sugar, salt, oregano, and basil and bring to a simmer. Reduce the heat to medium-low and cook, stirring occasionally and pressing on any larger pieces of tomato to break them up, for 15 to 20 minutes, until the sauce has reduced significantly; you should have about 3 cups of sauce. Add additional salt to taste. Remove from the heat and let cool to room temperature. Use immediately or transfer to a lidded container and refrigerate for up to 5 days.

DETROIT-STYLE PIZZA SAUCE

The maximalism of Detroit-style pies extends to the sauce—this one is jammy, thick, and distinctly sweet. For those of us who grew up eating at chain pizzerias, it's nostalgic in all the best ways. The heft makes it good for pan pizzas, but not so much for thin-crust pies, where it can weigh down the crust and make it soggy.

Makes 725 grams (3 cups)

25 grams (2 tablespoons) extra-virgin olive oil

4 garlic cloves, finely chopped

794 grams (one 28-ounce can) crushed tomatoes

16.5 grams (1 tablespoon plus 1 teaspoon) sugar

1 teaspoon fine salt, plus more to taste

In a medium saucepan over medium heat, heat the oil until shimmering. Stir in the garlic and cook, stirring, until fragrant, about 30 seconds. Add the tomatoes, sugar, and salt and bring to a simmer. Simmer, stirring occasionally, for about 20 minutes, until the sauce has reduced significantly; you should have 3 cups of sauce. Add additional salt to taste. Remove from the heat and let cool to room temperature. Use immediately or transfer to a lidded container and refrigerate for up to 5 days.

SPICY VODKA SAUCE

For occasions when you want the sauce to be the star, look to this one: It's decadent (see: heavy cream), fiery, and on the chunkier side. It's best for sturdier doughs such as the Sourdough Detroit (page 219) or Weeknight Detroit (page 207).

Makes 600 grams (2¼ cups)

25 grams (2 tablespoons) extra-virgin olive oil

1 medium yellow onion, diced (about 226 grams/8 ounces)

3 garlic cloves, minced

¾ teaspoon red pepper flakes

43 grams (3 tablespoons) vodka (optional)

794 grams (one 28-ounce can) whole peeled tomatoes, crushed by hand

76 grams (⅓ cup) heavy cream

Fine salt and freshly ground black pepper

In a large saucepan over medium heat, heat the oil until shimmering. Add the onion and garlic and sauté until softened, about 3 minutes. Add the red pepper flakes and stir until fragrant, about 30 seconds. Add the vodka, if using, and scrape the bottom of the pan to release any stuck-on browned bits. Add the tomatoes and bring to a boil. Reduce the heat and simmer, stirring occasionally, until the sauce has reduced significantly and is thick, 25 to 30 minutes. Add the heavy cream and stir to combine. Season the sauce with salt and pepper to taste. Simmer for an additional 5 to 10 minutes, until the sauce is somewhat thickened. Remove from the heat and let cool to room temperature. Use immediately or transfer to a lidded container and refrigerate for up to 3 days.

PARMESAN BÉCHAMEL

This is the classic choice for any pizza that leans savory and rich instead of bright and sweet. It's a thicker béchamel that doesn't run off the pizza, even in the heat of the oven. The Cacio e Pepe pie (page 229) is a great example of how and where to use it, but don't discount the power of combining béchamel with tomato sauce—it works for lasagna!

Makes 624 grams (2⅓ cups)

56.5 grams (4 tablespoons) unsalted butter

60 grams (½ cup) unbleached all-purpose flour

454 grams (2 cups) whole milk, warm (85° to 90°F)

100 grams (3½ ounces) Parmigiano-Reggiano, finely grated (1¾ cups)

¾ teaspoon fine salt

½ teaspoon freshly ground black pepper

In a medium saucepan over medium heat, melt the butter. Add the flour and cook, whisking constantly, until the mixture looks pasty, smells nutty, and is a very light golden color, about 3 minutes. Whisk in the milk, ½ cup at a time, whisking to incorporate fully before adding more (this will prevent your sauce from getting lumpy). Continue cooking, whisking, until the sauce thickens, 2 to 3 minutes. Remove the pan from the heat and whisk in the Parmesan, salt, and pepper. Transfer to a bowl and press a piece of plastic wrap directly on the surface of the béchamel to prevent a skin from forming. Let sit at room temperature until ready to use, up to an hour. If you don't plan on using the béchamel within an hour of making it, place in an airtight container and refrigerate for up to 5 days. Whisk to loosen before using.

BASIL PESTO

Pesto is as friendly to pizza as it is to pasta, and this one is made especially for pizza: It's thick, so it doesn't run off the pizza, and it has more garlic than most, so we like it best when it's cooked. That said, it can absolutely be drizzled over finished pies, or served as a dipping sauce for the crust—just stir in a little more oil and lemon juice to get it to a drizzly consistency.

Makes 384 grams (1½ cups)

56 grams (4 cups) fresh basil leaves

2 garlic cloves, crushed

70 grams (½ cup) pine nuts, toasted

50 grams (1¾ ounces) Parmigiano-Reggiano, finely grated (¾ cup plus 2 tablespoons)

1 teaspoon fine salt

14 grams (1 tablespoon) lemon juice

100 grams (½ cup) extra-virgin olive oil

In a food processor, combine the basil, garlic, pine nuts, Parmesan, salt, and lemon juice and pulse to process until everything is finely chopped and starting to turn into a paste, about 30 seconds. With the machine running, slowly drizzle the oil into the basil mixture. Process until homogeneous and emulsified, about 1 minute. Use immediately or transfer to a lidded container and refrigerate for up to 5 days.

EXTRA SAUCE

Our sauce recipes make enough for several pizzas. Any extra can be frozen, ideally in portions for just one pizza (say, ½ cup), enabling you to thaw just the right amount you need. Even better than freezing: serving extra sauce on the side in ramekins to dip your crusts into. Extra points if you serve your side sauce warm.

THE CHEESE

Pizza and cheese are so inextricably linked that many pizza heads would be surprised to learn that there's an entire class—and long history—of cheeseless pies. In fact, the first Italian flatbreads to be called "pizza" were completely void of cheese and remained that way for years.

That's obviously not the case anymore. Now, if you don't get a great cheese pull when you lift a slice from a pie, are you even eating pizza? In many places, the answer is no. Detroit-style pies are defined by their heavy layer of Wisconsin brick, a highly meltable cow's milk cheese that tastes a lot like Muenster. Traditional Neapolitan pies feature the freshest mozzarella available, and New York City pies are finished with an end-to-end layer of shredded low-moisture mozz. There are good reasons to stick to these traditions. There are also good reasons to buck them.

Like everything else you put on your pizza, cheese is a personal choice, and despite what Neapolitans and Michiganders may tell you, there are no rules. But there are guidelines. Whatever cheese you choose will have an impact on not just the flavor, but also the texture, of your final pie.

CHEESE IS MOISTURE

So much of pizza making is a battle to get our crusts crispy—and sometimes, cheese is a saboteur. Hours-old balls of fresh mozzarella can be tempting, but these and other fresh cheeses (such as young ricottas) have a high water content. In the oven, that water escapes and can make your pie soggy, preventing the dough from fully baking. Sometimes this is exactly what you're going for (traditional Neapolitan pies are almost soupy in the center, which is why Italians eat them with a fork and knife). More often you want the cheese to be rich, stretchy, and anything but wet.

Enter low-moisture mozzarella. This, the MVP of pizza cheeses, contains less water than fresh mozzarella, and because it's been aged, it has a more assertive, saltier flavor (though as cheeses go, it's still pretty mild). It melts beautifully, it gives good cheese pull, and it's available widely in both blocks and shredded form. If you choose only one cheese to put on a pizza, it should probably be this one. Then again, if you choose to put only one cheese on a pizza, you're missing an opportunity.

CHEESES FOR TEXTURE, CHEESES FOR FLAVOR

Thinking of pizza as a multicheese affair is a good way to ensure that you get everything cheese has to offer—that is, both texture and flavor. Not every cheese provides both. Mozzarella has a subtle flavor—milky and light—but makes pizzas richer, and provides a hit of savory fat that offsets toppings like tomato sauce and pepperoni. Meanwhile, dry aged cheeses such as pecorino Romano or Parmesan don't provide any respite of milkiness at all; their power is all in the punchy, salty umami they pack.

A good rule of thumb is to choose multiple cheeses for every pizza: some that are primarily for texture/fat, some that are primarily for flavor. In this book you'll most often see a combination of low-moisture mozzarella and a hard cheese like pecorino Romano or Parmesan; what one cheese lacks, the other makes up for.

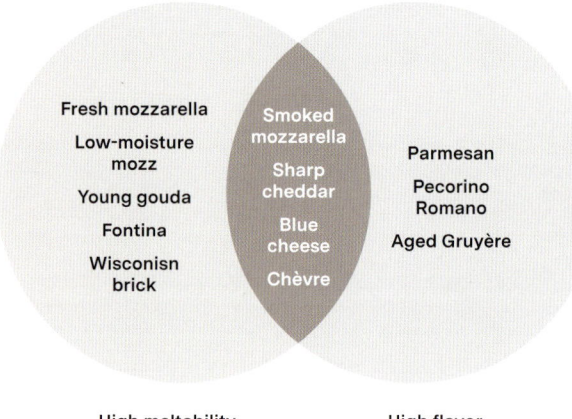

High meltability — High flavor

Fresh mozzarella, Low-moisture mozz, Young gouda, Fontina, Wisconisn brick | Smoked mozzarella, Sharp cheddar, Blue cheese, Chèvre | Parmesan, Pecorino Romano, Aged Gruyère

TO MELT OR TO FINISH

Taking the multicheese approach opens a question: When should the cheeses go on the pizza? Obviously any cheese you want to melt into stretchy pools on top of the pie (mozzarella, fontina, Monterey jack, cheddar) should be applied before the bake.

But don't sleep on cheeses that go on after the bake. Dry cheeses such as Parmesan can be sprinkled over the pie before or after the bake; often, we do both. Soft goat cheeses, spoonfuls of drained ricotta, crumbles of gorgonzola—all of these can go on before the bake, but they also add pops of flavor, and a level of *decadence*, to a just-baked pie. And while most forms of mozz go on a pizza prebake, balls of burrata or buffalo mozzarella are too precious (and wet) for that—tear them open and place them directly on a hot pie. It's the only way to achieve the rapturous interplay of crisp crust, creamy cheese.

TO SHRED OR TO TEAR

Shredded cheese is easy to distribute evenly and melts quickly; it's good for pizzas where you want an even blanket of cheese, such as mozzarella on a New York–

HOW TO MAKE A CHEESE-STUFFED CRUST

The children of the '90s will remember when Pizza Hut broke the culinary world with a cheese-stuffed pizza crust. They claimed it was so good "you'll eat it the wrong way"—and they were right. Want to try it at home? Follow these steps: On a well-floured surface, roll out your dough of choice—we think the Weeknight White (page 132) works great here—to about 15 inches in diameter. (Use a rolling pin for an evenly thin crust that will receive the cheese more easily.) After rolling, move the dough to a semolina-dusted peel (or use parchment for even easier loading). Cut sticks of string cheese into 2-inch pieces; you'll need about eight cheese sticks total. Place the cheese pieces along the outer rim of the pizza, 1 inch in from the edge. Moisten the outer edge of the dough with a little water, fold the dough over the cheese pieces, and press to seal. Top and bake your pizza as usual.

style pie. For other pies (such as Neapolitan), the move is to distribute the cheese less evenly, more sporadically, and so here we prefer to tear or slice our cheese into thin rectangular pieces, which melt into compelling puddles. If you go with shredded, avoid preshredded cheese, which is treated with anticaking agents and mold inhibitors, doesn't melt very well, and usually doesn't taste good. Looking for something as quick as preshredded but want great meltability? Get sliced brick mozzarella (or provolone) from the deli case.

The recipes in this book assume that hard cheeses such as Parmigiano-Reggiano and pecorino Romano are shredded on a fine rasp-style grater, and that softer cheeses such as mozzarella and cheddar are shredded less fine, on a box grater. If you use the small blades on a box grater to shred your Parm, use only half the volume the recipe calls for (Parm grated with a rasp-style grater is lighter and more feathery, and takes up more space than other grated Parm). If you're measuring by weight, no adjustment is necessary.

WHERE DOES THE CHEESE GO?

The cheese goes on top of the sauce! Well, most of the time.

A layer of melted cheese placed on the dough itself can act as moisture insurance on pizzas where the toppings are especially wet. The classic example here is Detroit-style pizza, which has a generous layer of thick, cooked tomato sauce, and a layer of brick cheese beneath it, keeping the crust from sogging out. Cheeses that experience a lot of spread in the oven (mostly high-moisture cheeses) also benefit from being placed right on top of the dough—they'll spread less there than on slippery sauce. On many of our white pizzas, we put a layer of cheese right on the dough because it acts as a sort of glue for the other toppings.

Cheese—specifically, grated Parm—can also go in all the unexpected places. Sprinkle some on the outer ring of the crust, or put a thin layer of it on the underside of a pan pizza; in both places you'll end up with frico—a layer of golden, crispy Parm—baked right into your pie.

AVOIDING CHEESE BREAKAGE

A perennial challenge for pizza bakers, especially those who bake New York–style pies, is "cheese breakage" (also called "splitting"). The term refers to that moment when the fat and protein components of cheese separate under high heat, producing a pool of grease atop a layer of milk solids and proteins. This is such a common occurrence in pizza that a lot of us just think that's how the cheese on pizza is supposed to be—and to be honest, we don't worry about it too much ourselves. But cheese that doesn't break is stretchier and creamier and less greasy, so it's not unreasonable to try to avoid breakage where possible.

In our testing we've found that the degree to which cheese breaks varies by cheese type (whole milk versus part skim), manufacturer, size of cheese (chunks versus grated), and length of bake. If you're struggling with some breakage and bothered by it, here are some things that might help:

Cut, don't grate. Cubing cheese delays the melt slightly, increasing the window of time before the cheese breaks and the weeping begins.

Change the cheese. Different mozzarella producers have different qualities and standards. Sometimes all that's required is a brand change to solve the breaking.

Go part skim. While we love the flavor of whole milk, it does tend to have more pooling fat. Try cutting your whole-milk mozzarella with some part skim.

Bake it hot and fast. The longer your pizza stays in the oven, the more likely it is your cheese will separate. So anything you can do to bake your pizzas hotter and faster will help. Check your setup: Are you preheating long enough? Can you swap out the stone and use a pizza steel instead? Anything that shortens the bake time will reduce the amount of cheese breakage.

Delay the cheese. If you really can't stand to see your cheese break, slide your pizzas into the oven with no cheese at all. Halfway through baking, pull out your pizza, apply the cheese, then continue baking. You'll lose some heat, but your cheese will stay beautifully intact.

THE TOPPINGS

Pizza does not strictly need toppings—it can be just crust and sauce, if you want to really take it down to the studs. But for most of us, pizza is a blank canvas too compelling to ignore. It begs for glistening cups of charred pepperoni, meaty slices of roasted mushroom. Name something, and somebody has put it on a pizza: fried chicken, spicy tofu, chocolate chip cookie dough, peanut butter and jelly. (Some of these have gone off better than others.)

The best pizza toppings are bursts of salt, acid, or sweetness—pops of flavor that contrast and complement the crust, sauce, and cheese. They should keep things interesting. Briny olives, salty anchovies, sharp and sweet red onions—these all bounce off the richness of the cheese and bring the flavors of a pizza into sharp relief. That's when things go well, anyway. But we've all had pizzas where the toppings ruined the whole damn pie.

It usually happens like this: Somebody (it's usually your brother-in-law, let's be honest) gets their pizza ready for the oven. It's shaped, it's sauced, it's covered with cheese. But right before they load it into the oven, they throw a fistful of sliced raw vegetables—bell peppers, mushrooms, chopped onion—over the whole thing. It all happens so fast, and the pizza is in the oven before you can stop them.

You know how this story ends. The vegetables, which never had a chance to cook in the short time the pizza is in the oven, come out lukewarm and crunchy. And yet they're also kind of soggy, because vegetables (especially those mushrooms) give off water as they cook, and the water has pooled on top of the pie.

Vegetables that go onto a pizza raw will usually come out of the oven raw. So remember this rule: **Every vegetable—yes, all of them!—needs to be given some TLC before it goes on your pizza.** It needs to be chopped, torn, wilted, squeezed, sautéed, salted, roasted—*something*. The information below will point you in the right direction.

And meats? Some of them are low maintenance—many cured meats like pepperoni and soppressata just need to be laid on top of a pizza (presuming they are presliced). But anything raw such as bacon and ground meat requires a calculation: Will the pizza be in the oven long enough to cook the meat through? How thick are the bacon slices? How big are the meatballs? As with every kind of topping, these questions are in service of two things: achieving the right texture and ensuring the topping is thoroughly cooked. Answer correctly and the toppings will enhance your pizza, not ruin it.

ANCHOVIES, OLIVES, AND CAPERS

These can go on a pizza with almost no prep. Drain olives and capers before putting on a pie (and for the love of dentistry, make sure the olives are pitted); you can slice the olives if you want to, but unless they're large it's not necessary. Lay anchovies down as full fillets, or chop or tear them into smaller pieces; smaller pieces allow for better distribution. You should rinse and pat dry salt-packed anchovies before putting them on your pizza, but the oil-packed ones can go straight on.

BELL PEPPERS

To get silky strips of bell pepper on a pizza you have to cook it first. Roasting is great, but time intensive; we prefer to sauté sliced peppers quickly in olive oil, which makes them sweet and tender and gives them a little char. See the method on the Sausage and Peppers pizza (page 136), or go for the easiest and fastest option: roasted peppers straight from the jar.

BROCCOLI, BRUSSELS SPROUTS, CAULIFLOWER, CABBAGE

Hearty cruciferous vegetables are unlikely to cook fully during a pizza's stint in the oven. To precook them, you have options. One of our favorites is to make use of the oven as it preheats for the pizza: Cut the vegetables into bite-size pieces; toss them with olive oil, salt, and pepper; and roast on a baking sheet until they've softened and taken on a little char. This method requires a careful eye; because the oven is preheating, it's at an unknown temperature, so who knows how long the vegetables will take? But generally it doesn't take more than twenty minutes, because you're getting the oven ripping hot. Watch carefully that the vegetables don't burn.

We also like blanching, which softens the vegetables but doesn't char them. To blanch, cut the vegetables into small pieces. Bring a medium saucepan of salted water to a boil. Add the vegetables and cook until crisp-tender; this will depend on the size of the vegetables, but start checking at about three minutes. Drain and set aside. (See the method on our Broccoli and Cheese pie, page 135.)

If you slice them thinly enough, these vegetables can get tossed with olive oil and scattered right on a pizza before it goes in the oven (see the method on page 93). And a raw shredded cabbage and/or sprouts salad can also be great on top of a just-baked pie, but at minimum it should be dressed with a little olive oil and vinegar; shaved pecorino doesn't hurt, either.

EGGS

Eggs are fabulous on pizza. They're also frustrating. While it seems like it should be easy to just crack an egg on top of a pie and pull it out with a cooked white and a runny yolk, the reality is that the timing almost always gets messed up—the eggs are either undercooked or overcooked when the rest of the pizza is at its peak. The solution to this is to fry your eggs in a skillet while the pizza's cooking and slide them on top of the pizza when it's out of the oven. See our method for the Pesto, Asparagus, and Fried Egg pizza (page 168) for details.

GROUND MEAT, BACON, AND SAUSAGE

The main consideration with raw meat toppings is making sure they get fully cooked. When there's any doubt, we default to precooking ground meat, sausage, and meatballs before putting them on an unbaked pizza; see the methods on our Cheeseburger (page 79), Meatball Sub (page 215), and Sausage and Peppers (page 136) pies. When the sausage is in small enough pieces and the pizza has a long enough stint in the oven, we put the sausage on raw (see the Triple Fennel pizza on page 190). But bacon always gets precooked (any method works), then crumbled and sprinkled on the unbaked pizza—this ensures the bacon is cooked, but more importantly, *crispy*. All forms of meat require a delicate touch: You want to precook them enough to give them a head start, but not so much that they dry out in the oven while the pizza bakes. When precooking, go for *just* done, or even ever-so-slightly *under*-done, and let them finish cooking in the oven.

GREENS

Hearty greens like kale, collards, and chard should be wilted, squeezed, and chopped before going on a pizza. Start by stripping the leaves from the stems and tearing or chopping them into bite-size pieces. Wash them and shake them dry; a little water clinging to the leaves is a good thing. Warm some olive oil in a skillet (with or without garlic), then add the greens. Cook, stirring often, until they soften and wilt, which should take just two minutes or so. Season them, let them cool enough to handle, and squeeze with your hands to remove any excess water before chopping.

WHEN YOU *STAY* READY, YOU DON'T HAVE TO *GET* READY

Preparing your toppings might be the most time-consuming part of the pizza process. Onions take forever to caramelize; mushrooms can take fifteen minutes to cook down; zucchini needs thirty minutes to sit in its salt bath (jealous?). It's best to get ahead of this. Preparing your toppings in advance—we're talking twenty-four or forty-eight hours, even—will make your life so much easier. This applies to sauce and cheese, too. Having that stuff ready—sauce made, cheese prepped, toppings cooked—is the best way to have a stress-free pizza night.

Baby spinach, baby arugula, and other tender greens are the rare vegetable that can go on a pizza with almost zero prep: Just toss with a little oil first (see the Spinach and Artichoke pie, page 76). Tender greens are also delicious tossed in a vinaigrette and piled on top of a just-baked pie (see our Rossa with Kale Salad, page 183). Note that adult spinach should be treated like kale and other hearty greens.

MUSHROOMS

Nothing ruins a pizza faster than a scattering of raw mushrooms, which contain a ton of water that leaks out and turns the pizza into a soupy mess. Don't be the person who commits this crime: Cook your mushrooms before they go on your pizza. Sautéing with a little garlic and thyme (see the method on our Magic Mushroom pie, page 140) not only gets rid of the water but also gets the mushrooms golden brown and infuses them with flavor. Roasting your mushrooms (toss sliced mushrooms with olive oil, season with salt and pepper, spread in an even layer on a baking sheet, and roast in your preheating oven) is also a good method.

GARLIC AND ONIONS

Garlic can be thinly sliced and placed right on a pie before baking; the thinner the better (see our Rossa pie, page 68, for an example). Onions need a head start before being put on a pizza for two reasons: 1. Raw onions will exude water. 2. Cooked onions are mellow and sweet and just delicious. How far you take your onions is up to you. A quick sauté (see the method on our Amatriciana pie, page 94) softens the onions just enough but retains some of their bite; if you want, you can throw garlic in the pan, too. Caramelized onions (see recipe, page 63) are obviously taken to the extreme—they add a sweet, jammy character to a pizza. While raw onions should not be sprinkled on an uncooked pizza destined for the oven, they can be great as a crisp, sharp garnish—see our Cheeseburger pie (page 79) for a classic example.

PEPPERONI AND OTHER CURED MEATS

Pepperoni, soppressata, salami—all of these can be sliced thinly and put on a pie right before it hits the oven. Fully cooked cured meats can also go on *after* the pizza is baked (mortadella is a good example), but of course you'll lose any crispy edges; we love prosciutto both ways (see the Prosciutto and Hot Honey pie on page 167 for the crispy version). Treat pancetta like bacon and cook it before you put it on a pie (see the Amatriciana pizza, page 94).

SUMMER SQUASH AND ZUCCHINI

These are delicious on a pizza either shredded or in strips, but they have to be salted first to get all the water out. Plan for this—it takes about thirty minutes for the salt to do its job. Squeeze the squash/zucchini to finish extracting all the water, but be gentle—you don't want to pulverize it in your fists. See the method in our Zucchini, Ricotta Salata, and Pistachio Salsa Verde pizza (page 67).

WINTER SQUASH, POTATOES, AND SWEET POTATOES

Cubes of squash and potatoes are great on pizza (a perfect example of carb-on-carb magic), but they'll never fully cook in the time a pizza is in the oven. To avoid crunchy centers, give these vegetables a preroast. If you don't want to mess with that, you can slice these vegetables very thinly, soak (or blanch) them in salted water to soften them, then put them straight on an unbaked pie (see the Loaded Baked Potato pizza, page 211).

TOMATOES

The only tomatoes worth putting on a pizza (that is, that aren't in the sauce) are those that are at the absolute peak of season. Slice them thinly, sprinkle them with salt, and let them sit for fifteen minutes to release some of their juice. Dab-dry the tomatoes with a clean towel before putting on your pizza. Salting applies to small tomatoes, too—slice them in half, season lightly with salt, and let sit before using.

FIND YOUR PIZZA IN YOUR FRIDGE If you have leftovers, you have pizza toppings. That handful of roasted squash from Sunday night? The braised greens your kids didn't eat? The rotisserie chicken you bought on a whim? Throw it on a pizza with a little sauce and cheese and you've got a brand-new meal (and this time, your kids will eat it . . . maybe).

THE BAKE

*H*ome ovens are an entirely different species from the behemoths that pizzerias use. If the big deck ovens and wood-fired hearths of pizzerias are Ferraris—built for precision, heat, speed, and, let's face it, joy—the typical home oven is a Honda Accord. Dependable. Reliable. But nowhere near as powerful, and objectively less sleek. Despite this, it's entirely possible to make great pizza in a home oven; you just have to know your oven's challenges.

For the typical home oven, that challenge is simply heat—it will never get anywhere near as hot as a wood-fired masonry oven, which can reach 1000°F. Unaddressed, the impact of less heat will show up as pale crusts that don't puff, undercarriages that lack crispness, and toppings that appear more wilted than appetizing. That's the bad news. The good news is that there are some workarounds. No, your home oven will never be a Ferrari. But you can make it act like one. Here's how:

TURN UP THE HEAT

If there's only one rule you keep in mind when making pizza, let it be this: the hotter, the better. Commercial deck ovens can easily hit 650° or 700°F, and wood-burning masonry ovens get even hotter (many pizzaioli keep them roaring at 900°F). You'll be lucky to get your home oven to 500°F, but you have to try. **To emulate the heat of pro ovens, crank your oven as high as it'll go and preheat it for at least an hour before baking your first pizza.** Confirm the temperature by pointing an infrared thermometer toward your baking steel or stone—it should be at least 500°F. To speed up preheating, consider using the convection functionality if your oven has it. (See sidebar, page 48.)

LAY A NEW FLOOR

The floor of a pro pizza oven is usually made of stone, fire brick, or steel (in some deck ovens)—essentially, any material that can get ripping hot (that is, has high thermal mass) and can transfer that heat to a pizza via thermal conductivity. In these ovens, pizzas are cooked directly on the floor, where the shock of heat jolts the pizza into action, inspiring it to rise and puff (a process called "oven spring"). The hot floor also gives the bottom of the pizza deep leopard-spotted color and edge-to-edge crispness—two qualities that mark success (not to mention deliciousness) for almost every pizza style.

The floor of a typical home oven, on the other hand, is usually a thin metal plate, and isn't designed to have food directly placed on it. So home pizza bakers have to install their own "floor," in the form of a baking steel or stone.

We consider this nonnegotiable. Baking steels (thick, heavy slabs of metal) and stones (usually made of ceramic) both have exceptional thermal mass and conductivity, with steels significantly edging out stones on the conductivity front. They are the single most important tool for making good pizza at home, because it's the only way to really get a crisp and colored bottom crust. **Use a steel or stone every time you make pizza.**

Steels and stones must be heated thoroughly in order to transfer that heat to your pizza, so they should be in the oven during the entire preheat (at least an hour). Pizzas can be baked directly on them, or you can add a layer of parchment between dough and stone. Pan pizzas also benefit from being baked on steels and stones, but not if you're using a glass pan (note: you shouldn't be using a glass pan for pizza anyway). For more on steels and stones, see Tools (page 13).

FINISH OFF THE TOP

It's hard to replicate the kind of heat that's generated and circulates around pizzas baked in pro ovens, so we employ one other tool to get top-down heat when we need it: the broiler. Some bakers preheat their ovens (with stones) on the bake setting but switch to the broiler right before a pizza goes in; this way they simultaneously get a blast of heat from above (the broiler) and below (the preheated stone). We use a different tactic. **To give our crusts more color (and give our toppings a little char), we start our pizzas on the baking steel or stone, then move them up a rack, placing them under the broiler for the last minute or two of baking.** (More details about this below.) Note that this step is optional, and dependent on the style of pizza we're baking. For a Chicago tavern–style pizza, we don't find the broiling step necessary. On the other hand, we like to broil Neapolitan, New Haven, New American, and even our Roman tonda pizzas in an attempt to replicate the crispness and/or char endemic to those styles.

THE CONVECTION OPTION

Large wood- or coal-fired masonry ovens have an advantage that other ovens don't: airflow. In a typical masonry pizza oven, air is constantly drawn in and pulled along the oven's walls and ceiling before exiting. This vortex of hot air helps cook and color a pizza from all directions and, when combined with high heat and long fermentation, gives pies the coveted leopard spotting on the crust. The moving air also wicks moisture, helping to crisp toppings. A masonry oven's shape is also an advantage: The low, curved interior emanates heat from all sides, cooking the pizza from both the bottom and the top. Home ovens don't have the benefit of this airflow, but most have a setting that emulates it: convection. If you're having trouble getting color on your crust, try baking with the convection fan on. It won't be as effective as a masonry oven, but it will help; at the very least, your pies will bake faster.

BAKE, TURN, BROIL

The moment you slide your pizza into the oven may seem like the moment you can take a breath, sit back, and wait for your pizza to be done. But in fact, this is the most hands-on part of pizza making. Throughout baking you want to keep a close eye on your pizza—turning it, monitoring the puff and color, checking the undercarriage, and, when the bottom is cooked to your liking, transferring it from stone to broiler for a final blast of heat on top. It's a process that feels more like cooking than baking. Here's what it looks like for a round hearth-baked pizza in a conventional home oven:

Load. Transfer your dough to a peel and make any adjustments to fix the shape (see page 29). Check that your pizza isn't sticking by giving the peel a little shake—a slightly jerky back-and-forth to ensure your pizza will slide off without catching. If you're using parchment, you probably won't have any issues. If you're using semolina or flour and your pizza isn't moving freely on the peel, gently lift the corner that's sticking and throw some more flour or semolina under it. Do this all around the pizza, wherever you see it sticking. (Work quickly here—the longer your pizza sits on the peel, the more likely it is to stick.) Open the oven door and reach the peel into the oven, lining up the edge of the peel with the far end of the stone. Swiftly and confidently tilt the peel about 20 degrees, dropping the far end of the pizza on the stone, and swiftly pull the peel back, depositing the pizza in place. Jiggling the pizza off the peel onto the stone can sometimes help the pizza release evenly.

Bake. Immediately close the oven door and let the pizza bake. The amount of time here is variable by recipe, anywhere from three minutes or so for the Neapolitan up to as many as six for the larger New York style. You don't *have* to spend these minutes sitting on the kitchen floor, watching your pizza bake through the oven door window, but it's what we usually do.

Turn. Around the halfway point of your estimated bake time, check on the pizza. Is it getting color in some spots but not others? You may be able to tell just by peeking through the window, but often you'll need to open the oven door to really get a good look. If your pizza is baking unevenly, it's time to turn it. Slide your peel under the pie and turn it 180 degrees, or turn it using a long pair of tongs. However you turn your pizza, do it quickly, then close the oven so that you don't lose too much heat. Continue baking the pizza, turning it every few minutes if necessary and checking the bottom by lifting the front slightly with your peel. At this point you are watching the pizza constantly, monitoring its oven spring, the crust color, and the level of melt (and color) on the cheese.

Broil. About two minutes before the end of the bake time (bake times will vary from dough to dough), assess the color of the crust and toppings. Have they browned enough? If not, use the peel (or tongs and a baking sheet) to transfer the pie to the top rack, a few inches from the broiler. Turn your oven from the bake setting to broil (if your oven has the option for a high or low broil, choose high). Broil your pizza for as long as it takes to give it the color you want. This may take only thirty seconds, or it might take two minutes. Do not walk away during this time—pizzas can go from browned to burned in a blink of an eye.

Unload. Remove your pizza and transfer it to a cooling rack. Avoid putting your baked pie on a cutting board—it will just turn your crisp crust soft and soggy. Instead, slide it onto a wire rack and let it rest for five minutes, until the cheese sets slightly, then transfer to a cutting board and slice.

Reset. Let your oven (and pizza steel or stone) reheat for a few minutes before baking the next pizza. Every time you bake a pizza you zap heat from both the oven and the pizza stone. Because of this, the sad reality is that your first pizza will usually be your best, but resetting between pies can help. If you have an infrared thermometer, use it to determine when you can bake your next pizza (you want the steel or stone to be 500°F). If you don't let the oven and pizza steel or stone recover after each pizza and instead make pizzas in quick succession, expect diminishing returns.

BAKING IN A TABLETOP OVEN

Nothing has changed at-home pizza making more than the advent of tabletop ovens. With their small footprint, masonry baking surface, and quick-heating chamber capable of reaching screaming-hot temperatures, these ovens have unlocked levels of flavor and texture that were formerly the sole domain of professionals.

But slinging restaurant-quality pies at 900°F isn't as easy as it seems—it requires practice, patience, and a willingness to sacrifice some dough. As anyone who's used a tabletop oven knows, you burn a lot of pizzas on the road to blistered success.

As we have learned (and burned), we've come around to the idea of thinking about heat in zones. There's the low zone (where we recommend beginners start), medium zone (what we think of as the sweet spot), and high zone (wear your track shoes!). Every pizza in this book can be baked in any of these zones; of course, since our recipes were written for home ovens, which run at a lower heat than tabletop ovens are even capable of, the time in which they cook will be greatly reduced. Pay close attention and practice—each zone can result in great pizza; you just need to know how to bake in it.

The low zone (550° to 650°F)

If you're just beginning to bake with a tabletop oven, start here. The low zone allows for slightly slower bakes, maximum crispness, and more selective char. We bake our pizzas a little longer in this zone, which allows moisture to leave the crust, giving it the "no-dip-tip" that's appropriate for some styles. This zone also allows time for the heat to penetrate a pizza with a thicker crust, such as a Detroit-style pie. In short, the baker has more control in this zone—the pizza-making process is less harried, more manageable. As they say, "slow is smooth, smooth is fast."

Can all pizzas be baked in the low zone? Yes. There is no liability or downside to baking in a slightly lower-and-slower fashion (remember that we're still working at hotter temperatures than in the home oven). The only caveat is that at lower temperatures you may see slightly less edge crust puff and char. But even if a true, high-heat Neapolitan pizza is your goal, we recommend that you train here before proceeding to the medium and high zones.

To bake on low, we first like to preheat the oven *past* the temperature we ultimately want to bake at (checking with an infrared thermometer to confirm, even if the unit has its own temperature probe). Then we reduce the heat and let the stone settle to our desired temperature. This method ensures that the stone is fully preheated, requiring less recovery time between pizzas.

The medium zone (650° to 750°F)

Once you feel like you're crushing it in the low zone, you may want to shoot for more char on the toppings, underside, and crust. You may also want to try shorter bake times, which keep cheeses pliable and milky (especially in the case of fresh mozzarella). And you may chase a textural sweet spot between a floppy Neapolitan and the fully crispy bottom crust you get with an extended bake. Welcome to the medium zone. This is the tabletop zone we like best.

As with the other zones, we like to fully preheat the stone, overshooting our target temperature, then let the oven temperature fall off slightly before loading. Knowing that the heat has increased slightly from the low zone, you'll want to check the pizza sooner, rotating in the first minute or so, just to make sure that the bake isn't proceeding too quickly. As you get used to this zone, you may find you prefer to load at your zone temperature but then reduce the heat right after loading. This will ensure that the bottom crust gets the increased heat that you want, without blasting the toppings.

The high zone (750° to 850°F)

Welcome to the big leagues. If you're here, we sure hope that you gave low and medium a shot, because in this zone things move fast.

With high heat, things happen in seconds rather than minutes. Crusts instantly puff, vents of steam open, and toppings sizzle, all without delay. And that's the challenge. In the blink of an eye the pizza goes from *cowabunga* to *carbonized*. So how do you move quickly enough, rotating the pizza before it's even fully set or burnt? How do you anticipate what's happening on the side closest to heat, out of view? All of this takes practice.

Before we get to how, let's look at why high heat might be worth the risk. With high heat, long-fermented doughs such as our Neapolitan will char and develop beautiful "leopard spots." The quick bake will also leave enough moisture that a fork and knife might be necessary, as they are in Naples.

To work at high heat we recommend a couple of things. First, after loading, don't leave the oven. Don't stretch another dough. Definitely don't look at your phone. Ignore everything except what's in the oven—you should be watching the pizza like it's a child taking her first steps.

Within the first thirty seconds or so you'll want to slip the peel under the crust edge to check on the bottom and adjust as necessary (a turning peel—see Tools, page 14—is your best friend). It's not uncommon for the first pizza to color a little too rapidly, especially on the bottom; think of this like the first pancake rule. And that's our second tip: Plan for extras. Because while the high-wire act of high-heat baking comes with great opportunity, it also comes with a lot of risk. So plan accordingly: Make extra doughs, and give yourself the margin to flub a couple. With practice, it will happen less and less.

Our last rule for the high zone: Don't hang out there too long. While high heat does deliver some characteristics that are unique, we truly believe that most, if not all, of the benefits can be attained working on the high side of medium. There, you'll have just a little more margin for error, a slightly crispier result (when is that bad?), and more pies that don't need the edge crust cut off or apologized for.

THE FINISHING TOUCH

So you're at the finish line. Your pizza is cooling on a rack and all you have to do now is eat it. Congratulations. You've won! Eating pizza you've made yourself is always a win.

But what if you're going for gold? For us, the touches that we apply postbake make the difference between earning a finisher's medal and standing on the podium. It could be a shake of red pepper flakes or grated cheese, or a sprinkling of dried herbs. A squiggle of good olive oil. A little "snow" in the form of our best Microplaned pecorino. It could even be a bright vinaigrette or, if you want to go really elegant, piped dollops of ricotta. These additions contribute beauty, heat, umami, texture, and aromas that bloom when they meet the hot pie, but they also send a signal to the eater that the pizzaiolo (that's you!) cares. There are a lot of ways to lavish love on your pizza; the following are some of our favorites.

HOT HONEY

Almost every pizza tastes better with a little hot honey drizzled on it. Even if you don't drizzle it on a slice, it's great as a dip for any leftover crusts. This version has a bit of vinegar, giving it a bright edge.

Makes 525 grams (1½ cups)

56 grams (½ cup) chile peppers, such as serrano or Fresno, very thinly sliced

52 grams (¼ cup) white wine vinegar

504 grams (1½ cups) mild-flavored honey, such as clover

2 medium garlic cloves, very thinly sliced

6 grams (1 tablespoon) red pepper flakes

In a medium saucepan, combine the chiles and vinegar. Cook over medium heat, stirring, until the vinegar has cooked off and no liquid remains in the bottom of the pan, about 4 minutes.

Add the honey, garlic, and red pepper flakes. Bring to a low simmer and cook for 2 minutes.

Remove from the heat and let cool completely, then transfer to a jar with a tight-fitting lid. The honey will keep, refrigerated, for at least 1 month.

GARLICKY PANKO

A final sprinkling of richness (thank the olive oil), flavor (garlic!), and crunch.

Makes 97.5 grams (1 cup)

37.5 grams (3 tablespoons) extra-virgin olive oil

1 garlic clove, peeled and smashed

60 grams (1 cup) panko breadcrumbs

Fine salt and freshly ground black pepper

In a small skillet, combine the oil and garlic. Cook over medium heat until the garlic is sizzling and light golden brown, about 1 minute. Add the breadcrumbs and cook, stirring, until deep golden brown, about 7 minutes. Transfer to a bowl and season to taste with salt and pepper. Let cool to room temperature. The breadcrumbs will keep in a lidded container at room temperature for up to 1 week.

PISTACHIO SALSA VERDE

Pizza is a beautiful thing, but if we're being honest, it's not always *gorgeous*. For times when a splash of something emerald is needed to offset all the golden brown, this sauce comes to the rescue. It's also bright, rich, fresh, and crunchy all at once. (Try it on chicken and fish.)

Makes 127 grams (2/3 cup)

1/2 packed cup fresh flat-leaf parsley, leaves and tender stems

1/2 packed cup fresh basil leaves

30 grams (1/4 cup) roasted, unsalted shelled pistachios

1/2 teaspoon grated lemon zest

1 small garlic clove, finely grated

1/2 teaspoon red pepper flakes

1/4 teaspoon fine salt, plus more to taste

25 grams (2 tablespoons) fresh lemon juice

100 grams (1/2 cup) extra-virgin olive oil

Finely chop the parsley, basil, and pistachios. Transfer to a small bowl. Add the lemon zest, garlic, red pepper flakes, salt, lemon juice, and oil and stir to combine. Season with additional salt to taste.

Salsa verde is best eaten the day it's made. Store leftovers in a lidded container in the refrigerator for up to 2 days; bring to room temperature before using.

GIARDINIERA

You can be forgiven for thinking that giardiniera, a crunchy Italian condiment of pickled and marinated vegetables, is Midwestern—Chicagoans won't eat an Italian beef without it. Chicago giardiniera is spicy and often used as a condiment, whereas Italian giardiniera is pickled and can be a side dish. This version takes elements from both. Calabrian chile paste provides the heat here; dial it up or down according to your preference.

Makes 1 quart

For the vegetables:
250 grams (2½ cups) cauliflower florets, cut into 1½-inch pieces

2 small carrots, peeled and cut into ½-inch pieces (about 125 grams)

1 Fresno chile, cut into ¼-inch-thick rounds

1 serrano chile, cut into ¼-inch-thick rounds

½ medium yellow onion, cut into ½-inch pieces (about 113 grams)

2 stalks celery, cut on the diagonal into ½-inch-thick pieces (about 120 grams)

72 grams (¼ cup) fine salt

For the marinade:
150 grams (¾ cup) extra-virgin olive oil

65 grams (5 tablespoons) white wine vinegar

15 to 30 grams (1 to 2 tablespoons) Calabrian chile paste

2 grams (1 tablespoon) dried oregano

8 grams (2 teaspoons) sugar

1 teaspoon coarsely ground black pepper

3 garlic cloves, finely chopped

Pickle the vegetables: In a large bowl, combine the vegetables and salt. Add cool water just to cover the vegetables, then cover the bowl and let sit at room temperature for 24 hours.

Drain the liquid from the vegetables and rinse well in cold water to remove excess salt. Set aside.

Make the marinade: In a large bowl, stir together the oil, vinegar, chile paste, oregano, sugar, pepper, and garlic.

Add the vegetables and mix well, then use a slotted spoon to transfer the vegetables to a quart-size jar with a tight-fitting lid, pressing down so the vegetables are firmly packed into the jar. Pour as much of the marinade over the vegetables as will fit in the jar, making sure the vegetables are completely covered by the marinade.

Cover and let marinate in the refrigerator for 24 hours. Giardiniera will keep, refrigerated, for up to 1 month; let come to room temperature before serving.

RANCH

We all have that person in our life who can't eat pizza without ranch on the side. This recipe is for them, but also for the rest of us (we could probably stand to be more like them).

Makes 315 grams (1¼ cups)

113 grams (½ cup) full-fat sour cream

113 grams (½ cup) mayonnaise

28 grams (2 tablespoons) buttermilk, plus more as needed

25 grams (2 tablespoons) lemon juice, plus more to taste

1 teaspoon garlic powder

1 teaspoon onion powder

1 teaspoon freshly ground black pepper, plus more to taste

¾ teaspoon fine salt, plus more to taste

¼ cup fresh dill, tender leaves and stems, finely chopped

¼ cup fresh flat-leaf parsley, tender leaves and stems, finely chopped

½ cup finely chopped fresh chives

In a small bowl, stir together the sour cream, mayonnaise, buttermilk, lemon juice, garlic powder, onion powder, pepper, and salt. Stir in the dill, parsley, and chives and season to taste with additional pepper and salt.

To use as a salad dressing, add additional buttermilk by the tablespoon until thin enough to drizzle; season to taste with additional lemon juice, pepper, and salt.

The dressing will keep, covered, in the refrigerator for up to 3 days.

GARLIC CONFIT

To make this easier, use peeled garlic—no more squeezing garlic out of oily skins! You don't need to use your finest olive oil here.

Makes 150 grams (¾ cup) confit garlic cloves and 1 cup garlic oil

180 grams (about 6 ounces) peeled garlic cloves (about 36)

230 grams (1 cup) olive oil, plus more if needed

Preheat the oven to 300°F. Combine the garlic and oil in a small oven-safe baking dish or loaf pan. The garlic cloves need to be completely covered by the oil; if they aren't, add additional oil to cover (or choose a smaller vessel). Bake until the garlic cloves are very tender, about 1 hour 30 minutes.

Let the garlic cool to room temperature in the oil, then use right away or transfer the garlic and oil to a lidded jar and refrigerate for up to 2 weeks.

THE PIZZAS

59 Pizza Tonda
73 Chicago Tavern Style
87 New Haven Style
103 New York Style
119 Pizza alla Pala
131 Weeknight Pizza
159 Neapolitan
175 New American
193 Grandma
205 Weeknight Detroit
217 Sourdough Detroit

PIZZA TONDA

Pizza tonda (or pizza tonda Romana) is distinctively Roman, and a far cry from the pizzas that most Americans are used to. It's as thin as paper, rich with olive oil, and shatteringly crisp. So crisp, in fact, that its other name in Italian, scrocchiarella, literally means "to crunch." If pizza is truly garnished bread, this is a garnished cracker.

But—and this is important—it is garnished *lightly*. Unlike the other superthin dough in this book, the Chicago Tavern Style (page 73), pizza tonda gets a light coat of sauce and scattered toppings—an anchovy here, some pancetta there. The idea is to go light enough on the toppings that you can taste the olive oil, semolina, and salt in the dough and keep the crust's texture on point. If you weigh it down too much, the pizza will be less crisp—and with this crust, crisp is the whole point.

Tonda dough is unique in two ways. First, there's that olive oil. While other doughs merely get a splash—just enough oil to support tenderness and browning—the tonda gets almost 2 tablespoons. The result is a crust that's aromatic, crisp, and beautifully delicate. The other defining feature of this dough is the semolina. The coarsely milled product of durum wheat, semolina brings a butter-yellow color and textural crunch to pizza doughs. Again, where other doughs are hesitant, the tonda is bold, using beautifully golden semolina for 20 percent of the total flour.

Don't be afraid to be assertive with this dough. The low hydration means it won't stick to your counter and can take a beating. Put some muscle into the rolling and don't stop until it reaches the right size and thinness. (If you leave it thicker, it won't be as crispy.) Pizza tonda tends to bubble in the oven, and we think that's part of the charm, but if you want a flatter pie, you can prick the dough with a fork after you roll it out. (You can also carefully reach into the oven and pop any bubbles you see during the bake.)

Tonda is not a sharing pizza. In Rome, everybody gets their own pie, and that's what you'll want, too. These are light, snackable, habit-forming pizzas. Don't be surprised when you eat a whole pie and still want more.

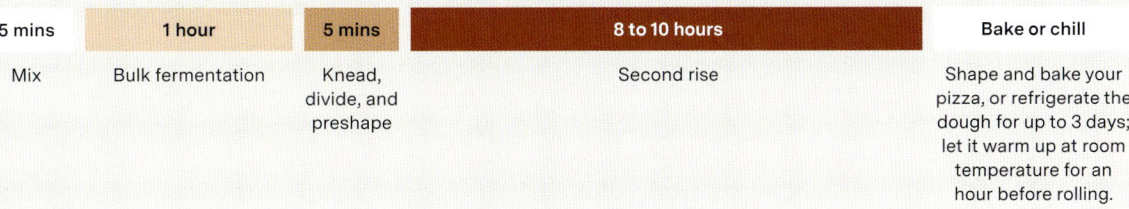

5 mins	1 hour	5 mins	8 to 10 hours	Bake or chill
Mix	Bulk fermentation	Knead, divide, and preshape	Second rise	Shape and bake your pizza, or refrigerate the dough for up to 3 days; let it warm up at room temperature for an hour before rolling.

Pizza Tonda/Roman-Style Dough

Makes 327 grams, enough for two superthin 12-inch pizzas

160 grams (1⅓ cups) unbleached all-purpose flour, plus more for dusting

41 grams (¼ cup) semolina flour

4.5 grams (¾ teaspoon) fine salt

¼ teaspoon instant yeast

21 grams (1 tablespoon plus 2 teaspoons) extra-virgin olive oil

99 grams (¼ cup plus 3 tablespoons) cool water (60° to 70°F)

Make the dough: In a medium bowl, combine the flours, salt, and yeast, then add the oil and water. Mix to combine, then use your hands to knead briefly in the bowl until homogeneous and no dry spots remain; the dough will be firm. Cover and let it rest at room temperature for 1 hour.

Transfer the dough to a lightly floured work surface and knead by hand until smooth, 2 minutes. Divide the dough into 2 equal pieces (about 163 grams per piece). Shape each piece into a tight ball and place seam side down in a lightly greased container. Cover tightly and let rise at room temperature for 8 to 10 hours. The dough is now ready to use in the recipes on the pages that follow, or it can be refrigerated for up to 3 days. Let refrigerated dough sit at room temperature while your oven preheats, at least 1 hour, before shaping.

Squash, Fontina, and Bacon

Makes one 12-inch pizza

1 honeynut squash (about 454 grams/1 pound), halved and seeded (an equal weight of another winter squash variety can be substituted)

25 grams (2 tablespoons) extra-virgin olive oil

Fine salt and freshly ground black pepper

All-purpose flour, for dusting

1 ball (about 163 grams) Pizza Tonda Dough (page 61)

Semolina flour or cornmeal, for dusting

26 grams (¼ cup) caramelized onions (see recipe, opposite page)

42 grams (1½ ounces) fontina, cut into ½-inch cubes

28 grams (1 ounce) cream cheese, at room temperature

28 grams (1 ounce) cooked bacon (about 3 strips), broken into 1-inch pieces

1 teaspoon fresh thyme leaves

Small chunk of pecorino Romano, for finishing

Hot Honey (page 52), for finishing (optional)

This is a habit-forming combination of toppings—the squash and onions are sweet, the cheese and bacon are salty, and the cream cheese provides a lush dairy element that pulls it all together. (Cream cheese on pizza! Who knew?) While these toppings will work on any crust, they are particularly suited for a crackery crust like the tonda.

Arrange oven racks in the lower and upper thirds of the oven. Place a baking steel or stone on the lower rack and preheat the oven to 500°F.

Place the squash halves on a rimmed baking sheet, cut side up, and drizzle the cut sides with the oil. Season with salt and pepper. Slide the pan into the preheating oven, setting it directly on the steel or stone, and let the squash roast until the flesh is tender enough that you can easily poke it with the tip of a sharp knife and it is lightly caramelized in spots, 45 minutes. Transfer to a wire rack and let cool. Keep the oven on. When the squash is cool enough to handle, scrape the flesh from the skin, discarding the skin. Measure out ½ cup roasted squash for your pizza; save the remainder for another use (or another pizza!).

Shape the pizza: Flour your work surface and place the dough on it. Flip it over so that both sides are coated with flour. With your hands, pat the dough into a 5-inch round.

Switch to a rolling pin and roll the dough into a 12-inch circle, flipping the dough occasionally to prevent sticking. If the dough springs back as you roll it, set it aside for 10 minutes to allow the gluten to relax, then try again. Lightly dust a peel or overturned baking sheet with semolina. Transfer the shaped dough to the peel. If the dough retracts when transferring it to the peel, gently stretch the edges to re-form it.

Dot the dough evenly with small mounds of caramelized onions, avoiding the edge, and top evenly with the fontina. Using two small spoons, dollop the cream cheese on the pizza, distributing it evenly. Scatter the bacon, squash, and thyme all over.

Bake: Use the peel to transfer the pizza onto the steel or stone (see Load, page 49), then bake for 3 to 4 minutes. Check the bottom of the crust—it should be spotted and charred in places, and the edge crust should start to have some color. If not, rotate the pizza and bake for another 1 to 2 minutes.

When the bottom has sufficient color, transfer the pizza to the top rack, switch the oven to broil, and broil for 2 to 3 minutes, until well charred in spots. (Don't walk away—pizza can go from well browned to burnt quickly.) Home ovens vary substantially, so use the visual cues and your own preferences to gauge when you've achieved the perfect bake.

Use the peel to remove the pizza from the oven and slide it onto a wire rack. Sprinkle with pepper and grate a snowdrift of pecorino over the top. Drizzle with hot honey, if using. Slice and serve.

CARAMELIZED ONIONS

Heat **1 tablespoon unsalted butter** in a large heavy-bottomed skillet over medium-high heat. When the butter has melted, add **454 grams (1 pound) thinly sliced yellow onions** and **½ teaspoon fine salt** to the skillet and stir to combine. Cover the skillet and cook, stirring occasionally, until the onions are completely soft and beginning to brown, about 10 minutes. Uncover, reduce the heat to medium-low, and add **2 tablespoons water** to the skillet. Continue to cook, stirring often and adding water 1 tablespoon at a time if the skillet gets dry, until the onions are silky and deeply golden brown, 25 to 30 minutes more. Remove from the heat and stir in **2 teaspoons balsamic vinegar**. Season to taste with additional salt. Makes 1 cup.

Zucchini, Ricotta Salata, and Pistachio Salsa Verde

Makes one 12-inch pizza

1 medium or 2 small zucchini (about 170 grams/6 ounces total)

¾ teaspoon fine salt

12.5 grams (1 tablespoon) extra-virgin olive oil, plus more for drizzling

28 grams (1 ounce) ricotta salata, thinly sliced

All-purpose flour, for dusting

1 ball (about 163 grams) Pizza Tonda Dough (page 61)

Semolina flour or cornmeal, for dusting

70 grams (2½ ounces) low-moisture whole-milk mozzarella, shredded (½ cup plus 2 tablespoons)

Pistachio Salsa Verde (page 53), for drizzling

Flaky salt, such as Maldon, for finishing (optional)

Red pepper flakes, for finishing (optional)

Pizza is a great place to put summer's bumper crop of zucchini (and other summer squash) to work. But it's also dangerous: If you don't salt it, let it sit, and then squeeze the water out of it, the zucchini will turn your pizza into a watery mess. Luckily you have an hour to kill while the oven heats up, which is time you can use to get all that water out, and also prep some salsa verde.

Arrange oven racks in the lower and upper thirds of the oven. Place a baking steel or stone on the lower rack and preheat the oven to 500°F for at least 1 hour.

Using a mandoline or a sharp knife, thinly slice the zucchini lengthwise into ribbons about ⅛ inch thick. Transfer to a medium bowl, add the salt, and gently toss to coat. Let sit at room temperature for 30 minutes. This will draw out the excess moisture from the zucchini. Using clean hands, squeeze as much liquid from the zucchini as you can; discard the liquid and return the zucchini to the bowl. Add the oil and ricotta salata and, using your hands, gently mix to combine, taking care not to break up the cheese too much.

Shape the pizza: Flour your work surface and place the dough on it. Flip it over so that both sides are coated with flour. With your hands, pat the dough into a 5-inch round.

Switch to a rolling pin and roll the dough into a 12-inch circle, flipping the dough occasionally to prevent sticking. If the dough springs back as you roll it, set it aside for 10 minutes to allow the gluten to relax, then try again. Lightly dust a peel or overturned baking sheet with semolina. Transfer the shaped dough to the peel. If the dough retracts when transferring it to the peel, gently stretch the edges to re-form it.

Top the pizza evenly with the mozzarella, avoiding the edge. Use your hands to separate the zucchini slices and drape them all over the pizza. Drizzle with a scant tablespoon additional oil.

Bake: Use the peel to transfer the pizza onto the steel or stone (see Load, page 49), then bake for 3 to 4 minutes. Check the bottom of the crust—it should be spotted and charred in places, and the edge crust should start to have some color. If not, rotate the pizza and bake for another 1 to 2 minutes.

When the bottom has sufficient color, use the peel to transfer the pizza to the top rack, switch the oven to broil, and broil for 2 to 3 minutes, until well charred in spots. (Don't walk away—pizza can go from perfectly charred to burnt quickly.) Home ovens vary substantially, so use the visual cues and your own preferences to gauge when you've achieved the perfect bake.

Use the peel to remove the pizza from the oven and slide it onto a wire rack. Spoon the salsa verde over the pizza, sprinkle with flaky salt and red pepper flakes, if using, then slice and serve.

Pizza Rossa

Makes one 12-inch pizza

All-purpose flour, for dusting

1 ball (about 163 grams) Pizza Tonda Dough (page 61)

Semolina flour or cornmeal, for dusting

130 grams (½ cup) No-Cook Pizza Sauce (page 34)

4 whole oil-packed anchovy fillets, torn into pieces (optional)

1 small garlic clove, very thinly sliced

25 grams (2 tablespoons) extra-virgin olive oil, divided

¾ teaspoon dried oregano

½ teaspoon red pepper flakes (optional)

A classic, simple pie, pizza rossa is almost unfathomably delicious. In the oven the tomato sauce reduces and concentrates, the bite of the garlic and anchovies softens, and the crust gets irresistibly crisp. This is a pie where every ingredient matters, because there's nowhere for them to hide—so break out the good olive oil, especially for the final drizzle at the end.

Arrange oven racks in the lower and upper thirds of the oven. Place a baking steel or stone on the lower rack and preheat the oven to 500°F for at least 1 hour.

Shape the pizza: Flour your work surface and place the dough on it. Flip it over so that both sides are coated with flour. With your hands, pat the dough into a 5-inch round.

Switch to a rolling pin and roll the dough into a 12-inch circle, flipping the dough occasionally to prevent sticking. If the dough springs back as you roll it, set it aside for 10 minutes to allow the gluten to relax, then try again. Lightly dust a peel or overturned baking sheet with semolina. Transfer the shaped dough to the peel. If the dough retracts when transferring it to the peel, gently stretch the edges to re-form it.

Spread the sauce evenly over the dough, leaving a ½-inch border. Evenly distribute the anchovy pieces, if using, and the garlic all over the pizza. Drizzle on half of the oil.

Bake: Use the peel to transfer the pizza onto the steel or stone (see Load, page 49), then bake for 3 to 4 minutes. Check the bottom of the crust—it should be spotted and charred in places, and the edge crust should start to have some color. If not, rotate the pizza and bake for another 1 to 2 minutes.

When the bottom has sufficient color, use the peel to transfer the pizza to the top rack, switch the oven to broil, and broil for 2 to 3 minutes, until well charred in spots. (Don't walk away—pizza can go from perfectly charred to burnt quickly.) Home ovens vary substantially, so use the visual cues and your own preferences to gauge when you've achieved the perfect bake.

Use the peel to remove the pizza from the oven and slide it onto a wire rack. Drizzle with the remaining oil and sprinkle with the oregano and red pepper flakes, if using, then slice and serve.

Soppressata and Salad

Makes one 12-inch pizza

For the vinaigrette:

12 grams (1 tablespoon) finely diced shallot

9 grams (2 teaspoons) red wine vinegar

8 grams (2 teaspoons) extra-virgin olive oil

¼ teaspoon honey

½ teaspoon dried oregano

¼ teaspoon garlic powder

¼ teaspoon fine salt

¼ teaspoon black pepper

For the pizza:

All-purpose flour, for dusting

1 ball (about 163 grams) Pizza Tonda Dough (page 61)

Semolina flour or cornmeal, for dusting

12.5 grams (1 tablespoon) extra-virgin olive oil

75 grams (2½ ounces) soppressata salami, thinly sliced (about 10 slices)

50 grams (1½ cups) mixed tender and bitter greens such as arugula, endive, watercress, and/or radicchio, torn into bite-size pieces

Small chunk of Parmigiano-Reggiano, for shaving

Lemon wedge, for squeezing (optional)

Here, a thin layer of soppressata is placed right on the dough where a red sauce would usually be. As the pizza bakes in the oven, the salami gets beautifully crisp—the perfect salty foil for a bright salad dressed in a classic vinaigrette.

Arrange oven racks in the lower and upper thirds of the oven. Place a baking steel or stone on the lower rack and preheat the oven to 500°F for at least 1 hour.

Make the vinaigrette: In a large bowl, whisk together the shallot, vinegar, oil, honey, oregano, garlic powder, salt, and pepper. Set aside.

Shape the pizza: Flour your work surface and place the dough on it. Flip it over so that both sides are coated with flour. With your hands, pat the dough into a 5-inch round.

Switch to a rolling pin and roll the dough into a 12-inch circle, flipping the dough occasionally to prevent sticking. If the dough springs back as you roll it, set it aside for 10 minutes to allow the gluten to relax, then try again. Lightly dust a peel with semolina. Transfer the shaped dough to the peel. If the dough retracts when transferring it to the peel, gently stretch the edges to re-form it.

Drizzle the dough with the oil and lay the soppressata over the dough in a single layer, leaving a ½-inch border.

Bake: Use the peel to transfer the pizza onto the steel or stone (see Load, page 49), then bake for 3 to 4 minutes. Check the bottom of the crust—it should be spotted and charred in places, and the edge crust should start to have some color. If not, rotate the pizza and bake for another 1 to 2 minutes.

When the bottom has sufficient color, use the peel to transfer the pizza to the top rack, switch the oven to broil, and broil for 2 to 3 minutes, until well charred in spots. (Don't walk away—pizza can go from perfectly charred to burnt quickly.) Home ovens vary substantially, so use the visual cues and your own preferences to gauge when you've achieved the perfect bake.

Use the peel to remove the pizza from the oven and slide it onto a wire rack. Add the greens to the bowl with the vinaigrette and toss until each leaf is coated. Pile the dressed greens on top of the pizza and use a vegetable peeler to shave Parmesan over the greens. Squeeze a lemon wedge over the top, if desired, then slice and serve.

CHICAGO TAVERN STYLE

At first glance Chicago's cracker-thin pies seem like the opposite of that city's other signature pizza style, deep-dish. But the doughs are more similar than they may first appear. Both are enriched with butter; both incorporate a little cornmeal for crunch; and both have a flakiness that gives off pastry vibes. And while a tavern-style pie obviously can't hold as much cheese as Chicago deep-dish (no pizza can), the toppings *are* piled on in a maximalist way: edge to edge, so that there's really no outer crust to speak of.

You'd think only a tough dough—Bears jersey, ready to tailgate—could hold such a thick layer of toppings. But no. A Chicago tavern pizza is a pie that plays opposites, the decadent toppings offset by a crust so crisp and thin that it seems pulled from a pâtisserie. To achieve this texture, we use cornmeal for tenderness (its nonglutinous status keeps things from getting chewy). And unlike the pizza tonda (page 59), which is enriched with olive oil, here we use butter. While butter may seem out of place in pizza, it's effective—we work it in as one would for a tender biscuit or scone, coating the flour particles by rubbing it in prior to adding any liquid.

But perhaps the most notable and unusual step that's taken with this style of pizza is the drying. After rolling the pies into thin rounds, the unbaked, untopped dough is set aside to dry for several hours, losing as much as 10 percent of its moisture in the process.

A hot baking surface is critical here—preheat your oven (steel or stone in place) for at least an hour. If you have an infrared thermometer, this is a great time to use it; you want your stone to be at least 500°F. When your pie comes out of the oven, cut it into 2-inch squares, the way it's served in classic Chicago bars.

As the name suggests, this pizza is obviously great with beer (Old Style, if you want to get really authentic). When it comes to toppings, we lean into the pizza's roots as a bar snack. We like it topped with something a little spicy (like giardiniera) and/or meaty (see the cheeseburger pie, complete with special sauce). Figure one pizza per person or, if it's the weekend, one pizza per bottle of beer.

10 mins	30 mins	10 mins	8 to 12 hours (or up to 3 days)
Mix and divide	Rest	Roll	Refrigerate

Chicago Tavern-Style Dough

Makes 332 grams, enough for two 12-inch pizzas

103 grams (¾ cup plus 2½ tablespoons) cool water (60° to 70°F)

6 grams (1½ teaspoons) sugar

6 grams (1 teaspoon) fine salt

Scant ¼ teaspoon instant yeast

160 grams (1 cup plus 5 tablespoons) unbleached all-purpose flour, plus more for dusting

28 grams (3 tablespoons plus 1 teaspoon) cornmeal

28 grams (2 tablespoons) unsalted butter, cold

Make the dough: In a small bowl, whisk together the water, sugar, salt, and yeast. In a medium bowl, combine the flour and cornmeal and stir to mix, then add the cold butter and, using your fingers, work the butter into the flour until fully distributed and the mixture looks like coarse sand.

Add the wet ingredients to the dry and mix until homogeneous; the dough will be rough and clumpy, and that's OK. Lightly flour your work surface, turn the dough out onto it, and divide into 2 equal pieces (about 166 grams per piece). Loosely shape each piece into a ball, cover, and let it rest at room temperature for 30 minutes.

Shape the pizza: Generously flour your work surface and line a baking sheet with parchment paper. Working with one piece of dough at a time, roll into a 13-inch circle (it will spring back slightly so you'll end up with a 12-inch round of dough). Transfer to the prepared baking sheet. Repeat with the second piece of dough, then transfer to a sheet of parchment paper and stack on the baking sheet on top of the first.

Cover the rounds loosely with plastic wrap or a loose-fitting cover to slow the drying process and refrigerate for 8 to 12 hours. The dough pieces will become dry and leathery—this is normal. The trick here is to dry the dough while also keeping it pliable. (The rounds can be kept in the fridge for up to 3 days. To store it longer than 12 hours and up to 3 days, cover tightly with plastic or a cover to prevent the rounds from becoming brittle.)

Remove the dough rounds from the fridge. The dough is now ready to use in the recipes that follow.

Spinach and Artichoke

Makes one 12-inch pizza

1 round (about 166 grams) Chicago Tavern-Style Dough (page 75)

113 grams (4 ounces) low-moisture whole-milk mozzarella, shredded (1 cup)

1 garlic clove, thinly sliced

170 grams (one 6-ounce jar) marinated artichokes, drained, squeezed dry, and chopped

85 grams (3 ounces) cream cheese, softened

57 grams (2 ounces) fresh baby spinach (about 2 cups)

12.5 grams (1 tablespoon) extra-virgin olive oil

¼ teaspoon fine salt

½ teaspoon freshly ground black pepper

28 grams (1 ounce) Parmigiano-Reggiano, finely grated (½ cup)

Red pepper flakes, for finishing (optional)

All the elements of spinach-artichoke dip are accounted for here, including the cream cheese—a surprisingly great option for many pizzas, not just ones based on party dips. Because none of the toppings need to be prepped in advance, it's quick to assemble on a weeknight. Obviously it's also perfect for game day.

Arrange a rack in the center of the oven. Place a baking steel or stone on the rack and preheat the oven to 475°F for at least 1 hour.

Place the dough round on a pizza peel or the back of an overturned baking sheet. Distribute the mozzarella evenly over the dough, edge to edge. Scatter the garlic over, then the artichokes. Using two spoons, spoon small dollops of the cream cheese all over the pizza.

In a medium bowl, combine the spinach, oil, salt, and black pepper and toss to coat the spinach with the oil. Pile the spinach mixture on the pizza (it will look like a lot but will shrink as it cooks).

Bake: Use the peel to transfer the pizza onto the steel or stone (see Load, page 49), then bake for 7 to 10 minutes, until both the bottom and top of the pizza are deeply browned and it looks crackery around the edges.

Use the peel to remove the pizza from the oven and slide it onto a wire rack. Sprinkle with the Parmesan and red pepper flakes, if using. To serve, transfer to a cutting board and cut into 1½- to 2-inch squares.

Cheeseburger

Makes one 12-inch pizza

12.5 grams (1 tablespoon) extra-virgin olive oil

170 grams (6 ounces) ground beef (80% lean)

½ teaspoon fine salt, plus more to taste

½ teaspoon freshly ground black pepper, plus more to taste

85 grams (3 ounces) yellow American cheese, chopped or torn into small pieces

29 grams (2 tablespoons) mayonnaise

1½ teaspoons ketchup

1½ teaspoons chopped cornichons

1 teaspoon cornichon brine

1 round (about 166 grams) Chicago Tavern-Style Dough (page 75)

124 grams (½ cup) Chicago Tavern-Style Pizza Sauce (page 35)

85 grams (3 ounces) low-moisture whole-milk mozzarella, shredded (¾ cup)

70 grams (2½ ounces) shredded iceberg lettuce (about 1 cup)

28 grams (1 ounce) white onion, thinly sliced (about ⅓ cup)

Some cheeseburger pizzas stop at ground beef and cheese, but this one goes all the way: It has the shredded iceberg, the crunchy onions, and best of all, the special sauce. Take care with the ground beef when you precook it—you want it cooked but not overly so, because it gets cooked a second time on top of the pizza.

Arrange a rack in the center of the oven. Place a baking steel or stone on the rack and preheat the oven to 475°F for at least 1 hour.

Heat the oil in a large skillet over medium-high heat. Add the ground beef, season with the salt and pepper, and cook, breaking the meat into pieces with a wooden spoon or spatula, until browned and crispy, 8 to 10 minutes. Use a slotted spoon to transfer to a bowl, then add the American cheese and stir until melted.

Make the burger sauce: In a small bowl, stir together the mayonnaise, ketchup, cornichons, and cornichon brine. Season to taste with pepper. Set aside.

Place the dough round on a pizza peel or the back of an overturned baking sheet. Spread the pizza sauce all the way to the edges of the dough, then distribute the mozzarella evenly over the sauce, edge to edge. Evenly distribute the ground beef over the cheese.

Bake: Use the peel to load the pizza onto the steel or stone (see Load, page 49), then bake for 7 to 10 minutes, until both the bottom and top of the pizza are deeply browned and it looks crackery around the edges.

Use the peel to remove the pizza from the oven and slide it onto a wire rack. Immediately top with the lettuce and onion and drizzle the burger sauce over. To serve, transfer to a cutting board and cut into 1½- to 2-inch squares.

Sausage and Giardiniera

Makes one 12-inch pizza

1 round (about 166 grams) Chicago Tavern-Style Dough (page 75)

124 grams (½ cup) Chicago Tavern-Style Pizza Sauce (page 35)

113 grams (4 ounces) low-moisture whole-milk mozzarella, shredded (1 cup)

14 grams (½ ounce) finely grated Parmigiano-Reggiano (¼ cup)

114 grams (4 ounces) sweet Italian sausage, casings removed

50 grams (¼ cup) Chicago-style giardiniera, store-bought or homemade (page 54), drained, patted dry, and cut into ¼- to ½-inch pieces

¼ teaspoon fennel seed, coarsely chopped or coarsely ground

2 teaspoons dried oregano

We love anything that adds big flavor to a pizza without any prep, and this pie features two such ingredients: spicy, crunchy giardiniera and fennel-packed Italian sausage. Most store-bought Chicago-style giardiniera is more spicy than tart; for a version that's more pickled and dialed in to your personal spice tolerance, make your own (see page 54).

Arrange a rack in the center of the oven. Place a baking steel or stone on the rack and preheat the oven to 475°F for at least 1 hour.

Place the dough round on a pizza peel or the back of an overturned baking sheet. Spread the pizza sauce all the way to the edges of the dough and distribute the mozzarella and Parmesan evenly over the sauce, edge to edge. Pinch the raw sausage into ½-inch pieces and evenly distribute over the pizza, followed by the giardiniera, scattering evenly. Sprinkle all over with the fennel seed.

Bake: Use the peel to load the pizza onto the steel or stone (see Load, page 49), then bake for 7 to 10 minutes, until both the bottom and top of the pizza are deeply browned and it looks crackery around the edges.

Use the peel to remove the pizza from the oven and slide it onto a wire rack. Immediately top with the oregano. To serve, transfer to a cutting board and cut into 1½- to 2-inch squares.

Calabrian Chile and Cheese

Makes one 12-inch pizza

1 round (about 166 grams) Chicago Tavern-Style Dough (page 75)

124 grams (½ cup) Chicago Tavern-Style Pizza Sauce (page 35)

113 grams (4 ounces) low-moisture whole-milk mozzarella, shredded (1 cup)

28 grams (2 tablespoons) chopped Calabrian chiles in oil

14 grams (½ ounce) finely grated Parmigiano-Reggiano (¼ cup)

Calabrian chiles are our go-to hot pepper because of where they sit on the flavor matrix: They offer a perfect balance of heat, fruitiness, and acidity. (Also, you can't beat the color.) You could put these chiles on literally any pizza in this book, where they'd serve as a flavor-enhancing condiment. But here they get the full spotlight (albeit mellowed by cheese) and become the star of the show.

Arrange a rack in the center of the oven. Place a baking steel or stone on the rack and preheat the oven to 475°F for at least 1 hour.

Place the dough round on a pizza peel or the back of an overturned baking sheet. Spread the pizza sauce all the way to the edges of the dough, then distribute the mozzarella evenly over the sauce, edge to edge. Evenly distribute the Calabrian chiles all over the cheese.

Use the peel to load the pizza onto the steel or stone (see Load, page 49), then bake for 7 to 10 minutes, until both the bottom and top of the pizza are deeply browned and it looks crackery around the edges.

Use the peel to remove the pizza from the oven and slide it onto a wire rack. Immediately shower with the Parmesan. To serve, transfer to a cutting board and cut into 1½- to 2-inch squares.

NEW HAVEN STYLE

Of all the pizzas we've tasted across the country, we find the crisp, crackery, coal-kissed pies in New Haven among the hardest to beat. They're also among the hardest to replicate. Our recipe uses bread flour to mimic the high-protein flours used at classic New Haven pizzerias such as Sally's and Frank Pepe (it's what makes the dough extensible enough to stretch thinly without tearing). We also keep the dough low in hydration, which helps ensure a maximally crisp crust—no purchase of a multiton coal-fired oven required.

New Haven pies don't have a puffy edge crust—they are thin edge to edge—so we recommend rolling this dough (see page 28). You may even want to start shaping by flattening the outer rim with your hands, just to ensure it remains as thin as the rest of the crust. Experienced bakers might enjoy the challenge of shaping this dough by hand entirely, but that's a flex you really don't need to attempt, especially the first few times you make it. The important thing is to get the pizza to the correct thinness and size, and a rolling pin is the best tool for that.

There are many forms a New Haven pie can take. The dough can be baked plain, with just olive oil and salt, and topped with what is essentially salad. Or it can get red sauce and cheese like any other pizza. The most famous New Haven pie is the clam pie, which is a tall order for home bakers—are you really going to shuck a bag of clams on a Friday night? Our solution (see page 100) is to pour garlic butter over high-quality canned clams and spoon it on the pizza right before it gets broiled. It's not the authentic New Haven clam pie, but it's a delicious homage.

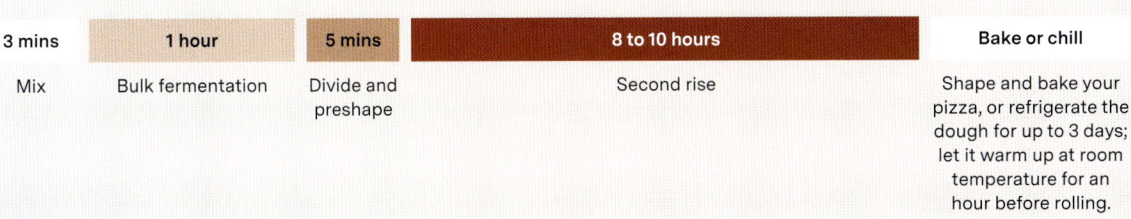

3 mins	1 hour	5 mins	8 to 10 hours	Bake or chill
Mix	Bulk fermentation	Divide and preshape	Second rise	Shape and bake your pizza, or refrigerate the dough for up to 3 days; let it warm up at room temperature for an hour before rolling.

New Haven–Style Dough

Makes 399 grams, enough for two 12-inch pizzas

240 grams (2 cups) unbleached bread flour, plus more for dusting

6 grams (1 teaspoon) fine salt

¼ teaspoon instant yeast

152 grams (⅔ cup) water, room temperature (70° to 75°F)

Make the dough: In a medium bowl, whisk together the flour, salt, and yeast until well combined. Add the water and mix until combined and homogeneous. Then use your hands to knead it in the bowl until smooth, 2 to 3 minutes. Cover and place in a warm spot (70° to 75°F) to rest for 1 hour.

Transfer the dough to a lightly floured work surface and divide into 2 equal pieces (about 199 grams per piece). Form each piece into a tight ball and place seam side down in a lightly greased container. Cover tightly and let rise at room temperature for 8 to 10 hours. The dough is now ready to use on the pages that follow, or it can be refrigerated for up to 3 days. Let refrigerated dough rest at room temperature while your oven preheats, at least 1 hour.

Cheese

Makes one 12-inch pizza

Bread flour or all-purpose flour, for dusting

1 ball (about 199 grams) New Haven–Style Dough (page 89)

Semolina flour or cornmeal, for dusting

130 grams (½ cup) No-Cook Pizza Sauce (page 34)

57 grams (2 ounces) low-moisture whole-milk mozzarella, shredded (½ cup)

14 grams (½ ounce) finely grated pecorino Romano (¼ cup)

Dried oregano

Extra-virgin olive oil

The cheese pie is one of New Haven's two signatures (the clam pie is the other; see our version on page 100). But this cheese pie is anything but plain: The bright no-cook sauce and generous finish of pecorino Romano give it a stand-out savoriness, proving once again that simplicity wins.

Arrange racks in the lower and upper thirds of the oven. Place a baking steel or stone on the lower rack and preheat the oven to 500°F for at least 1 hour.

Shape the pizza: Flour your work surface and place the dough on it. Flip the dough over so that both sides are coated with flour. Pat and press to remove any bubbles and flatten and extend the dough into a round, starting first with the edges and working toward the center.

Switch to a rolling pin and roll to an even thickness of ⅛ inch and a rough 13-inch diameter. While rolling, flip the dough and flour the surface as necessary to prevent sticking. If the dough snaps back when rolling, set it aside for 10 minutes to allow the gluten to relax, then try again. Lightly dust a peel or an overturned baking sheet with semolina and transfer the dough to the peel. If the dough retracts when transferring it to the peel, gently stretch the edges to re-form it.

Evenly spread the sauce over the surface of the dough, leaving a ½-inch border, then distribute the mozzarella evenly over the sauce. Sprinkle on the pecorino and a few pinches of oregano, and drizzle a thin stream of oil over the pizza.

Bake: Use the peel to load the pizza onto the steel or stone (see Load, page 49), then bake for 5 minutes. Check the bottom of the crust—it should be spotted and charred in places, and the edge crust should start to have some color. If not, rotate the pizza and bake for another 1 to 2 minutes.

When the bottom has sufficient color, use the peel to transfer the pizza to the top rack, switch the oven to broil, and broil for 2 to 3 minutes, until well charred in spots. (Don't walk away—pizza can go from perfectly charred to burnt quickly.) Home ovens vary substantially, so use the visual cues and your own preferences to gauge when you've achieved the perfect bake.

Use the peel to remove the pizza from the oven and transfer to a wire rack. Let cool briefly, then slice and serve.

Brussels Sprouts and Smoked Mozzarella

Makes one 12-inch pizza

25 grams (2 tablespoons) extra-virgin olive oil, divided

220 grams (2 medium) shallots, sliced into ¼-inch rounds, rings separated

¾ teaspoon fine salt, plus more to taste

¾ teaspoon freshly ground black pepper, plus more to taste

28 grams (2 tablespoons) water

26 grams (2 tablespoons) apple cider vinegar

20 grams (1 tablespoon) maple syrup

1 small sprig fresh rosemary

70 grams (2½ ounces) Brussels sprouts, thinly sliced

Bread flour or all-purpose flour, for dusting

1 ball (about 199 grams) New Haven–Style Dough (page 89)

Semolina flour or cornmeal, for dusting

113 grams (4 ounces) smoked whole-milk mozzarella, thinly sliced into rounds

14 grams (½ ounce) Parmigiano-Reggiano, finely grated (¼ cup)

Mozzarella is usually a texture play—it's a little salty and milky, sure, but it's really on the pizza to add creaminess. Smoked mozz is an entirely different ballgame: it contributes texture but also the bold flavor of barbecue. Here the mozzarella's smokiness provides a flavorful base for the sweet-earthy Brussels sprouts and agrodolce shallots.

Arrange racks in the lower and upper thirds of your oven. Place a baking steel or stone on the lower rack and preheat the oven to 500°F for at least 1 hour.

Heat half of the oil in a large skillet over medium-high heat. Add the shallots, season with the salt and pepper, and cook, stirring, until browned and starting to soften, 3 to 4 minutes. Reduce the heat to medium and add the water, vinegar, maple syrup, and rosemary sprig and cook, stirring occasionally, until the liquid has reduced and the shallots are soft, about 3 minutes. Remove from the heat, discard the rosemary sprig, and set aside until ready to use.

In a small bowl, combine the Brussels sprouts, the remaining oil, and a few pinches each of salt and pepper and toss to coat. Set aside.

Shape the pizza: Flour your work surface and place the dough on it. Flip the dough over so that both sides are coated with flour. Pat and press to remove any bubbles and flatten and extend the round, starting first with the edges and working toward the center.

Switch to a rolling pin and roll to an even thickness of ⅛ inch and a rough 13-inch diameter. While rolling, flip the dough and flour the surface as necessary to prevent sticking. If the dough snaps back when rolling, set it aside for 10 minutes to allow the gluten to relax, then try again. Lightly dust a peel or an overturned baking sheet with semolina and transfer the dough to the peel. If the dough retracts when transferring it to the peel, gently stretch the edges to re-form it.

Evenly spread the shallots over the surface of the dough, leaving a ½-inch border, then arrange the mozzarella slices in a single layer. Top with the Brussels sprouts, distributing evenly.

Bake: Use the peel to transfer the pizza onto the steel or stone (see Load, page 49), then bake for 5 minutes. Check the bottom of the crust—it should be spotted and charred in places, and the edge crust should start to have some color. If not, rotate the pizza and bake for another 1 to 2 minutes.

When the bottom has sufficient color, use the peel to transfer the pizza to the top rack, switch the oven to broil, and broil for 2 to 3 minutes, until well charred in spots. (Don't walk away—pizza can go from perfectly charred to burnt quickly.) Home ovens vary substantially, so use the visual cues and your own preferences to gauge when you've achieved the perfect bake.

Use the peel to remove the pizza from the oven and transfer to a wire rack. Immediately top with the Parmesan, then let cool briefly. Slice and serve.

Amatriciana

Makes one 12-inch pizza

113 grams (4 ounces) pancetta, cut into ¼-inch cubes

1 small red onion, thinly sliced (about 140 grams/5 ounces)

½ teaspoon red pepper flakes, plus more for serving

Bread flour or all-purpose flour, for dusting

1 ball (about 199 grams) New Haven–Style Dough (page 89)

Semolina flour or cornmeal, for dusting

130 grams (½ cup) No-Cook Pizza Sauce (page 34)

28 grams (1 ounce) pecorino Romano, finely grated (½ cup), divided

Cured pork, tomatoes, and pecorino Romano are nonnegotiable on anything that calls itself Amatriciana. Here that pork is pancetta that's been irresistibly crisped up in a skillet, leaving a gold mine of rendered pancetta fat behind. To take advantage of that fat, we soften an onion in it and spread that mixture over the pie. It's not traditional, but once you try it, you'll never make Amatriciana without it.

Arrange racks in the lower and upper thirds of the oven. Place a baking steel or stone on the lower rack and preheat the oven to 500°F for at least 1 hour.

Put the pancetta in a medium skillet and cook over medium-low heat, stirring occasionally, until the fat has rendered out and the pancetta is browned and crispy, 10 to 15 minutes. Line a plate with paper towels, then use a slotted spoon to transfer the pancetta to the plate, leaving behind the fat in the pan.

Return the pan to medium heat. Add the onion and cook, stirring occasionally, until just starting to soften, about 2 minutes. Remove from the heat, add the red pepper flakes, and set aside until ready to use.

Shape the pizza: Flour your work surface and set the dough on it. Flip the dough over so that both sides are coated with flour. Pat and press to remove any bubbles and flatten and extend the round, starting first with the edges and working toward the center.

Switch to a rolling pin and roll to an even thickness of ⅛ inch and a rough 13-inch diameter. While rolling, flip the dough and flour the surface as necessary to prevent sticking. If the dough snaps back when rolling, set it aside for 10 minutes to allow the gluten to relax, then try again. Lightly dust a peel or an overturned baking sheet with semolina and transfer the dough to the peel. If the dough retracts when transferring it to the peel, gently stretch the edges to re-form it.

Evenly spread the sauce over the surface of the dough, leaving a ½-inch border, then distribute the pancetta, onion (along with any fat that remains in the pan), and half the pecorino evenly over the pizza.

Bake: Use the peel to transfer the pizza onto the steel or stone (see Load, page 49), then bake for 5 minutes. Check the bottom of the crust—it should be spotted and charred in places, and the edge crust should start to have some color. If not, rotate the pizza and bake for another 1 to 2 minutes.

When the bottom has sufficient color, use the peel to transfer the pizza to the top rack, switch the oven to broil, and broil for 2 to 3 minutes, until well charred in spots. (Don't walk away—pizza can go from perfectly charred to burnt quickly.) Home ovens vary substantially, so use the visual cues and your own preferences to gauge when you've achieved the perfect bake.

Use the peel to remove the pizza from the oven and transfer to a wire rack. Immediately top with the remaining pecorino and more red pepper flakes, if desired. Let cool briefly, then slice and serve.

Puttanesca

Makes one 12-inch pizza

Bread flour or all-purpose flour, for dusting

1 ball (about 199 grams) New Haven–Style Dough (page 89)

Semolina flour or cornmeal, for dusting

130 grams (½ cup) No-Cook Pizza Sauce (page 34)

113 grams (4 ounces) low-moisture whole-milk mozzarella, shredded (1 cup)

60 grams (¼ cup) pitted, chopped kalamata olives, or a mix of kalamata and green olives

9 grams (1 tablespoon) capers

5 whole oil-packed anchovy fillets, torn into thirds

2 grams (1 tablespoon) finely chopped fresh flat-leaf parsley

Finely ground black pepper, for finishing

Garlicky Panko (page 53), for finishing, optional

Look, a pizza that sports both olives *and* anchovies is going to be controversial for some folks—ask around before you serve it at a party. This pie is a good candidate for Garlicky Panko (page 53), which adds a nice crunch.

Arrange racks in the lower and upper thirds of your oven. Place a baking steel or stone on the lower rack and preheat the oven to 500°F for at least 1 hour.

Shape the pizza: Flour your work surface and set the dough on it. Flip the dough over so that both sides are coated with flour. Pat and press to remove any bubbles and flatten and extend the round, starting first with the edges and working toward the center.

Switch to a rolling pin and roll to an even thickness of ⅛ inch and a rough 13-inch diameter. While rolling, flip the dough and flour the surface as necessary to prevent sticking. If the dough snaps back when rolling, set it aside for 10 minutes to allow the gluten to relax, then try again. Lightly dust a peel or an overturned baking sheet with semolina and transfer the dough to the peel. If the dough retracts when transferring it to the peel, gently re-form it.

Evenly spread the sauce over the surface of the dough, leaving a ½-inch border. Distribute the cheese evenly over the sauce, then dot the pizza with the olives, capers, and anchovy pieces.

Bake: Use the peel to transfer the pizza onto the steel or stone (see Load, page 49), then bake for 5 minutes. Check the bottom of the crust—it should be spotted and charred in places, and the edge crust should start to have some color. If not, rotate the pizza and bake for another 1 to 2 minutes.

When the bottom has sufficient color, use the peel to transfer the pizza to the top rack, switch the oven to broil, and broil for 2 to 3 minutes, until well charred in spots. (Don't walk away—pizza can go from perfectly charred to burnt quickly.) Home ovens vary substantially, so use the visual cues and your own preferences to gauge when you've achieved the perfect bake.

Use the peel to remove the pizza from the oven and transfer to a wire rack. Let cool briefly, then sprinkle with the parsley, pepper, and panko (if using). Slice and serve.

Clam

Makes one 12-inch pizza

56 grams (4 tablespoons) unsalted butter

2 garlic cloves, minced

¼ teaspoon red pepper flakes

28 grams (2 tablespoons) fresh lemon juice

2 tablespoons chopped fresh flat-leaf parsley, plus ¼ cup fresh parsley leaves, for garnish

2 tablespoons chopped fresh oregano

184 grams (one 6.5-ounce can) chopped clams, drained

All-purpose flour, for dusting

1 ball (about 199 grams) New Haven–Style Dough (page 89)

Semolina flour or cornmeal, for dusting

75 grams (¼ cup) Parmesan Béchamel (page 37)

Freshly ground black pepper

Flaky salt, such as Maldon, for garnish

New Haven's signature pie (see its cohort, the Cheese pie, on page 90) is dependent on great, freshly shucked clams. We think that's a tall order for a home baker, so our method calls for adding canned clams (which are fully cooked) to the pizza halfway through the bake. Spooning buttery, spicy clams over a crispy crust isn't the way they do it in New Haven, but it delivers fresh, briny flavors just the same.

Arrange racks in the lower and upper thirds of your oven. Place a baking steel or stone on the lower rack and preheat the oven to 500°F for at least 1 hour.

In a small saucepan, melt the butter over medium-low heat. Add the garlic and red pepper flakes and cook for 45 seconds to 1 minute, until you can smell the garlic; don't let the garlic brown. Remove from the heat and add the lemon juice, chopped parsley, oregano, and clams. Set aside.

Shape the dough: Flour your work surface and place the dough on it. Flip the dough over so that both sides are coated with flour. Pat and press to remove any bubbles and flatten and extend the dough into a round, starting first with the edges and working toward the center.

Switch to a rolling pin and roll the dough to an even thickness of ⅛ inch and a rough 13-inch diameter. While rolling, flip the dough and flour the surface as necessary to prevent sticking. If the dough snaps back when rolling, set it aside for 10 minutes to allow the gluten to relax, then try again. Lightly dust a peel or an overturned baking sheet with semolina and transfer the dough to the peel. If the dough retracts when transferring it to the peel, gently stretch the edges to re-form it.

Gently spread the béchamel over the dough, leaving a ½-inch border. Sprinkle on some black pepper.

Bake: Use the peel to transfer the pizza onto the steel or stone (see Load, page 49), then bake for 5 minutes. Check the bottom of the crust—it should be spotted and charred in places, and the edge crust should start to have some color. If not, rotate the pizza and bake for another 1 to 2 minutes.

When the bottom has sufficient color, use the peel to transfer the pizza from the oven to your work surface (keeping it on the peel). Spoon the clam mixture over the entire pizza.

Use the peel to transfer the pizza to the top rack, switch the oven to broil, and broil for 2 to 3 minutes, until well charred in spots. (Don't walk away—pizza can go from perfectly charred to burnt quickly.) Home ovens vary substantially, so use the visual cues and your own preferences to gauge when you've achieved the perfect bake.

Use the peel to remove the pizza from the oven and transfer to a wire rack. Let cool briefly, then garnish with the parsley leaves and a sprinkling of flaky salt. Slice and serve.

NEW YORK STYLE

On a trip to New York during the writing of this book, we visited more than thirty slice shops. At each one we bought a couple of slices, took them to a park bench, and, starting at the crust end, ripped them open and stuck our noses in. Most of them smelled sweetly yeasty, a sign that the dough had fermented in the fridge the night before. A few smelled more sour, and those probably used sourdough culture instead of (or in addition to) yeast. Some slices didn't smell like anything at all, and those were typically the ones that tasted bland, too.

Did we look a little weird with our noses stuck in pizza crust? Probably. But in New York nobody bats an eyelash. And besides, we were on a mission to learn as much about these pizzas as possible so that we could write a recipe that replicates them. The formula we landed on honors the New York nonnegotiables: a little bit of sugar and oil in the dough, and a relatively low hydration. Bread flour is key here as it gives us just enough tug while also helping us achieve a thin but very sturdy pie. For the method, we follow in the footsteps of our favorite pizzerias: We mix on day one, divide and ball an hour later, then tuck the doughs in for a long overnight room-temperature fermentation before chilling or baking on day two. Once the doughs have had their room-temperature rise, they hold for a surprisingly long time in the fridge, which makes this a dough that can work easily with your schedule.

Any slice you get from a New York slice shop is twice baked: once to cook it through, and the second time to recrisp, remelt, and reheat (so it's screaming hot when you take your first bite). You can—and should!—do the same at home. Make a few pies, cut them into NYC-size slices (see diagram, page 111), and put them on the hot stone again right before eating. The result is shockingly authentic. One tester, a Vermonter who grew up in Brooklyn, was almost brought to tears when she first tasted it—and you know how hard it is to make a real New Yorker cry.

5 mins	1 hour	5 mins	8 to 10 hours	Bake or chill
Mix	Bulk fermentation	Divide and preshape	Second rise	Shape and bake your pizza, or refrigerate the dough for up to 3 days; let it warm up at room temperature for an hour before stretching.

New York–Style Dough

Makes 602 grams, enough for two 13-inch pizzas

360 grams (3 cups) unbleached bread flour, plus more for dusting

12 grams (scant 1 tablespoon) sugar

12 grams (2 teaspoons) fine salt

¼ teaspoon instant yeast

12 grams (scant 1 tablespoon) vegetable oil

206 grams (¾ cup plus 2½ tablespoons) cool water (60° to 70°F)

Make the dough: In a large bowl, combine the flour, sugar, salt, and yeast and stir to combine, then add the oil and water. Mix to combine, then knead the dough by hand in the bowl until you have a rough but cohesive dough. Cover and let the dough rest at room temperature for 1 hour.

On a lightly floured surface, divide the dough into 2 equal pieces (about 300 grams per piece). Form each piece into a tight ball and place seam side down in a lightly greased container. Cover tightly and let it rest at room temperature for 8 to 10 hours. The dough is now ready to use in the recipes on the pages that follow, or it can be refrigerated for up to 3 days. Let refrigerated dough rest at room temperature while your oven preheats, at least 1 hour.

Cheese

Makes one 13-inch pizza

All-purpose flour, for dusting

1 ball (about 301 grams) New York–Style Dough (page 105)

Semolina or cornmeal, for dusting

130 grams (½ cup) No-Cook Pizza Sauce, New York variation (page 34)

99 grams (3½ ounces) low-moisture whole-milk mozzarella, shredded (¾ cup)

6 grams (2 tablespoons) grated Parmigiano-Reggiano, plus more for topping

Red pepper flakes, for finishing

Dried oregano, for finishing

When it's hot and *very* crispy, and you've shaken the perfect amount of Parm, oregano, and red pepper flakes on it, a New York–style cheese slice is a life-affirming food. Just one oversized slice (see page 111) can remind you that there's good in the world, that pleasure is worth seeking out, and that the perfect meal really is the one you're holding and folding in your hands.

Arrange racks in the lower and upper thirds of the oven. Place a baking steel or stone on the lower rack and preheat the oven to 500°F for at least 1 hour.

Shape the pizza: Dust your work surface generously with flour. Place the dough on the work surface. Without distorting the round dough, flip it over so that both sides are coated with flour. Use your fingertips to gently depress the center of the dough (avoiding the outer edge), pressing out the gas and beginning to flatten and expand the dough into a round.

Continue using your fingertips to press the center of the dough outward until you have an 8-inch circle. Gently grab the dough on the east and west sides, careful to position your grip *over* the edge crust, and tug the dough in an east-west direction. Rotate the dough and repeat the tug. Continue rotating and tugging until the dough round measures about 10 inches. Lift the pizza from the work surface and use your knuckles to gently stretch the dough into a 12-inch round. Use two hands at once to gently move the dough in a circle, allowing gravity to do most of the work for you. If the dough resists stretching, let it rest for 5 to 10 minutes to allow the gluten to relax, then try again. If the dough is at all sticky, use more flour. Return the dough to the floured work surface and give a few more east-west tugs until the round measures 13 inches.

Lightly dust a peel or an overturned baking sheet with semolina and transfer the dough to the peel. If the dough retracts when transferring it to the peel, gently re-form it. Shimmy the dough on the peel to ensure it's not sticking; if it is, lift the edge of the crust and add more semolina.

Evenly spread the sauce over the surface of the dough, leaving a ½-inch border, then distribute the mozzarella and Parmesan evenly over the sauce.

Bake: Use the peel to transfer the pizza onto the steel or stone (see Load, page 49), then bake for 5 minutes. Check the bottom of the crust—it should be spotted and charred in places, and the edge crust should start to have some color. If not, rotate the pizza and bake for another 1 to 2 minutes.

When the bottom has sufficient color, use the peel to transfer the pizza to the top rack, switch the oven to broil, and broil for 2 to 3 minutes, until well charred in spots. (Don't walk away—pizza can go from perfectly charred to burnt quickly.) Home ovens vary substantially, so use the visual cues and your own preferences to gauge when you've achieved the perfect bake.

Use the peel to remove the pizza from the oven and slide it onto a wire rack to cool briefly. Sprinkle with more Parmesan, red pepper flakes, and oregano to taste. Cut the pizza into sixths, two "super slices," or one "mega slice" (see page 111) and serve.

Pepperoni and Jalapeño

Makes one 13-inch pizza

All-purpose flour, for dusting

1 ball (about 301 grams) New York–Style Dough (page 105)

Semolina or cornmeal, for dusting

130 grams (½ cup) No-Cook Pizza Sauce, New York variation (page 34)

99 grams (3½ ounces) low-moisture whole-milk mozzarella, shredded (¾ cup)

55 grams (2 ounces) cupping pepperoni (see sidebar, page 110)

½ to 1 small jalapeño pepper, thinly sliced

40 grams (2 tablespoons) Hot Honey (page 52), for finishing

A now-classic slice shop offering, specifically for hotheads. (For a less spicy version, use the lower amount of jalapeño and cut out the seeds.) Hot honey is a perfect finisher for this pie because it completes the flavor trifecta, making each slice hot *and* sweet *and* salty.

Arrange racks in the lower and upper thirds of the oven. Place a baking steel or stone on the lower rack and preheat the oven to 500°F for at least 1 hour.

Shape the dough: Dust your work surface generously with flour. Place the dough on the work surface and gently coat both sides with flour. Use your fingertips to gently depress the center of the dough (avoiding the outer edge), pressing out the gas and flattening the dough into a round.

Continue using your fingertips to press the center of the dough outward until you have an 8-inch circle. Gently grab the dough on the east and west sides, careful to position your grip *over* the edge crust, and tug the dough in an east-west direction. Rotate the dough and repeat the tug. Continue rotating and tugging until the dough round measures about 10 inches. Lift the pizza from the work surface and use your knuckles to gently stretch the dough into a 12-inch circle. Use two hands at once to gently move the dough in a circle, allowing gravity to do most of the work for you. If the dough resists stretching, let it rest for 5 to 10 minutes to allow the gluten to relax, then try again. If the dough is at all sticky, use more flour. Return the dough to the work surface and give a few more east-west tugs until the round measures 13 inches.

Lightly dust a peel or an overturned baking sheet with semolina and transfer the dough to the peel. If the dough retracts when transferring it to the peel, gently re-form it. Shimmy the dough on the peel to ensure it's not sticking; if it is, lift the edge of the crust and add more semolina.

Evenly spread the sauce over the surface of the dough, leaving a ½-inch border, then sprinkle the mozzarella over, distributing in an even layer, and top with the pepperoni and jalapeño slices.

Bake: Use the peel to transfer the pizza onto the steel or stone (see Load, page 49) then bake for 5 minutes. Check the bottom of the crust—it should be spotted and charred in places, and the edge crust should start to have some color. If not, rotate the pizza and bake for another 1 to 2 minutes.

When the bottom has sufficient color, use the peel to transfer the pizza to the top rack, switch the oven to broil, and broil for 2 to 3 minutes, until well charred in spots. (Don't walk away—pizza can go from perfectly charred to burnt quickly.) Home ovens vary substantially, so use the visual cues and your own preferences to gauge when you've achieved the perfect bake.

Use the peel to remove the pizza from the oven and slide it onto a wire rack to cool briefly. Drizzle the hot honey all over the pie, then cut into sixths, two "super slices," or one "mega slice" (see page 111) and serve.

WHAT IS PEPPERONI CUPPING, AND WHY DOES IT MATTER?

Pizza people, like tax preparers, engineers, and coffee nerds, notoriously sweat the details. Ask what cheese a pizza person likes and you'll get a dissertation on the difference between Grande and di Bufala. Wade into a discussion of dough? Prepare to hear a lot about hydration.

Enter pepperoni. Until a few years ago, the term "cupping" wasn't on anybody's radar. Now it's the topic of endless pizza forum threads.

But what is cupping, and should we care? Cupping is simply the upward-curling response some pepperoni has to heat. As the casing heats, it contracts, forming small perfect cups that pool with pepperoni juice. (Shots, anyone?)

It's not just about aesthetics. When pepperoni cups, it actually tastes better. As the pieces shrink and rise up, they crisp slightly along the rim. The result is a charred top, which balances perfectly against a softer middle (the portion of pepperoni that meets the sauce and cheese). Cupping is also a sign of quality. In general, pepperoni in a natural casing cups more easily than those in fiber casings. And, broadly speaking, sausage in a natural casing is made with more care. It's seasoned better. It's often lightly smoked. Put simply, it's superior.

A lot of pepperoni is now made specifically to cup (look for the word "cup" or "cupping" on the packaging). But what if your pepperoni isn't cupping? First, check that the pepperoni has a natural casing. Next, take a few slices and place them in a sauté pan, cooking until they curl toward the heat of the pan. If your pepperoni curls in the pan but not the oven, try increasing your oven temperature. Still no luck? Slice thickness might play a role. Overly thick or overly thin slices may resist cupping; try something in the middle and it should cup just right.

HOW TO CUT NEW YORK–STYLE "SUPER SLICES" AND ONE "MEGA SLICE"

New York slice shops make their pies big enough that each slice is a meal—if it doesn't hang over the paper plate it's served on, you deserve a refund. Most home ovens are too small to handle pizzas of this size, but you can still get NY-style slices out of a 13-inch pie. Here's how:

For two "super slices": Cut the edges off the ends of the pie (about 1½ inches off each side) so that you are left with a rectangle of pizza. Slice the rectangle in half on the diagonal into two "super slices."

For one "mega slice": Make a vertical cut about two inches from the left edge of the pie, then make another cut at about a 50-degree angle from the first one, creating a single "mega slice."

Caprese

Makes one 13-inch pizza

113 grams (4 ounces) fresh mozzarella, torn into bite-size pieces

28 grams (2 tablespoons) heavy cream

227 grams (8 ounces) cherry tomatoes, halved (1⅛ cups)

½ teaspoon fine salt

All-purpose flour, for dusting

1 ball (about 301 grams) New York–Style Dough (page 105)

Semolina or cornmeal, for dusting

96 grams (6 tablespoons) Basil Pesto (page 37)

99 grams (3½ ounces) low-moisture whole-milk mozzarella, shredded (¾ cup)

Small handful of fresh basil leaves, for finishing

12.5 grams (1 tablespoon) extra-virgin olive oil, for finishing

A few tricks help this pie reach maximum potential. Salting the fresh tomatoes purges them of excess water, and also ensures that they're well seasoned. Using pesto rather than tomato sauce gives the pie an herbal punch. And stirring cream into the torn mozzarella (a trick we learned from chef Abra Berens) gives it burrata's texture without burrata's price.

Arrange racks in the lower and upper thirds of the oven. Place a baking steel or stone on the lower rack and preheat the oven to 500°F for at least 1 hour.

Prepare the toppings: In a small bowl, combine the fresh mozzarella and heavy cream. Set aside. In a medium bowl, toss the tomatoes and salt and let stand at room temperature for 20 minutes. Drain the tomatoes and pat dry to remove excess moisture.

Shape the dough: Dust your work surface generously with flour. Place the dough on the work surface. Without distorting the round dough, flip it over so that both sides are coated with flour. Use your fingertips to gently depress the center of the dough (avoiding the outer edge), pressing out the gas and beginning to flatten and expand the dough into a round.

Continue using your fingertips to press the center of the dough outward until you have an 8-inch circle. Gently grab the dough on the east and west sides, careful to position your grip *over* the edge crust, so as not to deflate it. Use your hands to gently tug the dough in an east-west direction. Rotate the dough and repeat the tug. Continue rotating and tugging until the dough round measures about 10 inches. Lift the pizza from the work surface and use your knuckles to gently stretch the dough into a 12-inch circle. Use two hands at once to gently move the dough in a circle, allowing gravity to do most of the work for you, rather than pulling on the dough (pulling will stretch the center more than the edges). If the dough resists stretching, return it to your floured work surface and let it rest for 5 to 10 minutes to allow the gluten to relax, then try again. If the dough is at all sticky, use more flour. Return the dough to the floured work surface and give a few more east-west tugs until the round measures 13 inches.

Lightly dust a peel or an overturned baking sheet with semolina and transfer the dough to the peel. If the dough retracts when transferring it to the peel, gently re-form it. Shimmy the dough on the peel to ensure it's not sticking; if it is, lift the edge of the crust and add more semolina.

Recipe continues

Bake: Evenly spread the pesto over the surface of the dough, leaving a ½-inch border, then sprinkle the shredded mozzarella on top. Evenly top with the tomatoes. Use the peel to transfer the pizza onto the steel or stone (see Load, page 49) and bake for 6 to 8 minutes. Check the bottom of the crust—it should be spotted and charred in places, and the edge crust should start to have some color. If not, rotate the pizza and bake for another 1 to 2 minutes.

When the bottom has sufficient color, use the peel to transfer the pizza to the top rack, switch the oven to broil, and broil for 2 to 3 minutes, until well charred in spots. (Don't walk away—pizza can go from perfectly charred to burnt quickly.) Home ovens vary substantially, so use the visual cues and your own preferences to gauge when you've achieved the perfect bake.

Use the peel to remove the pizza from the oven and slide it onto a wire rack to cool briefly. Spoon over the fresh mozzarella-cream mixture, distributing evenly, and top with the basil leaves. Drizzle with oil, then cut into sixths, two "super slices," or one "mega slice" (see page 111) and serve.

Cheesy Greens Calzone

Makes one 10-inch calzone

12.5 grams (1 tablespoon) extra-virgin olive oil, plus more for brushing

½ medium yellow onion (about 86 grams/3 ounces), thinly sliced (about ⅔ cup)

4 garlic cloves, finely chopped

113 grams (4 ounces) kale, stemmed and chopped (about 5½ cups)

½ teaspoon fine salt

28 grams (2 tablespoons) water

57 grams (2 ounces) fresh baby spinach (about 2 cups)

All-purpose flour, for dusting

1 ball (about 301 grams) New York–Style Dough (page 105)

Semolina or cornmeal, for dusting

85 grams (3 ounces) low-moisture whole-milk mozzarella, shredded (¾ cup)

141 grams (5 ounces) whole-milk ricotta (½ cup plus 2 tablespoons)

14 grams (½ ounce) Parmigiano-Reggiano, finely grated (¼ cup)

Marinara Sauce (page 35), warmed, for dipping (optional)

There's only so much cheese you can fit on a pizza. But in a calzone you can triple down, which is what we do here, filling it with mozzarella, ricotta, and Parm. Take care with the seam and make sure it's airtight—this filling is opportunistic and will burst out of any gap it finds.

Arrange racks in the lower and upper thirds of the oven. Place a baking steel or stone on the lower rack and preheat the oven to 450°F for at least 1 hour.

Make the filling: Heat the oil in a large skillet over medium-high heat. Add the onion and cook, stirring frequently, until browned, about 4 minutes. Add the garlic and cook, stirring, until fragrant, 30 seconds. Add the kale, salt, and water and cook until the kale is wilted, about 2 minutes. Add the spinach and continue to cook until the spinach has wilted and all the liquid in the pan has evaporated, about 2 minutes. Remove from the heat and let cool before using.

Shape the dough: Dust your work surface generously with flour. Place the dough on the work surface. Without distorting the round dough, flip it over so that both sides are coated with flour. Use your fingertips to gently depress the center of the dough (avoiding the outer edge), pressing out the gas and beginning to flatten and expand the dough into a round.

Continue using your fingertips to press the center of the dough outward until you have an 8-inch circle. Gently grab the dough on the east and west sides, careful to position your grip *over* the edge crust, and tug the dough in an east-west direction. Rotate the dough and repeat the tug. Continue rotating and tugging until the dough round measures about 10 inches. Lift the pizza from the work surface and use your knuckles to gently stretch the dough into a 12-inch circle. Use two hands at once to gently move the dough in a circle, allowing gravity to do most of the work for you. If the dough resists stretching, let it rest for 5 to 10 minutes to allow the gluten to relax, then try again. If the dough is at all sticky, use more flour. Return the dough to the floured work surface and give a few more east-west tugs until the round measures 13 inches.

Lightly dust a peel or an overturned baking sheet with semolina and transfer the shaped dough to the peel. If the dough retracts when transferring it to the peel, gently re-form it. Shimmy the dough on the peel to ensure it's not sticking; if it is, lift the edge of the crust and add more semolina.

Spoon the cooked greens on half of the dough round, leaving a 1½-inch border. Top with the mozzarella, ricotta, and Parmesan. Fold the dough round over the filling to enclose, forming a half-moon, and crimp to seal.

Bake: Use the peel to transfer the calzone onto the steel or stone (see Load, page 49) and bake for 4 minutes. Use the peel to transfer the calzone to the top rack and continue to bake until deeply golden, 6 to 8 minutes. Use the peel to remove the calzone from the oven and slide it onto a wire rack. Brush a thin layer of olive oil all over the calzone and let cool for 5 minutes before serving. To serve, cut into wedges. If you'd like, serve with warm marinara sauce alongside, for dipping.

PIZZA ALLA PALA

Pizza alla pala hails from Rome, but it couldn't be more different from the other Roman pizza in this book, pizza tonda (page 59). Whereas the tonda is thin and crackery, pizza alla pala is a high-hydration dough that bakes up into a crisp cloudlike thing akin to ciabatta.

In Rome, pizza alla pala (which, when baked in a pan, is known as pizza in teglia) takes several forms. The simplest preparation, called pizza bianca, is topped with nothing other than olive oil and salt, and it's absolutely dreamy this way: light, crisp, salty, aromatic. (There's a reason you see so many people eating them out of waxed paper sleeves as they stroll the Campo de' Fiori.)

But pizza alla pala doesn't stop there. It can be split open horizontally and made into a panino stuffed with everything from oil-packed tuna to the classic Roman combination of mortadella, burrata, and toasted pistachios. Or pizza alla pala can be topped without being split, turning it into essentially an open-faced sandwich. That's the approach used by one of Rome's most famous pizzerias, Gabriele Bonci's Pizzarium, and it's the approach we've taken in the pages that follow.

This is the time to grab the good stuff. Pizza alla pala is a canvas for the freshest, crispest salads, the creamiest ricotta, and the finest (and thinnest!) prosciutto you can afford. Use the best-quality ingredients you can find, and pizza alla pala becomes an unbeatable lunch. Cut into thin slices, it's also a great cocktail hour snack.

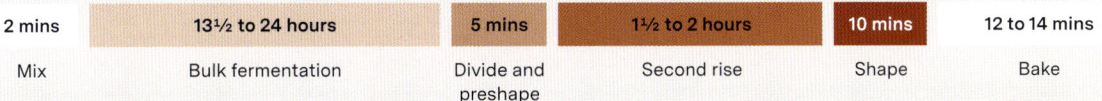

2 mins	13½ to 24 hours	5 mins	1½ to 2 hours	10 mins	12 to 14 mins
Mix	Bulk fermentation	Divide and preshape	Second rise	Shape	Bake

Pizza Bianca Dough

Makes 720 grams, enough for two 16 × 5-inch pizzas

360 grams (3 cups) unbleached all-purpose flour, plus more for dusting

21 grams (2 tablespoons) semolina flour, plus more for shaping

9 grams (1½ teaspoons) fine salt

2 grams (¾ teaspoon) instant yeast

303 grams (1 cup plus ⅓ cup) room-temperature water (70° to 75°F)

25 grams (2 tablespoons) extra-virgin olive oil, plus more for brushing

Flaky salt, such as Maldon, for sprinkling

Make the dough: In a large bowl or the bowl of a stand mixer fitted with the dough hook, combine the flours, salt, and yeast and stir briefly to combine. Add the water and stir until you have a shaggy, sticky dough with no dry, floury patches, about 1 minute. Gather the dough into a rough ball. Cover and let it rest at room temperature for 30 minutes.

Uncover the dough and perform a bowl fold: Using a wet hand, grab a section of dough from one side, lift it up, then press it down into the middle. Repeat, turning the bowl 90 degrees (a quarter turn) after each stretch, until the dough won't elongate easily and forms a smooth, tight round ball, 10 to 15 times total. Turn the dough over, placing it seam side down in the bowl. Cover and let the dough rest at room temperature for at least 1 hour and up to 2 hours.

Perform a second bowl fold: Using a wet hand, perform another round of folds. Turn the dough over, placing it seam side down in the bowl. Cover and refrigerate the dough for 12 to 24 hours.

Preshape the dough: Transfer the dough to a lightly floured work surface and divide into 2 equal pieces (about 360 grams per piece). On another part of your work surface, create a bed of semolina flour.

Gently stretch each piece of dough into a rectangle, roughly 7 × 5 inches, with a long side parallel to you. Fold each piece like a letter along the long axis: First fold the top edge two-thirds of the way down, then fold the bottom edge upward to reach the top. After folding, each piece will measure roughly 7 × 3½ inches.

Transfer the dough pieces, seam side down, onto the bed of semolina. Cover and let it rest until it's relaxed enough to stretch, 1½ to 2 hours. An hour before baking, preheat the oven to 500°F with a baking steel or stone placed on the center rack.

Shape the dough: Working with one piece at a time, lift the dough briefly to release it from the surface. (Add additional semolina if it's sticking.) Heavily dust the top of the dough with additional semolina. Using your fingertips, dimple the dough from end to end. (Press firmly but not so hard that you press through the dough.) Lift the dough from your work surface and let gravity elongate it to roughly 16 inches in length. Transfer to a large piece of parchment paper, leaving room for the second piece. Stretch the dough to form a rectangular flatbread measuring roughly 16 × 5 inches. Repeat with the second piece of dough, placing it next to the first on the parchment.

Drizzle each piece of dough with 1 tablespoon (12.5 grams) of the oil and sprinkle with flaky salt. Transfer the parchment and dough onto a peel.

Bake: Use the peel to load the dough (still on the parchment) onto the steel or stone (see Load, page 49) and bake until golden brown and crispy, 12 to 14 minutes.

Remove the pizzas from the oven and transfer to a wire rack to cool briefly. Eat right away, or let cool slightly and top (see the recipes on the pages that follow).

Prosciutto and Arugula

Makes two pizzas; serves 6 to 8

1½ teaspoons freshly squeezed lemon juice

1 teaspoon Dijon mustard

19 grams (1½ tablespoons) extra-virgin olive oil

Fine salt and freshly ground black pepper

90 grams (3 cups) baby arugula

12 thin slices (about 200 grams) prosciutto di Parma

2 fully baked Pizza Bianca (page 121)

Small chunk of Parmigiano-Reggiano, for shaving

½ teaspoon finely grated lemon zest

Flaky salt, such as Maldon, for finishing

Pizza sometimes gets a bad rap as a lunch food—too heavy, too nap-inducing. But this pizza upends that. It's essentially a perfect, classic salad that is even more perfect because it's on top of pizza. Get the thinnest prosciutto you can find, and wait to dress the salad until the moment you're ready to eat.

In a medium bowl, whisk together the lemon juice and mustard. Gradually whisk in the oil. Season to taste with salt and pepper. Add the arugula and toss to coat.

Arrange the prosciutto on top of the pizzas, dividing evenly. Top with the dressed arugula, dividing evenly. Using a vegetable peeler, shave Parmesan over the pizzas to taste. Sprinkle with the lemon zest and flaky salt to taste. To serve, cut crosswise into thick slices.

Ricotta and Pistachio Salsa Verde

Makes two pizzas; serves 6 to 8

340 grams (12 ounces) whole-milk ricotta (1½ cups)

14 grams (1 tablespoon) heavy cream

½ teaspoon fine salt

¼ teaspoon freshly ground black pepper

2 fully baked Pizza Bianca (page 121)

48 grams (½ cup) Pistachio Salsa Verde (page 53)

Here the light airiness of the dough is offset by something a little richer: ricotta that's been whizzed in a food processor with cream for ultimate lushness, and spoonfuls of bright and crunchy salsa verde.

Combine the ricotta and heavy cream in the bowl of a food processor fitted with the steel blade and process until smooth. Season with the salt and pepper.

Dollop some of the ricotta on top of each pizza, dividing evenly. Top with dollops of salsa verde. To serve, cut crosswise into thick slices.

Tonnato and Tomato

Makes two pizzas; serves 6 to 8

400 grams (14 ounces) cherry tomatoes (about 3 cups), sliced into thirds

14 grams (1 tablespoon) red wine vinegar

¼ cup thinly sliced fresh basil leaves, plus 10 whole leaves for garnish

25 grams (2 tablespoons) extra-virgin olive oil

Fine salt and freshly ground black pepper

230 grams (1 cup) Tonnato Sauce (recipe follows)

2 fully baked Pizza Bianca (page 121)

This one isn't for everybody—if you have an aversion to canned tuna, blending it with mayonnaise, anchovies, and capers probably isn't going to help. But for those of us who love it, this is a special pizza: a layer of creamy tonnato on the bottom, and a bright tomato salad on top. It's a bit messy, which is why we cut the tomatoes into thirds—it helps prevent them from rolling off.

In a medium bowl, combine the tomatoes, vinegar, sliced basil, and oil and toss to coat. Season to taste with salt and pepper.

Spread some of the tonnato sauce on top of each pizza, dividing evenly. Top with the tomato mixture, dividing evenly, and garnish each pizza with half the basil leaves. To serve, cut crosswise into thick slices.

TONNATO SAUCE

Makes about 390 grams (1½ cups)

284 grams (two 5-ounce cans) oil-packed tuna, such as Genova or Tonnino, drained

100 grams (½ cup) mayonnaise

18 grams oil-packed anchovies (about 4 fillets)

24 grams (2 tablespoons) capers, drained

100 grams (½ cup) extra-virgin olive oil

Fine salt and freshly ground black pepper

In the bowl of a food processor fitted with the steel blade, combine the tuna, mayonnaise, anchovies, and capers and process just until smooth. With the processor running, stream in the oil until incorporated. Transfer to a bowl and season to taste with salt and pepper. The tonnato will keep, refrigerated, for 1 week.

Potato

Makes two pizzas; serves 6 to 8

Fine salt and freshly ground black pepper

454 grams (1 pound) Yukon Gold potatoes, sliced about ⅛ inch thick (about 2½ cups)

1 small onion (about 120 grams/4¼ ounces), thinly sliced (1 cup)

75 grams (6 tablespoons) extra-virgin olive oil, divided

1 batch (720 grams) Pizza Bianca Dough (page 121), prepared through the shaping step

Flaky salt, such as Maldon, for sprinkling

1 tablespoon coarsley chopped fresh rosemary

Grated pecorino Romano, for serving

Potatoes on pizza might seem like too much starch. Trust us, it's not. From the dough you get chewy caramelized flavors; from the potatoes you get a chip-like crispness around the edges and a soft creaminess in the center. A tiny bit of onion adds sweetness and the rosemary adds woodsy depth. You'll want for nothing with this pie—except another slice.

This recipe is different from the others in this chapter in that the potatoes go on the pizza *before* it's baked. So prep the dough through the shaping step, then proceed below.

Preheat the oven to 500°F with a steel or stone on the lower rack.

Bring a medium pot of water to a boil. Add 1 tablespoon salt to the water, then add the potatoes and onion. Return to a boil and cook until the potatoes are just tender but still firm, about 1 minute. Drain, then spread the potatoes and onion on a kitchen towel and gently pat dry. Transfer to a bowl, add 50 grams (¼ cup) of the oil, season generously with salt and pepper, and gently stir to coat.

Drizzle each shaped, dimpled piece of dough with 12.5 grams (1 tablespoon) of the remaining oil and sprinkle with flaky salt. Transfer the pizza (still on the parchment) onto a peel. Divide the potato mixture between the two prepared doughs, spreading the potatoes in an even layer almost to the edges. Sprinkle each with some of the rosemary.

Bake: Load the dough (still on the parchment) onto the preheated steel or stone (see Load, page 49) and bake until golden brown and crispy, 15 to 16 minutes.

Using tongs, grab the edge of the parchment paper and slide the parchment and pizza onto the peel. Transfer to a wire rack and let cool for 5 minutes, then shower with freshly grated pecorino to taste. To serve, cut crosswise into slices and eat hot or at room temperature.

WEEKNIGHT PIZZA

When the words "weeknight" and "pizza" are put together, the context is usually pizza that's nabbed from the freezer, or delivered by a surly teenager to your front door. Though we love both of those things, neither is what we mean. When we say "weeknight pizza," we're referring to homemade pizza that you can get on the table for dinner—even if you don't give a single thought to dinner until 5 p.m.

Granted, a little foresight never hurts. Though the weeknight doughs in this chapter can be on the table in as little as two and a half hours (most of it downtime), their real superpower is that they can be kept in the refrigerator for twenty-four hours. This means that with just a little planning ahead you can always be an hour or so away from hot, homemade pizza—even on a Wednesday night.

Choose between our classic weeknight white dough, which has a spoonful of olive oil for flavor and richness, and the weeknight wheat, which gets a distinct nuttiness from a hefty dose of whole grains. Both bake up light, crispy, puffy around the rim, and almost shockingly tender throughout (especially if you take the 00 flour option).

These doughs are easy to shape by hand using the pressing method (see page 27), or—even easier—they can be rolled out with a rolling pin (see page 28). You'll have a puffier edge crust if you press it, but hey, maybe you don't want that—maybe you want less crust, more room for toppings. That's fine. It's a weeknight. It's been a long day. Make the pizza you want!

A little trivia: We originally developed this dough for the grill, but it worked so well in the oven, too, that it quickly became our go-to for pizza in a hurry. It's still our choice for grilled pizzas (see page 154), even when—*especially* when—you top it with nothing but olive oil and salt.

Weeknight White

5 mins	1 hour 30 mins	5 mins	20 mins to 1 hour	Bake or chill
Mix	Bulk fermentation	Divide and preshape	Second rise	Shape and bake your pizza, or refrigerate the dough for up to 24 hours; let it warm up at room temperature for an hour before stretching.

Weeknight Wheat

5 mins	1½ to 2 hours	5 mins	1 to 2 hours	Bake or chill
Mix	Bulk fermentation	Divide and preshape	Second rise	Shape and bake your pizza, or refrigerate the dough for up to 24 hours; let it warm up at room temperature for an hour before stretching.

Weeknight White Dough

Makes 551.5 grams, enough for two 11-inch pizzas

300 grams (2½ cups) unbleached all-purpose flour or 00 flour, plus more for dusting

6 grams (1 teaspoon) fine salt

4.5 grams (1½ teaspoons) instant yeast

19 grams (1½ tablespoons) extra-virgin olive oil

222 grams (¾ cup plus 3 tablespoons and 2 teaspoons) lukewarm water (85° to 90°F)

Make the dough: In a large bowl, combine the flour, salt, and yeast, then add the oil and water. Mix to combine, then knead the dough by hand in the bowl until you have a rough but cohesive dough. Cover the bowl and let the dough rest at room temperature for 30 minutes.

Uncover the dough and perform a bowl fold: With a wet hand (which will help keep the dough from sticking to you), grab a section of dough from one side, lift it up, then press it down into the middle. Repeat, turning the bowl 90 degrees (a quarter turn) after each stretch, until the dough won't elongate easily and forms a smooth, tight round ball, 4 to 6 times total. Turn the dough over, placing it seam side down in the bowl. Cover and let the dough rise at room temperature (70° to 75°F) for 1 hour, until puffy but not necessarily doubled in size. Toward the end of the rising time, preheat the oven to 500°F with a baking steel or stone placed on a rack in the lower third and an empty oven rack in the upper third.

Divide the dough: On a lightly floured surface, divide the dough into 2 equal pieces (about 275 grams per piece). Form each piece into a tight ball and place seam side down in a lightly greased container. Cover with a lid and let it rest at room temperature while the oven preheats, 20 to 60 minutes. The dough is now ready to use in the recipes on the pages that follow. Alternatively, the dough can be refrigerated for up to 24 hours; remove the dough from the refrigerator 1 hour before shaping and baking your pizzas.

Weeknight Wheat Dough

Makes 548.5 grams, enough for two 11-inch pizzas

150 grams (1¼ cups) unbleached all-purpose flour or 00 flour, plus more for dusting

150 grams (1⅓ cups) whole wheat flour

7 grams (1⅛ teaspoons) fine salt

4.5 grams (1½ teaspoons) instant yeast

19 grams (1½ tablespoons) extra-virgin olive oil

218 grams (¾ cup plus 3 tablespoons) lukewarm water (85° to 90°F)

Make the dough: In a large bowl, combine the flours, salt, and yeast, then add the oil and water. Mix to combine, then knead the dough by hand in the bowl until you have a rough but cohesive dough. Cover the bowl and let the dough rest at room temperature for 30 minutes.

Uncover the dough and perform a bowl fold: With a wet hand (which will help keep the dough from sticking to you), grab a section of dough from one side, lift it up, then press it down into the middle. Repeat, turning the bowl 90 degrees (a quarter turn) after each stretch until the dough won't elongate easily, and forms a smooth, tight round ball, 4 to 6 times total. Cover and let the dough rise at room temperature (70° to 75°F) for 1 to 2 hours. Toward the end of the rising time, preheat the oven to 500°F with a baking steel or stone placed on a rack in the lower third and an empty oven rack in the upper third.

Divide the dough: On a lightly floured surface, divide the dough (about 274 grams per piece). Form each piece into a tight ball and place seam side down in a lightly greased container. Cover with a lid and let it rest at room temperature for 1 to 2 hours, until puffy but not necessarily doubled in size. The dough is now ready to use in the recipes on the pages that follow. Alternatively, the dough can be refrigerated for up to 24 hours; remove the dough from the refrigerator 1 hour before shaping and baking your pizzas.

Broccoli and Cheese

Makes one 11-inch pizza

Fine salt, for blanching water

90 grams (½ cup) small broccoli florets

All-purpose flour, for dusting

1 ball (about 274 grams) Weeknight White Dough (page 132) or Weeknight Wheat Dough (page 133)

Semolina or cornmeal, for dusting

76 grams (⅓ cup) full-fat sour cream

57 grams (2 ounces) Muenster, shredded (½ cup)

1 small shallot (about 28 grams/1 ounce), thinly sliced (¼ cup)

14 grams (½ ounce) Parmigiano-Reggiano, finely grated (¼ cup)

½ teaspoon freshly ground black pepper

This pie is the beautiful offspring of pizza and broccoli casserole (and they said that marriage would never work out!). Muenster and Parmigiano-Reggiano are the titular cheeses, but it's the sour cream that really drives home the casserole vibes.

Arrange racks in the lower and upper thirds of the oven. Place a baking steel or stone on the lower rack and preheat the oven to 500°F for at least 1 hour.

Bring a medium saucepan of salted water to a boil. Add the broccoli and cook until crisp-tender, 3 to 4 minutes. Drain and set aside.

Shape the pizza: Dust your work surface with flour and place the dough on it. Without distorting the round dough, flip it over so that both sides are coated with flour. Use your fingertips to gently depress the center of the dough, being careful not to touch the outer edge of the crust. This step is important—leaving the circumference untouched at this stage will result in a beautiful bubbly outer crust postbake. Continue using your fingertips to press the center of the dough outward until you have an 8-inch circle. Again, taking care not to touch the outermost edge of the crust, lift the pizza from the work surface and use your knuckles to gently stretch the dough into an 11-inch round. Use two hands at once to gently move the dough in a circle, allowing gravity to do most of the work for you, rather than pulling on the dough. If the dough resists stretching, return it to your floured work surface and let it rest for 5 to 10 minutes to allow the gluten to relax, then try again. If the dough is at all sticky, use more flour.

Lightly dust a peel or an overturned baking sheet with semolina and transfer the shaped dough to the peel. If the dough retracts when transferring it to the peel, gently re-form it. Shimmy the dough on the peel to ensure it's not sticking; if it is, lift the edge of the crust and add more semolina.

Evenly spread the sour cream over the surface of the dough (leaving a ½-inch border), then sprinkle the Muenster over it. Evenly top with the broccoli and shallot.

Bake: Use the peel to transfer the pizza onto the steel or stone (see Load, page 49), then bake for 3 to 4 minutes. Check the bottom of the crust—it should be spotted and charred in places, and the edge crust should have some color. If your pizza is still pale, rotate the pizza and bake for another 1 to 2 minutes.

When the bottom has sufficient color, use the peel to transfer the pizza to the top rack, switch the oven to broil, and broil for 2 to 3 minutes, until well charred in spots. (Don't walk away—pizza can go from perfectly charred to burnt quickly.) Home ovens vary tremendously, so use the visual cues and your own preferences to gauge when you've achieved the perfect bake.

Use the peel to remove the pizza from the oven and transfer to a wire rack. Sprinkle with the Parmesan and pepper, then slice and serve.

Sausage and Peppers

Makes one 11-inch pizza

12.5 grams (1 tablespoon) extra-virgin olive oil

1 small yellow bell pepper (about 140 grams/5 ounces), cored, halved, and thinly sliced

All-purpose flour, for dusting

1 ball (about 274 grams) Weeknight White Dough (page 132) or Weeknight Wheat Dough (page 133)

Semolina or cornmeal, for dusting

80 grams (⅓ cup) No-Cook Pizza Sauce (page 34)

57 grams (2 ounces) low-moisture whole-milk mozzarella, shredded (½ cup)

14 grams (½ ounce) Parmigiano-Reggiano, finely grated (¼ cup), plus more for topping

93 grams (1 link) cooked, smoked sausage, such as andouille, sliced into ¼-inch coins

42 grams (3 tablespoons) pickled jalapeño chiles, drained, patted dry, and coarsely chopped

Red pepper flakes, for finishing

Dried oregano, for finishing

Here's a true weeknight pizza with almost no prep: The sauce is no-cook, the sausage is precooked, and the pickled jalapeño peppers (you could use banana peppers, too) come straight from the jar.

Arrange racks in the lower and upper thirds of the oven. Place a baking steel or stone on the lower rack and preheat the oven to 500°F for at least 1 hour.

Heat the oil in a large skillet over medium-high heat. Add the bell pepper and sauté for 6 to 8 minutes, until charred on the edges and beginning to soften. Transfer to a bowl and cover with plastic wrap; let stand for 10 minutes.

Shape the pizza: Dust your work surface with flour and place the dough on it. Without distorting the round dough, flip it over so that both sides are coated with flour. Use your fingertips to gently depress the center of the dough, being careful not to touch the outer edge of the crust. This step is important—leaving the circumference untouched at this stage will result in a beautiful bubbly outer crust postbake. Continue using your fingertips to press the center of the dough outward until you have an 8-inch circle. Again, taking care not to touch the outermost edge of the crust, lift the pizza from the work surface and use your knuckles to gently stretch the dough into an 11-inch round. Use two hands at once to gently move the dough in a circle, allowing gravity to do most of the work for you, rather than pulling on the dough. If the dough resists stretching, return it to your floured work surface and let it rest for 5 to 10 minutes to allow the gluten to relax, then try again. If the dough is at all sticky, use more flour.

Lightly dust a peel or an overturned baking sheet with semolina and transfer the shaped dough to the peel. If the dough retracts when transferring it to the peel, gently re-form it. Shimmy the dough on the peel to ensure it's not sticking; if it is, lift the edge of the crust and add more semolina.

Evenly spread the sauce over the surface of the dough, leaving a ½-inch border, then distribute the mozzarella and Parmesan over the sauce. Evenly top with the sausage, bell pepper, and jalapeños.

Bake: Use the peel to transfer the pizza onto the steel or stone (see Load, page 49), then bake for 3 to 5 minutes. Check the bottom of the crust—it should be spotted and charred in places, and the edge crust should have some color. If not, rotate the pizza and bake for another 1 to 2 minutes.

When the bottom has sufficient color, use the peel to transfer the pizza to the top rack, switch the oven to broil, and broil for 1 to 2 minutes, until well charred in spots. (Don't walk away—pizza can go from perfectly charred to burnt quickly.) Home ovens vary tremendously, so use the visual cues and your own preferences to gauge when you've achieved the perfect bake.

Remove the pizza from the oven and let cool briefly on a wire rack before sprinkling with more Parmesan, red pepper flakes, and oregano. Slice and serve.

Quattro Formaggi

Makes one 11-inch pizza

All-purpose flour, for dusting

1 ball (about 274 grams) Weeknight White Dough (page 132) or Weeknight Wheat Dough (page 133)

Semolina or cornmeal, for dusting

57 grams (2 ounces) low-moisture whole-milk mozzarella, shredded (½ cup)

43 grams (1½ ounces) fontina, cut into ½-inch cubes

28 grams (1 ounce) gorgonzola, crumbled (about 3 tablespoons)

28 grams (1 ounce) Parmigiano-Reggiano, finely grated (½ cup)

1 small garlic clove, very thinly sliced

1 teaspoon dried oregano, for finishing

Hot Honey (page 52), for serving (optional)

A lot of four-cheese pizzas don't taste like anything. How is that possible? Because often the quartet of cheeses all taste and act the same. Here you get a symphony. Fontina and mozzarella add creaminess, the Parm is there for umami and salt, and the blue gorgonzola is there to be, well, blue (it definitely takes the lead, flavor-wise, and we like that). Anybody who has drizzled honey on Stilton knows that the hot honey here isn't *really* optional.

Arrange racks in the lower and upper thirds of the oven. Place a baking steel or stone on the lower rack and preheat the oven to 500°F for at least 1 hour.

Shape the pizza: Dust your work surface with flour and place the dough on it. Without distorting the round dough, flip it over so that both sides are coated with flour. Use your fingertips to gently depress the center of the dough, being careful not to touch the outer edge of the crust. This step is important—leaving the circumference untouched at this stage will result in a beautiful bubbly outer crust postbake. Continue using your fingertips to press the center of the dough outward until you have an 8-inch circle. Again, taking care not to touch the outermost edge of the crust, lift the pizza from the work surface and use your knuckles to gently stretch the dough into an 11-inch round. Use two hands at once to gently move the dough in a circle, allowing gravity to do most of the work for you, rather than pulling on the dough. If the dough resists stretching, return it to your floured work surface and let it rest for 5 to 10 minutes to allow the gluten to relax, then try again. If the dough is at all sticky, use more flour.

Lightly dust a peel or an overturned baking sheet with semolina and transfer the shaped dough to the peel. If the dough retracts when transferring it to the peel, gently re-form it. Shimmy the dough on the peel to ensure it's not sticking; if it is, lift the edge of the crust and add more semolina.

Evenly distribute the mozzarella, fontina, gorgonzola, and Parmesan over the surface of the dough, leaving a ½-inch border, then scatter the garlic over.

Bake: Use the peel to transfer the pizza onto the steel or stone (see Load, page 49), then bake for 3 to 4 minutes. Check the bottom of the crust—it should be spotted and charred in places, and the edge crust should have some color. If not, rotate the pizza and bake for another 1 to 2 minutes.

When the bottom has sufficient color, use the peel to transfer the pizza to the top rack, switch the oven to broil, and broil for 2 to 3 minutes, until well charred in spots. (Don't walk away—pizza can go from perfectly charred to burnt quickly.) Home ovens vary tremendously, so use the visual cues and your own preferences to gauge when you've achieved the perfect bake.

Use the peel to remove the pizza from the oven and slide it onto a wire rack. Sprinkle with the oregano, then drizzle hot honey over the pie (if using), slice, and serve.

Magic Mushroom

Makes one 11-inch pizza

12.5 grams (1 tablespoon) extra-virgin olive oil

255 grams (9 ounces) cremini or other mushrooms of your choosing, thinly sliced

14 grams (1 tablespoon) unsalted butter

1 teaspoon fresh thyme leaves

1 large garlic clove, finely chopped

9 grams (2 teaspoons) lemon juice

Fine salt, to taste

All-purpose flour, for dusting

1 ball (about 274 grams) Weeknight White Dough (page 132) or Weeknight Wheat Dough (page 133)

Semolina or cornmeal, for dusting

80 grams (⅓ cup) No-Cook Pizza Sauce (page 34)

57 grams (2 ounces) low-moisture whole-milk mozzarella, shredded (½ cup)

14 grams (½ ounce) pecorino Romano, finely grated (¼ cup), divided

1 tablespoon finely chopped fresh flat-leaf parsley

Any mushroom torn or cut into bite-size pieces will work on this pizza. A mix is particularly nice.

Arrange racks in the lower and upper thirds of the oven. Place a baking steel or stone on the lower rack and preheat the oven to 500°F for at least 1 hour.

Make the mushroom mixture: Heat the oil in a large skillet over medium-high heat until shimmering. Add the mushrooms and cook without stirring until the liquid has evaporated and most of the mushrooms are browned on one side, 3 to 5 minutes. Give them a toss and continue to cook until most of the mushrooms are golden brown, 3 to 4 minutes more. Lower the heat to medium and add the butter, thyme, and garlic. Cook, stirring, until the garlic and thyme are fragrant, about 1 minute. Remove from the heat and stir in the lemon juice and salt to taste. Set aside until ready to use.

Shape the pizza: Dust your work surface with flour and place the dough on it. Gently flip the dough over so that both sides are coated with flour. Use your fingertips to gently depress the center of the dough, being careful not to touch the outer edge of the crust. Continue using your fingertips to press the center of the dough outward until you have an 8-inch circle. Again, taking care not to touch the outermost edge of the crust, lift the pizza from the work surface and use your knuckles to gently stretch the dough into an 11-inch round. Use two hands at once to gently move the dough in a circle, allowing gravity to do most of the work for you. If the dough resists stretching, return it to your floured work surface and let it rest for 5 to 10 minutes to allow the gluten to relax, then try again. If the dough is at all sticky, use more flour.

Lightly dust a peel or an overturned baking sheet with semolina and transfer the shaped dough to the peel. If the dough retracts when transferring it to the peel, gently re-form it. Shimmy the dough on the peel to ensure it's not sticking; if it is, lift the edge of the crust and add more semolina.

Evenly spread the sauce over the surface of the dough, leaving a ½-inch border, then distribute the mozzarella and half of the pecorino over the sauce. Evenly top with the mushroom mixture.

Bake: Use the peel to transfer the pizza onto the steel or stone (see Load, page 49), then bake for 3 to 4 minutes. Check the bottom of the crust—it should be spotted and charred in places, and the edge crust should have some color. If not, rotate the pizza and bake for another 1 to 2 minutes.

When the bottom has sufficient color, use the peel to transfer the pizza to the top rack, switch the oven to broil, and broil for 2 to 3 minutes, until well charred in spots. (Don't walk away—pizza can go from perfectly charred to burnt quickly.) Home ovens vary tremendously, so use the visual cues and your own preferences to gauge when you've achieved the perfect bake.

Use the peel to remove the pizza from the oven and slide it onto a wire rack. Sprinkle with the remaining pecorino and parsley, then slice and serve.

SNACKING PIZZAS

Sometimes you just want a personal pan pizza. Perfect for after-school homework sessions, slumber parties, or weekend hangs, personal pizzas (or, as we prefer to call them, *snacking* pizzas) allow everyone to choose their own toppings. (For kids—and adults—who won't eat a pepperoni that's touched an onion, these are a godsend.)

To make snacking pizzas, prepare the Weeknight White Dough (page 132) or Weeknight Wheat Dough (page 133). On a lightly floured work surface, divide the dough into 6 equal pieces (about 90 grams per piece). Form each piece into a tight ball. Dust your surface generously with semolina or cornmeal and place the balls of dough seam side down on it, leaving room for the pieces to expand slightly. Cover the dough balls and let it rest for 60 to 90 minutes, until puffy and relaxed enough to stretch and shape.

Toward the end of the rise, preheat the oven to 500°F with one rack in the lowest position and another rack in the upper third. Grease two baking sheets with ½ teaspoon olive oil per pan, then wipe with a paper towel to remove any excess.

Shape the pizzas: Working with one piece of dough at a time on the semolina-dusted surface, lightly flour the top of the dough. Press the dough into a 4- to 5-inch round, working from the center to the edge and leaving a ¼-inch border untouched, then gently press, pull, and stretch the dough to a final diameter of about 5½ inches. If the dough resists stretching, set it aside to relax for 5 to 10 minutes before trying again.

Transfer the round of dough to the prepared baking sheet. Continue with the remaining pieces of dough, evenly spacing the stretched rounds on the baking sheet, three or four per sheet. Set one pan aside while you bake the first.

Bake: Top each dough round with 28 grams (1 ounce) sliced low-moisture whole-milk mozzarella so that it slightly overlaps the edge crust in places. Add four small dollops (about 20 grams/1 heaping tablespoon total) of No-Cook Pizza Sauce (page 34) onto each pizza. The sauce will not cover the cheese; do not spread it. Finish with your desired toppings and a generous dusting of grated Parmesan.

Place the baking sheet on the lower rack and bake the pizzas until the cheese is bubbling, the edges are taking on color, and the bottoms are golden brown, 8 to 12 minutes. If the tops are still pale, move the baking sheet to the upper rack, switch the oven to broil (broil on "high" if your oven provides the option), and cook for 1 to 2 minutes more, until well charred in spots. Home ovens vary greatly, so watch closely and use the visual cues to judge when you've achieved the perfect bake.

Remove the pizzas from the oven and transfer them to a wire rack to cool briefly before serving. Repeat with the remaining sheet of three pizzas.

Popeye

Makes one 11-inch pizza

75 grams (⅓ cup) whole-milk ricotta

15 grams (2 cloves) Garlic Confit (page 55), mashed to a paste, plus more cloves for garnish

¼ teaspoon fine salt, plus more to taste

¼ teaspoon freshly ground black pepper

42 grams (1½ ounces) fresh baby spinach (about 1½ cups)

¼ packed cup fresh basil leaves, chopped, plus small leaves for garnish

1 scallion (about 20 grams/¾ ounce), thinly sliced crosswise

8 grams (2 teaspoons) extra-virgin olive oil

All-purpose flour, for dusting

1 ball (about 274 grams) Weeknight White Dough (page 132) or Weeknight Wheat Dough (page 133)

Semolina flour or cornmeal, for dusting

57 grams (2 ounces) low-moisture whole-milk mozzarella, shredded (½ cup)

43 grams (1½ ounces) feta, crumbled (¼ cup)

1 teaspoon Garlic Confit oil, for finishing

Spinach is the defining feature of a Popeye pizza, of course, but this is sneakily also a three-cheese pie featuring ricotta (for creaminess), feta (big flavor), and mozzarella (for stretch!). If your ricotta is at all wet, place it in a fine-mesh sieve set over a bowl and let drain for 15 to 30 minutes before using. The fresh basil leaves seem like they should be optional, but here they really aren't: They add a vital freshness to the pie, not to mention some pretty greenery.

Arrange racks in the lower and upper thirds of the oven. Place a baking steel or stone on the lower rack and preheat the oven to 500°F for at least 1 hour.

In a small bowl, stir together the ricotta, mashed garlic confit, salt, and pepper. In a medium bowl, combine the spinach, chopped basil, and scallion. Drizzle with the olive oil and toss to coat.

Shape the pizza: Dust your work surface with flour and place the dough on it. Without distorting the round dough, flip it over so that both sides are coated with flour. Use your fingertips to gently depress the center of the dough, being careful not to touch the outer edge of the crust. This step is important—leaving the circumference untouched at this stage will result in a beautiful bubbly outer crust postbake. Continue using your fingertips to press the center of the dough outward until you have an 8-inch circle. Again, taking care not to touch the outermost edge of the crust, lift the pizza from the work surface and use your knuckles to gently stretch the dough into an 11-inch round. If the dough is at all sticky, use more flour. Use two hands at once to gently move the dough in a circle, allowing gravity to do most of the work for you, rather than pulling on the dough. If the dough resists stretching, return it to your floured work surface and let it rest for 5 to 10 minutes to allow the gluten to relax, then try again.

Lightly dust a peel or an overturned baking sheet with semolina and transfer the shaped dough to the peel. If the dough retracts when transferring it to the peel, gently re-form it. Shimmy the dough on the peel to ensure it's not sticking; if it is, lift the edge of the crust and add more semolina.

Spread the ricotta mixture over the dough in an even layer, leaving a ½-inch border. Top with the spinach mixture, piling it more heavily on the outer edge (but avoiding the crust), then distribute the mozzarella and feta over the spinach.

Bake: Use the peel to transfer the pizza onto the steel or stone (see Load, page 49), then bake for 3 to 4 minutes. Check the bottom of the crust—it should be spotted and charred in places, and the edge crust should have some color. If not, rotate the pizza and bake for another 1 to 2 minutes.

Recipe continues

When the bottom has sufficient color, use the peel to transfer the pizza to the top rack, switch the oven to broil, and broil for 2 to 3 minutes, until well charred in spots. (Don't walk away—pizza can go from perfectly charred to burnt quickly.) Home ovens vary tremendously, so use the visual cues and your own preferences to gauge when you've achieved the perfect bake.

Use the peel to remove the pizza from the oven and slide it onto a wire rack. Drizzle with the garlic confit oil and scatter whole basil leaves over. Top with additional whole confit garlic cloves. Slice and serve.

BBQ Chicken

Makes one 11-inch pizza

85 grams (3 ounces) cooked chicken, shredded (scant 1 cup)

95 grams (6 tablespoons) barbecue sauce, store-bought or homemade (recipe follows), divided

20 grams (¾ ounce) red onion, thinly sliced (¼ cup)

1 teaspoon apple cider vinegar

Fine salt and freshly ground black pepper

All-purpose flour, for dusting

1 ball (about 274 grams) Weeknight White Dough (page 132) or Weeknight Wheat Dough (page 133)

Semolina or cornmeal, for dusting

85 grams (3 ounces) low-moisture whole-milk mozzarella, shredded (¾ cup)

2 teaspoons chopped fresh cilantro, for finishing

Thanks to the innovation that came out of Southern and California pizzerias in the twentieth century, we now know that barbecue sauce—homemade or bottled—is as good a pizza sauce as any. This pie recreates the chicken version—which is to say the California version—of BBQ pizza, but if you've got pulled pork on hand, use it.

Arrange racks in the lower and upper thirds of the oven. Place a baking steel or stone on the lower rack and preheat the oven to 500°F for at least 1 hour.

In a small bowl, stir together the chicken and 32 grams (2 tablespoons) of the barbecue sauce until the chicken is coated. In a small bowl, toss the onion with the vinegar and season with a few pinches each of salt and pepper.

Shape the pizza: Dust your work surface with flour and place the dough on it. Without distorting the round dough, flip it over so that both sides are coated with flour. Use your fingertips to gently depress the center of the dough, being careful not to touch the outer edge of the crust. This step is important—leaving the circumference untouched at this stage will result in a beautiful bubbly outer crust postbake. Continue using your fingertips to press the center of the dough outward until you have an 8-inch circle. Again, taking care to not touch the outermost edge of the crust, lift the pizza from the work surface and use your knuckles to gently stretch the dough into an 11-inch round. If the dough is at all sticky, use more flour. Use two hands at once to gently move the dough in a circle, allowing gravity to do most of the work for you. If the dough resists stretching, return it to your floured work surface and let it rest for 5 to 10 minutes to allow the gluten to relax, then try again.

Lightly dust a peel or an overturned baking sheet with semolina and transfer the shaped dough to the peel. If the dough retracts when transferring it to the peel, gently re-form it. Shimmy the dough on the peel to ensure it's not sticking; if it is, lift the edge of the crust and add more semolina.

Spread the remaining barbecue sauce over the dough in an even layer, leaving a ½-inch border. Top with the chicken, then the mozzarella, then the onion, distributing evenly.

Bake: Use the peel to transfer the pizza onto the steel or stone (see Load, page 49), then bake for 3 to 4 minutes. Check the bottom of the crust—it should be spotted and charred in places, and the edge crust should have some color. If not, rotate the pizza and bake for another 1 to 2 minutes.

Recipe continues

When the bottom has sufficient color, use the peel to transfer the pizza to the top rack, switch the oven to broil, and broil for 2 to 3 minutes, until well charred in spots. (Don't walk away—pizza can go from perfectly charred to burnt quickly.) Home ovens vary tremendously, so use the visual cues and your own preferences to gauge when you've achieved the perfect bake.

Use the peel to remove the pizza from the oven and slide it onto a wire rack. Sprinkle with the cilantro, slice, and serve.

SIMPLE BARBECUE SAUCE

Makes 208 grams (⅔ cup)

- 160 grams (½ cup) ketchup
- 24 grams (2 packed tablespoons) light or dark brown sugar
- 15 grams (1 tablespoon) apple cider vinegar
- 1½ teaspoons paprika or smoked paprika
- 1 teaspoon chili powder
- 1 teaspoon Worcestershire sauce
- ¾ teaspoon garlic powder
- ¼ teaspoon onion powder
- Fine salt, to taste

In a small bowl, mix the ketchup, brown sugar, vinegar, paprika, chili powder, Worcestershire sauce, garlic powder, and onion powder until combined, then season to taste with salt.

Soppressata and Date

Makes one 11-inch pizza

All-purpose flour, for dusting

1 ball (about 274 grams) Weeknight White Dough (page 132) or Weeknight Wheat Dough (page 133)

Semolina or cornmeal, for dusting

75 grams (1/3 cup) No-Cook Pizza Sauce, New York variation (page 34)

85 grams (3 ounces) low-moisture whole-milk mozzarella, shredded (3/4 cup)

35 grams (2) Medjool dates, pitted and torn into 1/2-inch pieces

30 grams (15 pieces) thinly sliced soppressata salami (or other sliced salami of your choice)

Chili crisp, Hot Honey (page 52), and/or red pepper flakes, for serving (optional)

Crispy soppressata and sweet chewy dates are great toppings on a pizza, but it's the finishing sauce that really ties the two together and makes this pie sing. We offer two choices here, and it's hard to choose between them: the chili crisp offers more crunch, the hot honey more sweetness. If you've got both on hand, don't choose—drizzle on both.

Arrange racks in the lower and upper thirds of the oven. Place a baking steel or stone on the lower rack and preheat the oven to 500°F for at least 1 hour.

Shape the pizza: Dust your work surface with flour and place the dough on it. Without distorting the round dough, flip it over so that both sides are coated with flour. Use your fingertips to gently depress the center of the dough, being careful not to touch the outer edge of the crust. This step is important—leaving the circumference untouched at this stage will result in a beautiful bubbly outer crust postbake. Continue using your fingertips to press the center of the dough outward until you have an 8-inch circle. Again, taking care to not touch the outermost edge of the crust, lift the pizza from the work surface and use your knuckles to gently stretch the dough into an 11-inch round. If the dough is at all sticky, use more flour. Use two hands at once to gently move the dough in a circle, allowing gravity to do most of the work for you, rather than pulling. If the dough resists stretching, return it to your floured work surface and let it rest for 5 to 10 minutes to allow the gluten to relax, then try again.

Lightly dust a peel or an overturned baking sheet with semolina and transfer the shaped dough to the peel. If the dough retracts when transferring it to the peel, gently re-form it. Shimmy the dough on the peel to ensure it's not sticking; if it is, lift the edge of the crust and add more semolina.

Spread the sauce on the pizza in an even layer, leaving a 1/2-inch border. Distribute the mozzarella evenly over the pizza and top with the dates, then the soppressata, arranging the soppressata over the dates to protect them from burning in the oven.

Bake: Use the peel to transfer the pizza onto the steel or stone (see Load, page 49), then bake for 3 to 4 minutes. Check the bottom of the crust—it should be spotted and charred in places, and the edge crust should have some color. If not, rotate the pizza and bake for another 1 to 2 minutes.

When the bottom has sufficient color, use the peel to transfer the pizza to the top rack, switch the oven to broil, and broil for 2 to 3 minutes, until well charred in spots. (Don't walk away—pizza can go from perfectly charred to burnt quickly.) Home ovens vary tremendously, so use the visual cues and your own preferences to gauge when you've achieved the perfect bake.

Use the peel to remove the pizza from the oven and slide it onto a wire rack. Top with chili crisp, hot honey, and/or red pepper flakes (if using), then slice and serve.

Smoked Salmon

Makes one 11-inch pizza

100 grams (3½ ounces) cream cheese, at room temperature

39 grams (3 tablespoons) crème fraîche or sour cream

1 tablespoon chopped fresh dill, plus additional sprigs for garnish

½ teaspoon minced garlic

½ teaspoon finely grated lemon zest, plus a lemon wedge for squeezing

Fine salt and freshly ground black pepper

All-purpose flour, for dusting

1 ball (about 274 grams) Weeknight White Dough (page 132) or Weeknight Wheat Dough (page 133)

Semolina or cornmeal, for dusting

1 large egg (50 grams), beaten, for brushing

1½ teaspoons sesame or poppy seeds

57 grams (2 ounces) smoked salmon

12 grams (1 tablespoon) capers, drained

2 scallions (about 40 grams/1½ ounces), thinly sliced on the diagonal

Chili crisp, to taste (optional)

Crusting the dough with sesame seeds is a good move for a lot of pizzas; here it mimics a sesame bagel. Want to eat this pizza for brunch? Give the dough an overnight rest in the fridge (see page 29) and pull it out first thing on a weekend morning.

Arrange racks in the lower and upper thirds of the oven. Place a baking steel or stone on the lower rack and preheat the oven to 500°F for at least 1 hour.

In a small bowl, mix the cream cheese, crème fraîche, dill, garlic, and lemon zest until combined. Season to taste with salt and pepper and set aside.

Shape the pizza: Dust your work surface with flour and place the dough on it. Gently flip it over so that both sides are coated with flour. Use your fingertips to gently depress the center of the dough, being careful not to touch the outer edge of the crust. Continue using your fingertips to press the center of the dough outward until you have an 8-inch circle. Again, taking care to not touch the outermost edge of the crust, lift the pizza from the work surface and use your knuckles to gently stretch the dough into an 11-inch round. If the dough is at all sticky, use more flour. Use two hands at once to gently move the dough in a circle, allowing gravity to do most of the work for you. If the dough resists stretching, let it rest for 5 to 10 minutes to allow the gluten to relax, then try again.

Lightly dust a peel or an overturned baking sheet with semolina and transfer the shaped dough to the peel. If the dough retracts when transferring it to the peel, gently re-form it. Poke the surface of the crust all over with the tines of a fork (avoiding the edge); this will prevent it from puffing up in the oven during the parbaking step. Shimmy the dough on the peel to ensure it's not sticking; if it is, lift the edge of the crust and add more semolina. Brush the edge of the dough with the beaten egg and sprinkle with the sesame seeds.

Bake: Use the peel to transfer the pizza onto the steel or stone (see Load, page 49), then bake for 5 minutes. Use the peel to remove the parbaked dough from the oven and set on a work surface. Spread the cream cheese mixture over the pizza in an even layer, leaving a ½-inch border. Use the peel to return the pizza to the oven and bake for 1 minute. Check the bottom of the crust—it should be spotted and charred in places, and the edge crust should have some color. If not, rotate the pizza and bake for another minute.

When the bottom has sufficient color, use the peel to transfer the pizza to the top rack, switch the oven to broil, and broil for 1 minute, until lightly charred in spots and bubbling a bit. Home ovens vary substantially, so use the visual cues and your own preferences to gauge when you've achieved the perfect bake.

Remove the pizza from the oven and slide it onto a wire rack. Let cool briefly, then top with the salmon, dill sprigs, capers, and scallions. Drizzle with chili crisp, if using. Squeeze the lemon wedge over the pie, then slice and serve.

GRILLING PIZZA

Again and again we've said in this book that making pizza is often more like cooking than baking. Nowhere is that more true than when you're making pizzas outside on a hot grill. Like all live-fire cooking, grilling pizza requires paying close attention and making in-the-moment decisions: Where on the grill should the pizza be? How much longer should it sit there? When is the best time to flip? It's a much different and more hands-on process than baking a pizza in an oven. Many of us think it's a lot more fun.

Grilled pizzas are made like any other pizza up to the moment that they're shaped; then things go in a wildly different direction. Instead of topping the shaped pizza dough, you lay it on the grill naked. When the underside is golden and crisp, you take it off the grill; flip it over; top the grilled side with cheese, sauce, and toppings; then put it back on the grill to finish cooking. Because grills don't offer any top heat, the cheese doesn't get quite as melty, and the toppings definitely don't get charred. But these are just facts, not detriments. Grilled pizzas are a specific animal—they're crispy and smoky and one of the best foods to cook over a live fire. Here are some tips to keep in mind when you make them:

Create two zones of heat. If you're using a gas grill, turn some burners on medium-high and the rest on medium-low; if you're grilling over charcoal, bank the coals to one side, creating a hotter side and a cooler one. You'll use both zones to grill your pizza: the hotter one to get the crust crisp, the cooler one to warm the pizza through and melt the toppings.

Keep the pizza moving. The goal when grilling a pizza is to get a crisp, golden—and, sure, maybe even leopard-spotted—bottom crust. To do this your pizza needs to spend some time on the hot side of the grill. But not *too* much time, otherwise it will burn. So make that pizza dance! Move it from cool spots to hot spots and back again. Our method suggests starting on the cool side and keeping the pizza there for the majority of cooking, then moving it to the hot side to get some final color. But you could also go in the opposite direction, getting color first and finishing on the cooler side. Whatever route your pizza takes is fine, just as long as it travels, otherwise you'll end up with a pizza that's charred and bitter on the bottom and not yet melty on top.

Use a cheese that melts well. You'll be tempted to use gorgeous fresh mozzarella for your grilled pizzas. Why not, right? Here's why not: Fresh mozzarella melts best under high heat, especially heat from above. On a grill, you have neither of those things. Better to stick to low-moisture mozzarella, which melts much nicer under less hot conditions. Be sure to add that mozz to the pizza *first,* right on top of the hot dough—it will melt better that way.

Make the sauce *thick*. A lot of pizza sauces are too wet for grilled pizza. Because there's no top heat to coax evaporation, these wet sauces will *stay* wet, and make your grilled pizza soggy. (One way to test a sauce is to check its pourability. If it pours easily from a spoon, it's probably too thin.) Cooked sauces like the Marinara (page 35) or Detroit-Style Pizza Sauce (page 36) are good candidates to try.

Precook your toppings all the way. You remember the rules about prepping your pizza toppings, right? (See page 43 if you need a refresher.) Well, for grilled pizzas this rule is extra important. Toppings will not cook, will not lose any moisture, and certainly won't char on a grilled pizza. So cook them to exactly the texture you want them before you put them on the pie.

Put a lid on it. Whenever possible, close the lid of the grill. There's more opportunity to do this at the beginning of the process than at the end, when grilled pizzas need to be tended to almost constantly. But even then, if you have thirty seconds to spare, use that lid to trap some heat and help the cheese melt.

Don't walk away. It's easy to get distracted by the birds chirping in the trees and the dog digging up your hydrangeas and the nagging thought that you should probably apply more sunscreen (you definitely should), but when there's pizza on the grill you need to stay focused. These things cook quickly, and "deeply golden" turns into "irrevocably blackened" in seconds. So stay at the grill! Keep that pizza moving! A deer was going to get to those hydrangeas sooner or later anyway.

Grilled Pizza

Makes one 10-inch pizza

All-purpose flour, for dusting

1 ball (about 274 grams) Weeknight White Dough (page 132) or Weeknight Wheat Dough (page 133)

Neutral oil, for the grill grates

Cheese, sauce, and toppings of your choice

Grilled pizzas are unlike other pizzas—they're less melty, more smoky, and generally look and eat more like flatbreads. Use a thicker sauce here, and don't walk away from the grill—these pizzas require frequent tending. (For more information, see sidebar, page 154.)

Shape the pizza: Dust your work surface with flour and place the dough on it. Without distorting the round dough, flip it over so that both sides are coated with flour. Use your fingertips to gently depress the center of the dough, being careful not to touch the outer edge of the crust. This step is important—leaving the circumference untouched at this stage will result in a beautiful bubbly outer crust postbake. Continue using your fingertips to press the center of the dough outward until you have an 8-inch circle. Again, taking care not to touch the outermost edge of the crust, lift the pizza from the work surface and use your knuckles to gently stretch the dough into a 10-inch round. Use two hands at once to gently move the dough in a circle, allowing gravity to do most of the work for you, rather than pulling on the dough. If the dough resists stretching, return it to your floured work surface and let it rest for 5 to 10 minutes to allow the gluten to relax, then try again. If the dough is at all sticky, use more flour.

Prepare the grill: Set up a gas or charcoal grill for two-zone cooking (see details, page 154). Use a grill brush to remove any residue and clean the grates. For extra protection against sticking, saturate a wadded or folded paper towel with neutral oil, then use tongs to rub it over the grill grate.

Grill the pizza: Transfer the dough to the cooler part of the grill, cover the grill, and cook for 4 minutes, or until the bottom crust is golden brown.

Remove the dough from the grill using a grill spatula, peel, or tongs and transfer to a cutting board. Gently flip the dough over, so that the cooked side is facing up. Add your toppings, cheese first, to the cooked side of the dough, then use the peel or spatula to transfer the dough back to the cooler part of the grill. Cover and cook for an additional 4 minutes, or until the bottom crust is golden and the cheese is melted.

Check the bottom of the pizza. If it could use more color, move your pizza toward the hotter section of the grill and cook, watching carefully, until the pizza is the color and crispness you're going for.

Remove the pizza from the grill and transfer to a wire rack (this will prevent the crust from getting soggy). Let cool for a few minutes, then transfer to the cutting board, slice, and serve.

NEAPOLITAN

Neapolitan pizza—mother of all pizzas, holy grail of so many pizza bakers—is defined by its plushness: a true Neapolitan pie has a pillowy, puffy, oven-kissed edge crust (the legendary "cornicione"); is traditionally made with 00 flour, which gives it a marked tenderness; and sports a soft, almost soupy middle that can really only be eaten with a fork and knife. There's nothing crisp about a traditional Neapolitan pie. Don't even look for a no-dip tip.

Figuring out how to achieve those distinctive characteristics in an American home oven is the obsession of many bakers. But there's a problem. In Naples they cook their pies in 900°F wood-fired ovens, where the pizzas cook—and even get a few leopard spots of char—in ninety seconds or less. No home oven will get even close to this temperature, and cooking a Neapolitan pizza lower and slower isn't a clean solution—the longer the pizza is in the oven, the more the bottom will crisp up, and the less authentic your Neapolitan pizza becomes.

There are two solutions to this. If you're really going for authenticity, buy a tabletop oven, which can reach the temps you need and replicate Neapolitan pies with impressive success (see page 14). The other solution is to let go of authenticity and make something Neapolitan-ish. Baked in a hot home oven, the pizzas in this chapter will have a big, soft, puffy crust, and they will be vehicles for the simple and unbeatable combination of crushed San Marzano tomatoes and buffalo mozzarella. But the crust will be a little crisp, and you'll be able to eat it with your hands, by the slice. It's not strictly traditional Neapolitan pizza. Dare we say it might be better?

5 mins	1 hour	5 mins	8 to 10 hours	Bake or chill
Mix	Bulk fermentation	Divide and preshape	Second rise	Shape and bake your pizza, or refrigerate the dough for up to 3 days; let it warm up at room temperature for an hour before stretching.

Neapolitan Dough

Makes 555 grams, enough for two 10-inch pizzas

339 grams (scant 3 cups) 00 flour **or** 339 grams (2¾ cups plus 1 tablespoon) unbleached all-purpose flour, plus more for dusting

9 grams (1½ teaspoons) fine salt

¼ teaspoon instant yeast

207 grams (scant 1 cup) cold water (55° to 60°F)

In a medium bowl, combine the flour, salt, and yeast, then add the water. Mix to combine, then knead the dough by hand in the bowl until you have a rough but cohesive dough. Cover and let it rest at room temperature for 1 hour.

Lightly dust a work surface with flour and place the dough on it. Divide into 2 equal pieces (about 277 grams per piece). Tightly ball the dough, place seam side down in a lightly greased container, and cover tightly. Let rise at room temperature for 8 to 10 hours. At this point the dough is ready to use in the recipes that follow, or it can be refrigerated for up to 3 days. Let the refrigerated dough rest at room temperature while your oven preheats, at least 1 hour.

Margherita

Makes one 10½-inch pizza

00 or all-purpose flour, for dusting

1 ball (about 277 grams) Neapolitan Dough (page 161)

Semolina or cornmeal, for dusting

130 grams (½ cup) No-Cook Pizza Sauce (page 34)

Small handful of fresh basil leaves

86 grams (3 ounces) fresh mozzarella, torn into 1-inch pieces

12.5 grams (1 tablespoon) extra-virgin olive oil, for finishing

A Margherita pizza is a thing of beauty—and restraint. Just enough sauce, just enough fresh mozzarella, and a few leaves of fresh basil are all it needs.

Arrange oven racks in the lower and upper thirds of the oven. Place a baking steel or stone on the lower rack and preheat the oven as hot as it will go (500° to 550°F) for at least 1 hour.

Shape the pizza: Dust one section of your work surface generously with flour; dust another section of your work surface lightly with flour. Place the dough on the more heavily floured section of your work surface. Without distorting the round dough, flip it over so that both sides are coated with flour. Move the dough to the less floured section of your work surface. Use your fingertips to gently depress the center of the dough, being careful to leave a 1-inch border for the outer edge of the crust. This step is important—leaving the circumference untouched at this stage will result in a beautiful bubbly outer crust postbake.

Continue using your fingertips to press the center of the dough outward until you have an 8-inch circle. Again, taking care not to touch the outermost edge of the crust, lift the pizza from the work surface and drape it over your knuckles. Use two hands at once to gently move the dough in a circle, allowing gravity to do most of the work for you, rather than pulling on the dough. Continue until the dough is about 10½ inches in diameter (if you want a pizza with a puffier outer edge, stretch to a smaller size, leaving a larger border). If the dough resists stretching, let it rest for 5 to 10 minutes, then try again. If the dough is at all sticky, use more flour.

Lightly dust a peel or an overturned baking sheet with semolina and transfer the shaped dough to the peel. If the dough retracts when transferring it to the peel, gently re-form it. Shimmy the dough on the peel to ensure it's not sticking; if it is, lift the edge of the crust and add more semolina.

Evenly dollop the sauce over the surface of the dough (leaving the outer edge bare), then scatter the basil leaves over the sauce. Evenly top with the mozzarella.

Bake: Use the peel to transfer the pizza to the steel or stone (see Load, page 49), then bake for 3 to 4 minutes. Check the bottom of the crust—it should be spotted and charred in places, and the edge crust should have some color. If not, rotate the pizza and bake for another 1 to 2 minutes.

When the bottom has sufficient color, use the peel to transfer the pizza to the top rack, switch the oven to broil, and broil for 2 to 3 minutes, until well charred in spots. (Don't walk away—pizza can go from perfectly charred to burnt quickly.) Home ovens vary tremendously, so use the visual cues and your own preferences to gauge when you've achieved the perfect bake.

Use the peel to remove the pizza from the oven and transfer to a wire rack. Drizzle with the oil. Slice (scissors work best here) and serve.

Prosciutto and Hot Honey

Makes one 10½-inch pizza

00 or all-purpose flour, for dusting

1 ball (about 277 grams) Neapolitan Dough (page 161)

Semolina or cornmeal, for dusting

80 grams (⅓ cup) No-Cook Pizza Sauce (page 34)

86 grams (3 ounces) fresh mozzarella, torn into 1-inch pieces

57 grams (2 ounces) prosciutto, thinly sliced

40 grams (2 tablespoons) Hot Honey (page 52), for finishing

Small handful of fresh basil leaves

Whereas on other pizzas we drape thin slices of prosciutto over the finished pie (see the Prosciutto and Arugula pizza, page 122), here we put the prosciutto on *before* the bake. In the oven the prosciutto crisps up in places—a counterpoint to the tender dough and creamy mozzarella.

Arrange oven racks in the lower and upper thirds of the oven. Place a baking steel or stone on the lower rack and preheat your oven as hot as it will go (500° to 550°F) for at least 1 hour.

Shape the pizza: Dust one section of your work surface generously with flour; dust another section of your work surface lightly with flour. Place the dough on the more heavily floured section of your work surface. Without distorting the round dough, flip it over so that both sides are coated with flour. Move the dough to the less floured section of your work surface. Use your fingertips to gently depress the center of the dough, being careful to leave a 1-inch border for the outer edge of the crust.

Continue using your fingertips to press the center of the dough outward until you have an 8-inch circle. Again, taking care not to touch the outermost edge of the crust, lift the pizza from the work surface and drape it over your knuckles. Use two hands at once to gently move the dough in a circle, allowing gravity to do most of the work for you, rather than pulling on the dough. Continue until the dough is about 10½ inches in diameter (if you want a pizza with a puffier outer edge, stretch to a smaller size, leaving a larger border). If the dough resists stretching, let it rest for 5 to 10 minutes, then try again. If the dough is at all sticky, use more flour.

Lightly dust a peel or an overturned baking sheet with semolina and transfer the shaped dough to the peel. If the dough retracts when transferring it to the peel, gently re-form it. Shimmy the dough on the peel to ensure it's not sticking; if it is, lift the edge of the crust and add more semolina.

Evenly spread the sauce over the surface of the dough (leaving the outer edge bare), then evenly distribute the mozzarella over the sauce. Drape the prosciutto all over the pizza, crumpling it slightly to create mounds that will crisp up in the oven.

Bake: Use the peel to transfer the pizza to the steel or stone (see Load, page 49), then bake for 3 to 4 minutes. Check the bottom of the crust—it should be spotted and charred in places, and the edge crust should have some color. If not, rotate the pizza and bake for another 1 to 2 minutes.

When the bottom has sufficient color, use the peel to transfer the pizza to the top rack, switch the oven to broil, and broil for 2 to 3 minutes, until well charred in spots. Home ovens vary tremendously, so use the visual cues and your own preferences to gauge when you've achieved the perfect bake.

Remove the pizza from the oven and transfer to a wire rack. Drizzle the hot honey on the pie and scatter the basil leaves over it. Slice (scissors work best here) and serve.

Pesto, Asparagus, and Fried Egg

Makes one 10½-inch pizza

00 or all-purpose flour, for dusting

1 ball (about 277 grams) Neapolitan Dough (page 161)

Semolina or cornmeal, for dusting

80 grams (⅓ cup) Basil Pesto (page 37), divided

57 grams (2 ounces) fresh mozzarella, sliced into ¼-inch rounds

57 grams (2 ounces) thin asparagus, trimmed and thinly sliced crosswise

12.5 grams (1 tablespoon) extra-virgin olive oil

2 large eggs

Fine salt and freshly ground black pepper

2 tablespoons finely grated Parmigiano-Reggiano, for serving

Lemon wedges, for serving

Getting the eggs right—set whites, runny yolks—is important for this pizza, which is why we fry them separately, then slide them onto the pie. Right before serving, the yolks get mixed with the pesto to form the pizza's sauce.

Arrange oven racks in the lower and upper thirds of the oven. Place a baking steel or stone on the lower rack and preheat your oven as hot as it will go (500° to 550°F) for at least 1 hour.

Shape the pizza: Dust one section of your work surface generously with flour; dust another section of your work surface lightly with flour. Place the dough on the more heavily floured section of your work surface. Without distorting the round dough, flip it over so that both sides are coated with flour. Move the dough to the less floured section of your work surface. Use your fingertips to gently depress the center of the dough, being careful to leave a 1-inch border for the outer edge of the crust. This step is important—leaving the circumference untouched at this stage will result in a beautiful bubbly outer crust postbake.

Continue using your fingertips to press the center of the dough outward until you have an 8-inch circle. Again, taking care not to touch the outermost edge of the crust, lift the pizza from the work surface and drape it over your knuckles. Use two hands at once to gently move the dough in a circle, allowing gravity to do most of the work for you, rather than pulling on the dough. Continue until the dough is about 10½ inches in diameter (if you want a pizza with a puffier outer edge, stretch to a smaller size, leaving a larger border). If the dough resists stretching, return it to your floured work surface and let it rest for 5 to 10 minutes to allow the gluten to relax, then try again. If the dough is at all sticky, use more flour.

Lightly dust a peel or an overturned baking sheet with semolina and transfer the shaped dough to the peel. If the dough retracts when transferring it to the peel, gently re-form it. Shimmy the dough on the peel to ensure it's not sticking; if it is, lift the edge of the crust and add more semolina.

Evenly spread all but 1 tablespoon of the pesto over the surface of the dough (leaving the outer edge bare), then evenly distribute the mozzarella over the pesto. In a medium bowl, mix the asparagus and reserved pesto to coat, then evenly distribute the asparagus over the pizza.

Bake: Use the peel to transfer the pizza to the steel or stone (see Load, page 49), then bake for 3 to 4 minutes. Check the bottom of the crust—it should be spotted and charred in places, and the edge crust should have some color. If not, rotate the pizza and bake for another 1 to 2 minutes.

Recipe continues

When the bottom has sufficient color, use the peel to transfer the pizza to the top rack, switch the oven to broil, and broil for 2 to 3 minutes, until well charred in spots. (Don't walk away—pizza can go from perfectly charred to burnt quickly.) Home ovens vary tremendously, so use the visual cues and your own preferences to gauge when you've achieved the perfect bake.

Use the peel to remove the pizza from the oven and transfer to a wire rack. Heat the oil in a medium skillet over medium-high heat. Crack the eggs into the pan, season with salt and pepper, cover, and fry until the whites are set but the yolks are still runny, 3 to 4 minutes. Slide the eggs onto the pizza and dust with the Parmesan and additional pepper. Use a fork to pierce the yolks of the eggs and smear them over the surface of the pizza. Slice (scissors work best here) and serve with lemon wedges alongside for squeezing over.

Mortazza

Makes one large sandwich; serves 1 to 3 people

00 or all-purpose flour, for dusting

1 ball (about 277 grams) Neapolitan Dough (page 161)

Semolina or cornmeal, for dusting

Extra-virgin olive oil, for brushing and drizzling

113 grams (4 ounces) burrata, buffalo milk mozzarella, or whole-milk ricotta

113 grams (4 ounces) mortadella, thinly sliced

1 lemon

Roasted and salted pistachios, coarsely chopped, to taste

Finely grated pecorino Romano or Parmigiano-Reggiano, to taste

Freshly grated nutmeg, to taste

Red pepper flakes, to taste

Flaky salt, such as Maldon, to taste

Pizza e mortazza is a beloved snack in Italy composed of pizza bianca that's been split and stuffed with a thin layer of mortadella. That version is simple, slender, and understated; this version is exactly the opposite. Instead of pizza bianca, we fold (as best we can!) an entire Neapolitan crust over fistfuls of cheese, mortadella, and roasted pistachios. Definitely a meal and not a snack, one can feed at least two people, maybe three.

Arrange oven racks in the lower and upper thirds of the oven. Place a baking steel or stone on the lower rack and preheat your oven as hot as it will go (500° to 550°F) for at least 1 hour.

Shape the pizza: Dust one section of your work surface generously with flour; dust another section of your work surface lightly with flour. Place the dough on the more heavily floured section of your work surface. Without distorting the round dough, flip it over so that both sides are coated with flour. Move the dough to the less floured section of your work surface. Use your fingertips to gently depress the center of the dough, being careful to leave a 1-inch border for the outer edge of the crust. This step is important—leaving the circumference untouched at this stage will result in a beautiful bubbly outer crust postbake.

Continue using your fingertips to press the center of the dough outward until you have an 8-inch circle. Again, taking care not to touch the outermost edge of the crust, lift the pizza from the work surface and drape it over your knuckles. Use two hands at once to gently move the dough in a circle, allowing gravity to do most of the work for you, rather than pulling on the dough. Continue until your dough is 9½ inches in diameter. If the dough resists stretching, return it to your floured work surface and let it rest for 5 to 10 minutes to allow the gluten to relax, then try again. If the dough is at all sticky, use more flour.

Lightly dust a peel or an overturned baking sheet with semolina and transfer the shaped dough to the peel. If the dough retracts when transferring it to the peel, gently re-form it. Shimmy the dough on the peel to ensure it's not sticking; if it is, lift the edge of the crust and add more semolina.

Brush the surface of the dough all over with oil. Fold the round in half to make a semicircle.

Bake: Use the peel to transfer the dough to the steel or stone (see Load, page 49), then bake for 4 to 5 minutes. Check the bottom of the crust—it should be spotted and charred in places; the top should also have some color. If not, rotate and bake for another 1 to 2 minutes.

Recipe continues

When the bottom has sufficient color, use the peel to transfer the dough to the top rack, switch the oven to broil, and broil for 2 to 3 minutes, until golden brown, puffed, and charred in spots. (Don't walk away—pizza can go from perfectly charred to burnt quickly.) Home ovens vary tremendously, so use the visual cues and your own preferences to gauge when you've achieved the perfect bake.

Use the peel to remove the dough from the oven and transfer to a wire rack.

Assemble the sandwich: Gently open the dough pocket with your fingers, being careful of the steam. Tear open the burrata and evenly distribute it onto the bottom half of the dough. (If using mozzarella, tear into large pieces; if using ricotta, spoon it onto the bottom half of the dough.) Layer on the mortadella, folding and rolling the individual slices so the ruffled edges face outward. Zest the lemon over the mortadella to taste, then squeeze a bit of lemon juice directly on top. Sprinkle with pistachios, then grate the pecorino or Parmesan over the top. Finish with nutmeg, pepper flakes, and flaky salt, then drizzle with oil.

Fold the mortadella pizza sandwich in half, closing the pocket, and brush with more olive oil. Sprinkle more pistachios and pecorino on top and serve.

NEW AMERICAN

The pursuit of a recipe that embodies the spirit of American pizza *now* is a tricky one—pizza is as regional here as it is in Italy, and there is no one American style that dominates. But there *is* a national pastime that has taken hold and unites all 50 states, and that's an infatuation with bread—good bread, baked at home. Since we see pizza as just another form of great bread, we wanted to write a recipe that reflects the kind of bread that has captivated America: long-fermented, partially whole grain, with a crisp bottom, an open crumb structure, and a nice dark bake.

We use a mix of flours for this recipe: bread flour for strength and a thin, crisp crust, and a little whole grain (we like wheat, but rye or spelt would also work well) for flavor and color. The whole grain flour also amps up the fermentation process, giving us the floral and acidic flavors we're looking for. We add just a touch of honey, a little olive oil, and a tiny amount of (optional) sourdough culture to amplify those flavors. We don't want the dough to be sour, but we do want it to be robust.

The result looks and eats like an amalgam of several pizza styles. It has the char of New Haven style; the crispy, slightly sweet, oil-enriched notes of New York style; and a touch of Neapolitan puff. Like the best sourdough loaves, we like a strong bake on these pies, to make them crisp and add notes of char. And because the dough is so flavorful, we aren't shy about piling it with bold toppings of all kinds: bitter greens, pickled chiles, caramelized onions. This is one crust you don't have to worry about overpowering. In fact, the bolder, the better.

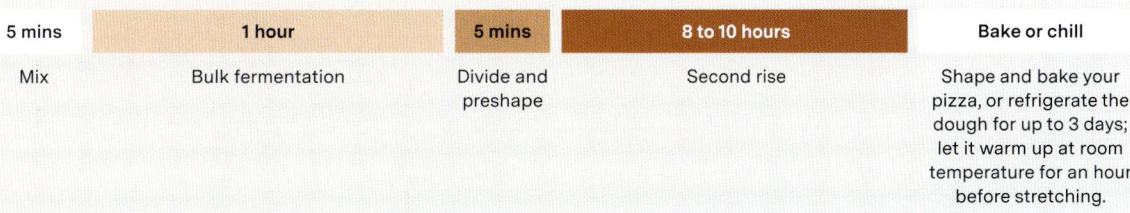

5 mins	1 hour	5 mins	8 to 10 hours	Bake or chill
Mix	Bulk fermentation	Divide and preshape	Second rise	Shape and bake your pizza, or refrigerate the dough for up to 3 days; let it warm up at room temperature for an hour before stretching.

New American Dough

Makes 705 grams, enough for two 13-inch pizzas

367 grams (3 cups plus 1 tablespoon) unbleached bread flour, plus more for dusting

45 grams (6 tablespoons) whole wheat flour

12 grams (2 teaspoons) fine salt

¼ teaspoon instant yeast

12.5 grams (1 tablespoon) extra-virgin olive oil

8 grams (1½ teaspoons) sourdough culture (optional)

7 grams (1 teaspoon) honey

253 grams (1 cup plus 2 tablespoons) cool water (60° to 70°F)

In a large bowl, combine the flours, salt, and yeast, then add the oil, sourdough culture (if using), honey, and water. Mix to combine, then knead the dough by hand in the bowl until you have a rough but cohesive dough. Cover and let it rest at room temperature for 1 hour.

Lightly dust a work surface with flour and place the dough on it. Divide into 2 equal pieces (about 352 grams per piece). Tightly ball the dough, place seam side down in a lightly greased container, and cover tightly. Let rise at room temperature for 8 to 10 hours. At this point the dough is ready to use in the recipes that follow, or it can be refrigerated for up to 3 days. Let the refrigerated dough rest at room temperature while your oven preheats, at least 1 hour.

Corn, Cheese, and Chiles

Makes one 13-inch pizza

85 grams (3 ounces) whole milk ricotta (⅓ cup)

15 grams (1 tablespoon) sour cream

½ teaspoon fine salt

Bread or all-purpose flour, for dusting

1 ball (about 352 grams) New American Dough (page 177)

Semolina flour or cornmeal, for dusting

113 grams (4 ounces) low-moisture whole-milk mozzarella, shredded (1 cup)

100 grams (¾ cup) fresh corn kernels (from 1 ear of corn)

2 scallions, thinly sliced on the bias

45 grams (1½ ounces) pickled jalapeño chiles

12.5 grams (1 tablespoon) extra-virgin olive oil

28 grams (1 ounce) aged cotija cheese, crumbled (3 tablespoons)

¼ cup fresh cilantro leaves

½ teaspoon freshly ground black pepper

Here we take inspiration from Mexican elote and pair corn with something creamy (we use sour cream instead of mayonnaise), spicy (our choice is pickled jalapeños), and salty. Just like elote, we finish this pizza with a layer of cotija.

Arrange oven racks in the lower and upper thirds of the oven. Place a baking steel or stone on the lower rack and preheat the oven to 500°F for at least 1 hour.

In a small bowl, stir together the ricotta, sour cream, and salt.

Shape the dough: Dust your work surface generously with flour and place the dough on it. Without distorting the round dough, flip it over so that both sides are coated with flour. Use your fingertips to gently depress the center of the dough (avoiding the outer edge), pressing out the gas and beginning to flatten and expand the dough into a round.

Continue using your fingertips to press the center of the dough outward until you have an 8-inch circle. Gently grab the dough on the east and west sides, being careful to position your grip *over* the edge crust, so as not to deflate it. Use your hands to gently tug the dough in an east-west direction. Rotate the dough and repeat the tug. Continue rotating and tugging until the dough round measures about 10 inches. Lift the pizza from the work surface and use your knuckles to gently stretch the dough into a 12-inch round. Use two hands at once to gently move the dough in a circle, allowing gravity to do most of the work. If the dough resists stretching, return it to your floured work surface and let it rest for 5 to 10 minutes, then try again. If the dough is at all sticky, use more flour. Return the dough to the floured work surface and give a few more east-west tugs until the round measures 13 inches.

Lightly dust a peel or an overturned baking sheet with semolina and transfer the shaped dough to the peel. If the dough retracts when transferring it to the peel, gently re-form it. Shimmy the dough on the peel to ensure it's not sticking; if it is, lift the edge of the crust and add more semolina.

Dollop the ricotta mixture over the stretched dough, leaving a ½-inch border. Distribute the mozzarella over the ricotta in an even layer and top with the corn, scallions, and pickled jalapeños. Drizzle with the oil.

Bake: Use the peel to transfer the pizza onto the steel or stone (see Load, page 49) and bake for 5 to 7 minutes. Check the bottom of the crust—it should be spotted and charred in places, and the edge crust should have some color. If not, rotate the pizza and bake for another 1 to 2 minutes.

When the bottom has sufficient color, use the peel to transfer the pizza to the top rack, switch the oven to broil, and broil for 2 to 3 minutes, until well charred in spots. (Don't walk away—pizza can go from well browned to burnt quickly.)

Use the peel to remove the pizza from the oven and slide it onto a wire rack to cool briefly. Top with the cotija, cilantro, and pepper, then slice and serve.

Rossa with Kale Salad

Makes one 13-inch pizza

15 grams (2 cloves) Garlic Confit (page 55), mashed to a paste

28 grams (2 tablespoons) Garlic Confit oil (page 55)

2 teaspoons lemon juice

¼ teaspoon fine salt

Freshly ground black pepper, to taste

171 grams (6 ounces) baby kale or mature kale, stemmed and torn into bite-size pieces (about 8 cups)

Bread or all-purpose flour, for dusting

1 ball (about 352 grams) New American Dough (page 177)

Semolina flour or cornmeal, for dusting

215 grams (¾ cup) No-Cook Pizza Sauce (page 34)

2 garlic cloves, sliced paper thin

Extra-virgin olive oil, for drizzling

2 tablespoons Garlicky Panko (page 53)

Small chunk of Parmigiano-Reggiano, for shaving

It was a pizzeria (Franny's, in Brooklyn) that popularized the kale salad in the early aughts, so it was inevitable that we'd start putting the salad right on the pizza itself. We like baby kale here because it's softer and sweeter, but mature kale that's been stripped off its stem and torn into bite-size pieces also works. Either way, you don't need to worry about the flavor of the kale dominating; with three forms of garlic, there's plenty going on to balance it.

Arrange oven racks in the lower and upper thirds of the oven. Place a baking steel or stone on the lower rack and preheat the oven to 500°F for at least 1 hour.

In a large bowl combine the garlic confit paste, garlic oil, lemon juice, salt, and a few cranks of pepper. Add the kale to the bowl, but do not toss.

Shape the dough: Dust your work surface generously with flour and place the dough on it. Without distorting the round dough, flip it over so that both sides are coated with flour. Use your fingertips to gently depress the center of the dough (avoiding the outer edge), pressing out the gas and beginning to flatten and expand the dough into a round.

Continue using your fingertips to press the center of the dough outward until you have an 8-inch circle. Gently grab the dough on the east and west sides, being careful to position your grip *over* the edge crust, so as not to deflate it. Use your hands to gently tug the dough in an east-west direction. Rotate the dough and repeat the tug. Continue rotating and tugging until the dough round measures about 10 inches. Lift the pizza from the work surface and use your knuckles to gently stretch the dough into a 12-inch round. Use two hands at once to gently move the dough in a circle, allowing gravity to do most of the work for you, rather than pulling on the dough. If the dough resists stretching, return it to your floured work surface and let it rest for 5 to 10 minutes to allow the gluten to relax, then try again. If the dough is at all sticky, use more flour. Return the dough to the floured work surface and give a few more east-west tugs until the round measures 13 inches.

Lightly dust a peel or an overturned baking sheet with semolina and transfer the shaped dough to the peel. If the dough retracts when transferring it to the peel, gently re-form it. Shimmy the dough on the peel to ensure it's not sticking; if it is, lift the edge of the crust and add more semolina.

Spread the sauce on the dough in an even layer, avoiding the edges. Scatter the sliced raw garlic on top of the sauce.

Recipe continues

Bake: Use the peel to transfer the pizza onto the steel or stone (see Load, page 49) and bake for 5 to 7 minutes. Check the bottom of the crust—it should be spotted and charred in places, and the edge crust should have some color. If not, rotate the pizza and bake for another 1 to 2 minutes.

When the bottom has sufficient color, use the peel to transfer the pizza to the top rack, switch the oven to broil, and broil for 2 to 3 minutes, until well charred in spots. (Don't walk away—pizza can go from well browned to burnt quickly.) Home ovens vary substantially, so use the visual cues and your own preferences to gauge when you've achieved the perfect bake.

Use the peel to remove the pizza from the oven and slide it onto a wire rack to cool briefly. Drizzle with a little oil.

Add the garlicky panko to the bowl with the kale and toss to coat the kale with the dressing. Pile the kale on top of the pizza, then use a vegetable peeler to shave Parmesan over the kale. Slice and serve.

French Onion

Makes one 13-inch pizza

Ingredients

25 grams (2 tablespoons) extra-virgin olive oil

1 medium leek (about 150 grams/5 ounces), halved lengthwise and sliced crosswise into ¼-inch half-moons, washed and drained (about 2 cups)

1 medium yellow onion (about 225 grams/ 8 ounces), sliced ¼ inch thick (about 2½ cups)

2 small shallots (about 90 grams/3 ounces), thinly sliced (about 1 cup)

½ teaspoon fine salt, plus more to taste

2 to 3 sprigs fresh thyme, plus 1 teaspoon chopped fresh thyme leaves

57 grams (¼ cup) dry sherry or chicken stock

Freshly ground black pepper, to taste

Bread or all-purpose flour, for dusting

1 ball (about 352 grams) New American Dough (page 177)

Semolina flour or cornmeal, for dusting

14 grams (½ ounce) Parmigiano-Reggiano, finely grated (¼ cup)

Caramelizing the trio of onions, leeks, and shallots that this pie calls for takes forty minutes, and yes, that's a bit of a chore. But for this pizza, it's worth it—the result takes the pie to sweet-and-savory umami depths that not even French onion soup can reach. So put on a podcast and start stirring; you need a way to pass the preheat hour anyway.

Arrange oven racks in the lower and upper thirds of the oven. Place a baking steel or stone on the lower rack and preheat the oven to 500°F for at least 1 hour.

Heat the oil in a large skillet over medium-high heat. Add the leek, onion, shallots, salt, and thyme sprigs and cook, stirring frequently, until the mixture begins to brown and soften, about 5 minutes. Reduce the heat to low and continue cooking, stirring every so often, until the onions are deeply caramelized and jammy, 35 to 40 minutes. Add the sherry and use a wooden spoon to scrape up any browned bits on the bottom of the pan, then cook briefly until the liquid has evaporated. Remove the thyme stems and discard; let the onion mixture cool, then season to taste with additional salt and pepper. The onions can be made ahead; let cool and store in a covered container in the refrigerator for up to 1 week.

Shape the dough: Dust your work surface generously with flour and place the dough on it. Without distorting the round dough, flip it over so that both sides are coated with flour. Use your fingertips to gently depress the center of the dough (avoiding the outer edge), pressing out the gas and beginning to flatten and expand the dough into a round.

Continue using your fingertips to press the center of the dough outward until you have an 8-inch circle. Gently grab the dough on the east and west sides, being careful to position your grip *over* the edge crust, so as not to deflate it. Use your hands to gently tug the dough in an east-west direction. Rotate the dough and repeat the tug. Continue rotating and tugging until the dough round measures about 10 inches. Lift the pizza from the work surface and use your knuckles to gently stretch the dough into a 12-inch round. Use two hands at once to gently move the dough in a circle, allowing gravity to do most of the work for you, rather than pulling on the dough. If the dough resists stretching, return it to your floured work surface and let it rest for 5 to 10 minutes to allow the gluten to relax, then try again. If the dough is at all sticky, use more flour. Return the dough to the floured work surface and give a few more east-west tugs until the round measures 13 inches.

Lightly dust a peel or an overturned baking sheet with semolina and transfer the shaped dough to the peel. If the dough retracts when transferring it to the peel, gently re-form it. Shimmy the dough on the peel to ensure it's not sticking; if it is, lift the edge of the crust and add more semolina.

Ingredients and recipe continue

142 grams (5 ounces) Gruyère, sliced into ¼-inch-thick slices

Flaky salt, such as Maldon, to finish

Sprinkle the Parmesan on the dough, leaving a ½-inch border. Scatter the cooled onion mixture over the top. Place the slices of Gruyère on top (it won't cover the entire surface).

Bake: Use the peel to transfer the pizza onto the steel or stone (see Load, page 49). Bake for 5 to 7 minutes. Check the bottom of the crust—it should be spotted and charred in places, and the edge crust should have some color. If not, rotate the pizza and bake for another 1 to 2 minutes.

When the bottom has sufficient color, use the peel to transfer the pizza to the top rack, switch the oven to broil, and broil for 2 to 3 minutes, until well charred in spots. (Don't walk away—pizza can go from well browned to burnt quickly.) Home ovens vary substantially, so use the visual cues and your own preferences to gauge when you've achieved the perfect bake.

Use the peel to remove the pizza from the oven and slide it onto a wire rack to cool briefly. Top with the chopped thyme leaves, a sprinkle of flaky salt, and a few grinds of pepper. Slice and serve.

Triple Fennel

Makes one 13-inch pizza

25 grams (2 tablespoons) extra-virgin olive oil, divided

1 teaspoon fennel seeds

2 small bulbs fennel (about 400 grams/ 14 ounces), halved and thinly shaved into ⅛-inch pieces, fronds reserved, divided

½ teaspoon fine salt, divided

14 grams (1 tablespoon) Pernod (optional, for more intense anise flavor)

1 teaspoon lemon juice

⅛ teaspoon freshly ground black pepper

2 tablespoons chopped fennel fronds

2 tablespoons finely chopped fresh flat-leaf parsley

Bread or all-purpose flour, for dusting

1 ball (about 352 grams) New American Dough (page 177)

Semolina flour or cornmeal, for dusting

85 grams (3 ounces) fontina, shredded (¾ cup)

14 grams (½ ounce) Parmigiano-Reggiano, finely grated (¼ cup)

140 grams (5 ounces) pork fennel sausage or sweet Italian sausage, casings removed

When fennel is cooked down, it gets as sweet as an onion; left raw, it's crunchy and refreshing and almost juicy. On this pizza you get fennel both ways, as well as in a third form, via fennel seeds, which punctuate the Italian sausage with their perfume.

Arrange oven racks in the lower and upper thirds of the oven. Place a baking steel or stone on the lower rack and preheat the oven to 500°F for at least 1 hour.

In a large sauté pan, heat 1 tablespoon of the oil over medium heat. Add the fennel seeds and toast for 1 minute, until fragrant. Add half of the shaved fennel and ¼ teaspoon of the salt and cook, stirring occasionally, until the fennel begins to soften, about 5 minutes. Reduce the heat to medium-low, add the Pernod (if using), and continue cooking until the fennel is browned and caramelized, 10 to 12 minutes. Transfer to a bowl and let cool.

In a separate medium bowl, whisk together the remaining 1 tablespoon oil, the lemon juice, the remaining salt, and the pepper. Add the remaining raw shaved fennel, fennel fronds, and parsley to the bowl but do not toss. Set aside.

Shape the dough: Dust your work surface generously with flour and place the dough on it. Without distorting the round dough, flip it over so that both sides are coated with flour. Use your fingertips to gently depress the center of the dough (avoiding the outer edge), pressing out the gas and beginning to flatten and expand the dough into a round.

Continue using your fingertips to press the center of the dough outward until you have an 8-inch circle. Gently grab the dough on the east and west sides, being careful to position your grip *over* the edge crust, so as not to deflate it. Use your hands to gently tug the dough in an east-west direction. Rotate the dough and repeat the tug. Continue rotating and tugging until the dough round measures about 10 inches. Lift the pizza from the work surface and use your knuckles to gently stretch the dough into a 12-inch circle. Use two hands at once to gently move the dough in a circle, allowing gravity to do most of the work for you, rather than pulling on the dough. If the dough resists stretching, return it to your floured work surface and let it rest for 5 to 10 minutes to allow the gluten to relax, then try again. If the dough is at all sticky, use more flour. Return the dough to the floured work surface and give a few more east-west tugs until the round measures 13 inches.

Lightly dust a peel or an overturned baking sheet with semolina and transfer the shaped dough to the peel. If the dough retracts when transferring it to the peel, gently re-form it. Shimmy the dough on the peel to ensure it's not sticking; if it is, lift the edge of the crust and add more semolina.

Scatter the fontina and Parmesan evenly over the pizza, leaving a ½-inch border. Top with the cooled, caramelized fennel mixture, then dot with ½-inch pieces of raw sausage.

Bake: Use the peel to transfer the pizza onto the steel or stone (see Load, page 49) and bake for 5 to 7 minutes. Check the bottom of the crust—it should be spotted and charred in places, and the edge crust should have some color. If not, rotate the pizza and bake for another 1 to 2 minutes.

When the bottom has sufficient color, use the peel to transfer the pizza to the top rack, switch the oven to broil, and broil for 2 to 3 minutes, until the sausage is well browned and cooked through. (Don't walk away—pizza can go from well browned to burnt quickly.) Home ovens vary substantially, so use the visual cues and your own preferences to gauge when you've achieved the perfect bake.

Use the peel to remove the pizza from the oven and slide it onto a wire rack to cool briefly. Toss the shaved raw fennel with the dressing to coat, then pile the fennel salad on top of the pizza. Slice and serve.

GRANDMA

Grandma pizza can be traced to Long Island pizza shops, where pizzaioli started emulating a style of pie their parents and grandparents made at home: thin and simple, baked in a square, oiled pan. At first these pies were just for the pizzeria's staff; they were probably considered too humble to appeal to customers. But once they were offered for sale, Grandma slices developed a loyal fan base. In the twenty-first century, they've become downright trendy.

This is an in-between style of pizza: not as thin as New York style, not as thick as Detroit or Sicilian. It eats just as light as our Detroit style, and the thin edge crust is crispy enough to have a little snap. (We like to bake our Grandma pies in dark anodized pans, which gives them the crispiest crusts.) Grandma slices go down easy, and you can eat a lot of them, just like an Italian grandmother would want you to.

Because they live somewhere between thick and thin, Grandma pies work with a wide range of toppings. The dough is hearty enough that you can load it up with, say, breaded chicken and blue cheese (see page 196) or piles of roasted tomatoes and garlic confit (see page 200). But it's also a style that shines when topped simply. The classic version features just some no-cook sauce and mozzarella (many traditional recipes put the cheese right on the crust, like a Detroit-style pie), and the Tricolore (page 199) is topped with only mozzarella and thick stripes of marinara and pesto. These pies are closest to the ones that Italian home cooks have kept in rotation for decades; they're probably the pies that will secure a place in your rotation, too.

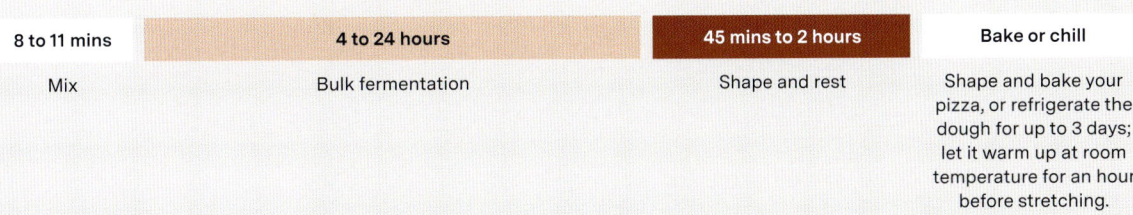

8 to 11 mins	4 to 24 hours	45 mins to 2 hours	Bake or chill
Mix	Bulk fermentation	Shape and rest	Shape and bake your pizza, or refrigerate the dough for up to 3 days; let it warm up at room temperature for an hour before stretching.

Grandma Dough

Makes 772 grams, enough for one 14-inch square pizza

450 grams (3¾ cups) unbleached all-purpose flour

8 grams (1¼ teaspoons) fine salt

6 grams (2 teaspoons) instant yeast

283 grams (1¼ cups) lukewarm water (85° to 90°F)

25 grams (2 tablespoons) extra-virgin olive oil

Make the dough: In the bowl of a stand mixer fitted with the dough hook (or in a large bowl with the handle of a wooden spoon) combine the flour, salt, yeast, water, and oil and mix on low speed until combined. Scrape the sides of the bowl and mix on medium-low speed until you have a smooth, elastic dough, 5 to 6 minutes. If mixing by hand, stir to combine, then transfer the dough to a floured work surface and knead until smooth and elastic, 10 to 11 minutes.

Place the dough in a large (at least 5-quart) bowl, cover, and refrigerate for at least 4 hours (or up to 24 hours). The dough is now ready to use in the recipes on the pages that follow.

Buffalo Chicken

Makes one large pizza; serves 10 to 12

37.5 grams (3 tablespoons) extra-virgin olive oil

1 batch (772 grams) Grandma Dough (page 195)

142 grams (½ cup) hot sauce (such as Frank's RedHot)

56 grams (4 tablespoons) unsalted butter

2 garlic cloves, smashed

Dash of Worcestershire sauce

200 grams (7 ounces) Monterey Jack cheese, shredded (about 2 cups)

350 grams (12 ounces) breaded, cooked chicken cutlets or nuggets, thawed if frozen, cut into bite-size pieces

130 grams (½ cup) Blue Cheese Dressing (recipe follows)

175 grams (1½ cups) very thinly sliced celery (about 2 stalks)

Pizza and wings are as compatible as peanut butter and chocolate, and here we combine them. In lieu of actual wings (we draw a hard line when it comes to putting anything with bones on a pie), we go for breaded chicken cutlets.

Position a rack in the lower third of the oven. Place a baking steel or stone on the rack and preheat the oven to 500°F for at least 1 hour.

Shape the pizza: Drizzle the oil into a 14-inch square Grandma-style pizza pan or an 18 × 13-inch rimmed baking sheet and spread to coat the pan completely. Transfer the dough to the pan and turn it once to coat both sides with oil. After coating the dough in oil, press to the edges of the pan, dimpling it with your fingertips in the process. The dough may start to resist; if that happens, just cover and let it rest for 15 minutes to allow the gluten to relax, then repeat the dimpling and pressing. At this point the dough should reach the edges of the pan; if it doesn't, give it one more 15-minute rest before repeating a third and final time. Cover and let it rest at room temperature until it has puffed slightly, at least 40 minutes or, for a slightly lighter pie, up to 1½ hours.

While the dough rests, make the buffalo sauce: In a small saucepan, combine the hot sauce, butter, garlic, and Worcestershire sauce. Bring to a simmer and cook for 1 minute, then remove and discard the garlic cloves; you will have about ⅔ cup sauce. Let cool.

Spread ⅓ cup of the buffalo sauce all over the dough, spreading all the way to the edges. Distribute the cheese evenly over the dough, all the way to the edges. Arrange the chicken on top, spacing evenly.

Bake: Slide the pan onto the steel or stone and bake for 12 to 15 minutes, until the cheese is bubbly and the crust is golden brown. Remove from the oven, run a dull knife around the edge of the pan, then slide the pizza out of the pan onto a wire rack and let cool for 5 minutes.

Drizzle with ½ cup of the blue cheese dressing and the remaining ⅓ cup buffalo sauce, then top with the celery, distributing evenly. Cut into squares (scissors work best here) and serve with more blue cheese dressing for dipping.

BLUE CHEESE DRESSING

Makes about 270 grams (1 cup)

75 grams (⅓ cup) sour cream

75 grams (⅓ cup) mayonnaise

60 grams (¼ cup) buttermilk

60 grams (2 ounces) Danish blue cheese, crumbled

1 to 2 teaspoons apple cider vinegar

Fine salt and freshly ground black pepper

In a small bowl stir together the sour cream, mayonnaise, buttermilk, and blue cheese. Season to taste with vinegar, salt, and pepper. Use right away, or cover and refrigerate for up to 1 week.

Tricolore

Makes one large pizza; serves 10 to 12

37.5 grams (3 tablespoons) extra-virgin olive oil

1 batch (772 grams) Grandma Dough (page 195)

340 grams (12 ounces) low-moisture whole-milk mozzarella, shredded (3 cups)

325 grams (1⅓ cups) Marinara Sauce (page 35)

128 grams (½ cup) Basil Pesto (page 37)

Grated Parmigiano-Reggiano or pecorino Romano, for finishing

Dried oregano, for finishing (optional)

Red pepper flakes, for finishing (optional)

The Tricolore allegedly honors Italy because the colors of the toppings mirror the colors of the Italian flag. But we think it celebrates Italy in a more meaningful way, by showcasing some of that country's greatest contributions to the world: perfect marinara sauce, bright and garlicky pesto, and creamy mozzarella cheese.

Position a rack in the bottom third of the oven. Place a baking steel or stone on the rack and preheat the oven to 500°F for at least 1 hour.

Shape the pizza: Drizzle the oil into a 14-inch square Grandma-style pizza pan or an 18 × 13-inch rimmed baking sheet and spread to coat the pan completely. Transfer the dough to the pan and turn it once to coat both sides with oil. After coating the dough in oil, press to the edges of the pan, dimpling it with your fingertips in the process. The dough may start to resist and shrink back; if that happens, just cover and let it rest for 15 minutes to allow the gluten to relax, then repeat the dimpling and pressing. At this point the dough should reach the edges of the pan; if it doesn't, give it one more 15-minute rest before repeating a third and final time.

Cover and let it rest at room temperature until it has puffed slightly, at least 40 minutes or, for a slightly lighter pie, up to 1½ hours.

Top the crust with the cheese, spreading it all the way to the edges of the pan, then dollop or spread the marinara sauce and basil pesto in alternating 1-inch-wide stripes diagonally across the dough, leaving a bit of space in between for the cheese to show through.

Bake: Slide the pan onto the steel or stone and bake for 12 to 15 minutes, until the cheese is bubbly and the crust is golden. Remove from the oven, run a dull knife around the edge of the pan, then slide the pizza out of the pan onto a wire rack and let cool for 5 minutes.

Shower with Parmesan to taste and sprinkle with oregano and red pepper flakes, if using. Cut into squares (scissors work best here) and serve.

Roasted Cherry Tomato and Garlic Confit

Makes one large pizza; serves 10 to 12

625 grams (4 cups) cherry tomatoes

87.5 grams (¼ cup plus 3 tablespoons) extra-virgin olive oil, divided

45 grams (3 tablespoons) capers, drained (optional)

2 teaspoons fresh oregano leaves or 1 teaspoon dried

1 teaspoon fine salt, plus more to taste

Freshly ground black pepper, to taste

60 grams (2½ tablespoons) mashed Garlic Confit (page 55), divided

1 batch (772 grams) Grandma Dough (page 195)

250 grams (8.8 ounces) whole-milk ricotta (1 cup)

42 grams (1½ ounces) Parmigiano-Reggiano, finely grated (¾ cup)

120 grams (4¼ ounces) low-moisture whole-milk mozzarella, grated (about 1 cup)

25 grams (2 tablespoons) Garlic Confit oil (page 55), for finishing

4 grams (¼ cup) fresh flat-leaf parsley leaves

Roasted tomatoes and ricotta are a late summer rite of passage, and here both are put to best use: The tomatoes are roasted until they're slumped and extra sweet, and the ricotta is spooned on at the end, providing a cool contrast. Though the garlic confit requires an extra step, it's a worthwhile one: You'll never be sad to have it in the fridge to schmear on toast or slip under the skin of a chicken before roasting, and the garlic confit oil is a great topping for most pizzas, or a base for a vinaigrette.

Position racks in the lower and upper thirds of the oven. Place a baking steel or stone on the lower rack and preheat the oven to 500°F for at least 1 hour.

Make the roasted tomatoes: In a large bowl, combine the tomatoes, 50 grams (¼ cup) of the olive oil, the capers (if using), and oregano. Season with the salt and pepper. Spread the tomatoes on a rimmed baking sheet. Turn the oven to broil and slide the baking sheet onto the top rack of the oven. Broil for 5 minutes, shake the pan to redistribute the tomatoes, then broil for another 3 to 5 minutes, until the tomatoes burst and begin to brown. Because broiler strength varies, keep a close eye on the tomatoes so they don't burn. Remove from the oven, transfer to a wire rack, and let cool slightly. Return the oven to the bake setting at 500°F. Scrape the tomatoes and any juices into a medium bowl and add 30 grams (1 heaping tablespoon) of the garlic confit.

Shape the pizza: Drizzle the remaining 37.5 grams (3 tablespoons) olive oil into a 14-inch square Grandma-style pizza pan or an 18 × 13-inch rimmed baking sheet and spread to coat the pan completely. Transfer the dough to the pan and turn it once to coat both sides with oil. After coating the dough in oil, press it to the edges of the pan, dimpling it with your fingertips in the process. The dough may start to resist and shrink back; if that happens, just cover and let it rest for 15 minutes to allow the gluten to relax, then repeat the dimpling and pressing. At this point the dough should reach the edges of the pan; if it doesn't, give it one more 15-minute rest before repeating a third and final time. Cover and let it rest at room temperature until it has puffed slightly, at least 40 minutes or, for a slightly lighter pie, up to 1½ hours.

In a medium bowl, stir together the ricotta and Parmesan. Add the remaining garlic confit, mashing it more as you stir it in, and season generously to taste with salt and pepper. Set aside.

Distribute the mozzarella over the dough, spreading it all the way to the edges. Dollop the roasted tomatoes over the dough.

Bake: Slide the pan onto the steel or stone and bake for 12 to 15 minutes, until the cheese is bubbly and the crust is golden. Remove from the oven, run a dull knife around the edge of the pan, then slide the pizza out of the pan onto a wire rack and let cool 5 minutes. Top with dollops of the ricotta mixture, spacing evenly, then drizzle with the garlic confit oil and scatter the parsley on top. Cut into squares (scissors work best here) and serve.

Eggplant Parm

Makes one large pizza; serves 10 to 12

540 grams (1 medium) eggplant, sliced crosswise into ½-inch-thick rounds

87.5 grams (¼ cup plus 3 tablespoons) extra-virgin olive oil, divided

Fine salt and freshly ground black pepper

1 batch (772 grams) Grandma Dough (page 195)

240 grams (8½ ounces) low-moisture whole-milk mozzarella, shredded (a generous 2 cups)

589 grams (2 cups) Marinara Sauce (page 35)

42 grams (1½ ounces) pecorino Romano, finely grated (¾ cup)

Fresh basil leaves, for garnish

50 grams (½ cup) Garlicky Panko (page 53)

Eggplant parm is one of the great slice shop flavors, but it's a laborious one to recreate at home—who in their right mind is going to fry a bunch of eggplant, *then* go through the process of making pizza? That's why we developed a shortcut: We roast the eggplant in the oven as it preheats, then shower the baked pizza in crispy, garlicky panko, emulating real eggplant parm with half the effort.

Position a rack in the bottom third of the oven with a baking steel or stone on the rack. Preheat the oven to 500°F for at least 1 hour.

Roast the eggplant: Brush the eggplant slices on both sides with 50 grams (¼ cup) of the oil, arrange in a single layer on a rimmed baking sheet, and season with salt and pepper. Slide the pan onto the baking steel or stone and roast for 8 minutes. Flip the eggplant slices over and continue to roast for an additional 7 to 8 minutes, until the eggplant is soft and golden brown on the underside. Remove from the oven and set aside.

Shape the pizza: Drizzle the remaining oil into a 14-inch square Grandma-style pizza pan or an 18 × 13-inch rimmed baking sheet and spread to coat the pan completely. Transfer the dough to the pan and turn it once to coat both sides with oil. After coating the dough in oil, press it to the edges of the pan, dimpling it with your fingertips in the process. The dough may start to resist and shrink back; if that happens, just cover and let it rest for 15 minutes to allow the gluten to relax, then repeat the dimpling and pressing. At this point, the dough should reach the edges of the pan; if it doesn't, give it one more 15-minute rest before repeating a third and final time. Cover and let it rest at room temperature until it has puffed slightly, at least 40 minutes or, for a slightly lighter pie, up to 1½ hours.

Evenly distribute the mozzarella on the dough, spreading it all the way to the edges of the pan, then dollop spoonfuls of sauce on the cheese and spread into an even layer all the way to the edges. Arrange the roasted eggplant slices on top.

Bake: Slide the pan onto the steel or stone and bake for 12 to 15 minutes, until the cheese is bubbly and the crust is golden. Remove from the oven, run a dull knife around the edge of the pan, then slide the pizza out of the pan onto a wire rack and let cool 5 minutes. Sprinkle with the pecorino, a few basil leaves, and the garlicky panko, then cut into squares (scissors work best here) and serve.

WEEKNIGHT DETROIT

We hate to get into a debate about thin crust versus thick crust, but facts are facts: If you're feeding a family of four (or more!) for dinner, thick-crust pan pizzas have an edge. A 13 × 9-inch pie can serve six people right out of the oven, assuming you don't have any particularly big eaters in the house (if there are teenagers involved, all bets are off). And if you're feeding a family on a weeknight, this recipe for Weeknight Detroit has an edge over our Sourdough Detroit (page 219), because it's fast—you can start it at noon, forget about it for most of the afternoon, and have it on the table for dinner.

And what a dinner it will be. Few regional pizzas are as craveable as Detroit. The fat square slices are beloved for the cheese (traditionally Wisconsin brick), which gets spread directly onto the parbaked dough, and the sweet and tangy sauce. As it bakes, the cheese at the edge of the pan forms a lacy, crispy, salty cheese skirt, called frico, that makes this pizza even more lovable.

This recipe is as flexible as our other weeknight doughs (pages 132 and 133). You can bring the dough to the bulk fermentation stage (while it's still in the bowl) or even to the shaped stage (when it has been pressed in the pan) and stick it in the fridge. It can hang out there for up to twenty-four hours, at which point all you need to do is take it out, let it come to room temperature, and proceed with the recipe.

About the bake: These pies are parbaked before they're topped and finished. This allows the dough to rise in the oven unencumbered, making for a much lighter and taller pizza than it would be otherwise. If baked from the outset with a full blanket of sauce and cheese, the pizza would not only be denser, but also soggy.

You'll notice that we have no anxiety about loading these pies up with heavier toppings such as meatballs and potatoes—that's because the parbake ensures the dough won't buckle underneath them. But the top isn't the only place these pizzas excel; a lot of folks think the golden, crispy bottom is the best part. If you want to go the extra mile, sprinkle a layer of sesame seeds or finely shredded Parm on the bottom of the pan before you press the dough into it—it adds flavor and makes the bottom of the pie even crispier.

5 mins	1½ to 2 hours	Chill or shape and bake
Mix	Bulk fermentation	Shape and bake your pizza, or refrigerate the dough for up to 24 hours; let it warm up at room temperature for an hour before stretching.

Weeknight Detroit Dough

Makes 669 grams, enough for one 13 × 9-inch pizza

360 grams (3 cups) unbleached bread flour

9 grams (1½ teaspoons) fine salt

3 grams (1 teaspoon) instant yeast

270 grams (1 cup plus 3 tablespoons) lukewarm water (85° to 90°F)

15 grams (1 generous tablespoon) extra-virgin olive oil

Make the dough: In a large bowl, mix together the flour, salt, and yeast until well combined. Add the water and oil. Mix until thoroughly combined and homogeneous; don't be afraid to stir vigorously to incorporate the dry ingredients. If the dough feels dry, add a scant tablespoon of water. Cover the dough and let it rest at room temperature for 15 minutes.

Uncover the dough and perform a bowl fold: Use a wet hand to grab a section of dough from one side, lift it up, then press it down into the middle. Repeat, turning the bowl 90 degrees (a quarter turn) after each stretch, 3 to 6 times total, until the dough won't elongate easily. Turn the dough over, placing it seam side down in the bowl. Cover and let it rest at room temperature for 15 minutes.

Repeat the bowl fold: After the second bowl fold, the dough should be smoother and feel tighter. Cover the dough and allow it to rest at room temperature for 1 to 1½ hours, until it's slightly puffy but not necessarily doubled in size.

The dough is now ready to use in the recipes on the pages that follow. Alternatively, after the second bowl fold (but before the room-temperature rest), cover the bowl tightly and transfer to the refrigerator for 8 to 24 hours. Remove from the refrigerator and allow the dough to come to room temperature for 1 hour before shaping and baking your pizza.

Garlicky Broccoli Rabe and Black Olive

Makes one 13 × 9-inch pizza

50 grams (4 tablespoons) extra-virgin olive oil, divided

1 batch (669 grams) Weeknight Detroit Dough (page 207)

18 grams (1 tablespoon) fine salt, plus more to taste

1 small bunch broccoli rabe (about 350 grams/ 12 ounces), ends trimmed

4 medium garlic cloves (about 20 grams), thinly sliced

¼ to ½ teaspoon red pepper flakes

½ teaspoon grated lemon zest

100 grams (1 cup) pitted black olives, such as kalamata, coarsely chopped

170 grams (6 ounces) low-moisture whole-milk mozzarella, shredded (1¼ cups)

70 grams (2½ ounces) Parmigiano-Reggiano, finely grated (1¼ cups)

Pizza is no stranger to bold flavors (looking at you, anchovies!), and here we've got two: briny, salty black olives and bitter broccoli rabe.

Position a rack in the bottom third of the oven. Place a baking steel or stone on the rack and preheat the oven to 500°F for at least 1 hour.

Shape the pizza: Coat a 13 × 9-inch Detroit-style pizza pan or metal baking pan with 1 tablespoon of the oil. Transfer the dough to the pan and turn once to coat in oil.

Gently press and stretch the dough, using your fingertips to dimple the surface and encourage it to cover the entire pan. If the dough resists, cover it, let it rest for 30 minutes, and try again. Cover the dough and let it rest for 45 to 60 minutes, until slightly puffy (there should be some bubbles on the surface and edges, but the dough will not have doubled in size).

While the dough rises, prepare the broccoli rabe: Add the salt to a large saucepan of water; it should taste salty. Bring it to a boil over high heat. Add the broccoli rabe and cook until tender (remove and taste a piece to check), 2 to 3 minutes. Drain the broccoli rabe and immediately rinse with cold water until cool, then gather into a bunch and squeeze firmly to remove the excess water. Transfer to a cutting board and cut into bite-size pieces.

Heat the remaining 3 tablespoons oil in a large skillet over medium heat. Add the garlic and red pepper flakes and cook, stirring, until the garlic begins to turn light golden, about 1 minute. Add the broccoli rabe and cook, stirring, until it starts to stick to the pan, 2 to 3 minutes. Remove from the heat and stir in the lemon zest. Season to taste with salt and let cool slightly. Stir in the olives.

Parbake the pizza: When the oven is fully preheated and the dough has risen, slide the pan onto the steel or stone and bake until the dough has set but has barely taken on any color, 10 to 12 minutes.

Remove the pan from the oven. Starting at the edges of the pan, sprinkle a thick layer of mozzarella over the dough, adding more where the dough meets the pan edge; it will sizzle on contact with the pan. Scatter the broccoli rabe over the parbaked dough, distributing it evenly. Top with the Parmesan, distributing the cheese all the way to the edges.

Slide the pan back onto the steel or stone and bake until the edges of the pizza are deeply colored and crisp, 12 to 14 minutes.

Remove the pan from the oven and use a dull knife to separate the crispy, cheesy edge of the pizza from the edge of the pan. With courage and conviction (and a large spatula to aid you), immediately slide the pizza out of the pan onto a wire rack (this will prevent the crust from getting soggy). Let cool for a few minutes, then transfer to a cutting board and cut into squares to serve.

Loaded Baked Potato

Makes one 13 × 9-inch pizza

25 grams (2 tablespoons) extra-virgin olive oil, divided

1 batch (669 grams) Weeknight Detroit Dough (page 207)

42 grams (2 tablespoons plus 1 teaspoon) fine salt, divided

454 grams (1 pound) Yukon Gold potatoes, scrubbed

170 grams (½ medium) onion, thinly sliced (about ½ cup)

1½ teaspoons finely chopped fresh rosemary

½ teaspoon red pepper flakes

113 grams (4 ounces) cooked thick-cut bacon, coarsely chopped (optional)

226 grams (8 ounces) sharp cheddar, shredded (2 cups)

57 grams (¼ cup) sour cream

14 grams (1 tablespoon) milk, heavy cream, or water

Finely chopped fresh chives, for sprinkling

There's a special place in heaven for potato pizzas (see the Potato pizza alla pala, page 129, for another take), and this one is especially lovely: The buttery-soft potatoes meld with the fluffy-yet-crispy crust.

Position a rack in the bottom third of the oven. Place a baking steel or stone on the rack and preheat the oven to 500°F for at least 1 hour.

Shape the pizza: Coat a 13 × 9-inch Detroit-style pizza pan or metal baking pan with 1 tablespoon of the oil. Transfer the dough to the pan and turn once to coat in oil.

Gently press and stretch the dough, using your fingertips to dimple the surface and encourage it to cover the entire pan. If the dough resists, cover it, let it rest for 30 minutes, and try again. Cover the dough and let it rest for 45 to 60 minutes, until slightly puffy (there should be some bubbles on the surface and edges, but the dough will not have doubled in size).

While the dough rises, prepare the topping: In a large bowl, combine 1 quart warm water with 2 tablespoons of the salt, stirring until the salt has dissolved. Slice the potatoes crosswise as thinly as possible (about ⅛ inch) and transfer to the salt water. Let the potatoes soak until you're ready to top the pizza. (Potatoes can soak at room temperature for up to 2 hours; any longer and the bowl should be transferred to the refrigerator, where they can soak up to 2 hours longer.)

Parbake the pizza: When the oven is fully preheated and the dough has risen, slide the pan onto the steel or stone and bake until the dough has set but has barely taken on any color, 10 to 12 minutes.

Remove the pan from the oven. Drain the potatoes well and pat them very dry with a clean kitchen towel. (Alternatively, bundle the potatoes in a clean kitchen towel and squeeze them dry.) Transfer the potatoes to a large bowl, along with the onion, the remaining 1 tablespoon oil, the rosemary, red pepper flakes, and the remaining 1 teaspoon salt. Toss to coat, then lay the potatoes on top of the parbaked dough, distributing them evenly in a single layer. Sprinkle the bacon evenly on top (if using), followed by the cheese, spreading it all the way to the edges of the pan.

Slide the pan back onto the steel or stone and bake until the edges of the pizza are deeply colored and crisp, 12 to 14 minutes.

Remove the pan from the oven and use a dull knife to separate the crispy, cheesy edge of the pizza from the edge of the pan. With courage and conviction (and a large spatula to aid you), immediately slide the pizza out of the pan onto a wire rack (this will prevent the crust from getting soggy). Let cool for a few minutes. Whisk together the sour cream and milk and drizzle over the pizza, then sprinkle with chives. Transfer to a cutting board and cut into squares to serve.

Roasted Pineapple, Ham, and Jalapeño

Makes one 13 × 9-inch pizza

12.5 grams (1 tablespoon) extra-virgin olive oil

1 batch (669 grams) Weeknight Detroit Dough (page 207)

283 grams (10 ounces) peeled, cored pineapple, cut into ¼-inch slices (about ½ of a fresh pineapple)

56 grams (2 ounces) pickled jalapeño chile rings, coarsely chopped (about ⅓ cup)

45 grams (2 tablespoons) Hot Honey (page 52), plus more for serving

4 tablespoons chopped fresh cilantro, divided

227 grams (8 ounces) low-moisture whole-milk mozzarella, shredded (2 cups)

250 grams (1 cup) Detroit-Style Pizza Sauce (page 36)

113 grams (4 ounces) ham, such as Black Forest, sliced crosswise into 1-inch-wide ribbons

This pie is topped with a chutney-like sauce of roasted pineapple, sliced jalapeños, hot honey, and cilantro. If that sounds like the type of thing that would be good slathered over a country ham, well, you aren't wrong—which is why we add slices of ham to this pie, too.

Position a rack in the bottom third of the oven. Place a baking steel or stone on the rack and preheat the oven to 500°F for at least 1 hour.

Shape the pizza: Coat a 13 × 9-inch Detroit-style pizza pan or metal baking pan with the oil. Transfer the dough to the pan and turn once to coat in oil.

Gently press and stretch the dough, using your fingertips to dimple the surface and encourage it to cover the entire pan. If the dough resists, cover it, let it rest for 30 minutes, and try again. Cover the dough and let it rest for 45 to 60 minutes, until slightly puffy (the dough will not have doubled in size).

While the dough rises, prepare the topping: Line a rimmed baking sheet with parchment paper and spread the pineapple on the pan in a single layer. Slide the pan onto the steel or stone and roast for 20 minutes, flipping the pineapple pieces halfway through roasting, until the pineapple pieces are browned and charred in spots. Remove from the oven, let cool slightly, then coarsely chop the pineapple into bite-size pieces. Transfer to a small bowl and add the jalapeños, hot honey, and 1 tablespoon of the cilantro. Stir to combine and set aside.

Parbake the pizza: When the oven is fully preheated and the dough has risen, slide the pan onto the steel or stone and bake until the dough has set but has barely taken on any color, 10 to 12 minutes.

Remove the pan from the oven. Starting at the edges of the pan, sprinkle half (113 grams/4 ounces) of the mozzarella in a thick layer where the dough meets the pan edge; it will sizzle on contact with the pan. Dollop the sauce over the pizza and spread evenly to the cheese border. Top with the ham ribbons, distributing evenly, followed by the pineapple-jalapeño mixture. Evenly cover the pizza with the remaining 113 grams (4 ounces) mozzarella.

Slide the pan back onto the steel or stone and bake for 12 to 14 minutes, until the cheesy edge and the top of the pizza are well browned.

Remove the pan from the oven, then use a dull knife to separate the crispy, cheesy edge of the pizza from the edge of the pan. With courage and conviction (and a large spatula to aid you), immediately slide the pizza out of the pan onto a wire rack (this will prevent the crust from getting soggy). Let cool for a few minutes, then top with the remaining 3 tablespoons cilantro. Transfer to a cutting board, cut into squares, and serve, with additional hot honey alongside for drizzling.

Meatball Sub

Makes one 13 × 9-inch pizza

12.5 grams (1 tablespoon) extra-virgin olive oil

1 batch (669 grams) Weeknight Detroit Dough (page 207)

454 grams (1 pound) ground beef (85% lean)

1 teaspoon garlic powder

56 grams (2 ounces) Parmigiano-Reggiano, finely grated (1 cup), divided

15 grams (½ cup plus 2 tablespoons) loosely packed fresh flat-leaf parsley leaves, finely chopped, divided

½ teaspoon fine salt

¼ teaspoon freshly ground black pepper

170 grams (6 ounces) provolone, shredded (about 1¼ cups)

375 grams (1½ cups) Detroit-Style Pizza Sauce (page 36)

To make sure the meatballs on this pie are fully cooked, we use the heat of the preheating oven to give them a jump-start. Keep an eye on them and remember that they'll go *back* in the oven after they're put on the pizza. You're trying to hit a sweet spot where the meatballs are cooked but still juicy.

Position a rack in the bottom third of the oven. Place a baking steel or stone on the rack and preheat the oven to 500°F for at least 1 hour.

Shape the pizza: Coat a 13 × 9-inch Detroit-style pizza pan or metal baking pan with the oil. Transfer the dough to the pan and turn once to coat in oil.

Gently press and stretch the dough, using your fingertips to dimple the surface and encourage it to cover the entire pan. If the dough resists, cover it, let it rest for 30 minutes, and try again. Cover the dough and let it rest for 45 to 60 minutes, until slightly puffy (there should be some bubbles on the surface and edges, but the dough will not have doubled in size).

While the dough rises, prepare the topping: Line a rimmed baking sheet with parchment paper. In a medium bowl, combine the beef, garlic powder, half of the Parmesan, ½ cup of the parsley, the salt, and pepper and mix until combined. Portion the mixture into 36 small meatballs (a rounded teaspoon scoop works well) and set on the prepared baking sheet.

Slide the pan onto the steel or stone and bake the meatballs for 5 to 7 minutes, until just cooked through. Transfer the pan to a wire rack and let cool.

Parbake the pizza: When the oven is fully preheated and the dough has risen, slide the pan onto the steel or stone and bake until the dough has set but has barely taken on any color, 10 to 12 minutes.

Remove the pan from the oven. Starting at the edges of the pan, sprinkle all but 2 tablespoons of the remaining Parmesan over the crust. Place the meatballs on top of the Parm, spacing them evenly, and press firmly into the dough. Distribute the provolone over the pizza in an even layer, applying it a bit more thickly around the edges of the pan. Dollop the sauce over the pizza.

Slide the pan back onto the steel or stone and bake for 12 to 14 minutes, until the edges are deeply colored.

Remove the pan from the oven and run a dull knife around the edge of the pan to separate the crispy, cheesy edge of the pizza from the edge of the pan. With courage and conviction (and a large spatula to aid you), immediately slide the pizza out of the pan onto a wire rack (this will prevent the crust from getting soggy). Sprinkle the remaining Parmesan and parsley on top, then cut into squares and serve.

SOURDOUGH DETROIT

Sourdough Detroit is a pizza that defies expectations. You might reasonably assume that the flavor of sourdough would get lost among all the other bold flavors of a Detroit pie, but in fact it turns out to be a natural partner—the tang of fermentation adds interest to the dough and enhances the toppings. And although these slices are thick and substantial, they're also pillowy, crispy, and light. You think you can't possibly eat two slices, but it turns out you can—and then keep going.

Dark, heavy anodized pans (particularly those made by LloydPans) are traditional for this style of pizza, and they really do make a difference. A regular 13 × 9-inch metal baking pan also works, but a dark anodized pan will give you a crispier pie with dramatic flames of golden frico. The sides and bottom of the pie almost fry in these pans, becoming impossibly crisp.

This is a sourdough pizza that is mixed and baked in a single day. (Yes, it's possible!) On first read the recipe may seem like a long process, but it's mostly hands-off: Mix the dough before breakfast and fold a few times during the first hour. Let the dough rise in a warm spot until midafternoon. Place the dough in an oiled pan and set to rise for an additional couple of hours before parbaking (this is key for the open structure of the crust), topping, and finishing. A vibrant, healthy starter is critical for the success of this pie, but if your sourdough isn't quite game-ready—or you just want an extra layer of assurance—add 1.5 grams (½ teaspoon) instant yeast to the dough at the mix stage.

5 mins	7 to 8 hours	45 mins to 1½ hours	22 to 26 mins
Mix	Bulk fermentation	Shape and rest	Bake

Sourdough Detroit Dough

Makes 807 grams, enough for one 13 × 9-inch pizza

360 grams (3 cups) unbleached bread flour

39 grams (¼ cup) semolina flour

10 grams (1¾ teaspoons) fine salt

1.5 grams (½ teaspoon) instant yeast (optional, see page 217)

99 grams (7 tablespoons) sourdough culture

29 grams (2 tablespoons plus 1 teaspoon) extra-virgin olive oil

268 grams (1 cup plus 3 tablespoons) water, warm (95° to 100°F)

Make the dough: In a large bowl (a 2-quart bowl or container with a lid works best), whisk together the flours and salt. (If your sourdough isn't vibrant and healthy, add the yeast at this stage.) Add the sourdough culture, oil, and water and mix until the mixture is thoroughly combined and homogeneous; there should be no dry patches or lumps. Cover and let it rest for 20 minutes.

Uncover the dough and perform a bowl fold: Use a wet hand to grab a section of dough from one side, lift it up, then press it down into the middle. Repeat, turning the bowl 90 degrees (a quarter turn) after each stretch, 8 to 12 times total, until the dough won't elongate easily. Turn the dough over, placing it seam side down in the bowl. Cover and let it rest at room temperature for 20 minutes.

Repeat the bowl fold: After the second bowl fold, the dough should be smoother and feel tighter. Cover the dough and let it rest for 20 minutes.

Repeat the bowl fold one final time: Cover the dough and let rise at warm room temperature until slightly puffy, 6 to 8 hours. The dough is now ready to use in the recipes on the pages that follow.

Motor City Classic

Makes one 13 × 9-inch pizza

12.5 grams
(1 tablespoon)
extra-virgin olive oil

1 batch (807 grams)
Sourdough Detroit
Dough (page 219)

340 grams (12 ounces)
brick cheese, shredded
(3 cups) **or** 170 grams
(6 ounces) low-moisture
whole-milk mozzarella,
shredded (1½ cups)
plus 170 grams
(6 ounces) cheddar,
shredded (1½ cups)

350 grams (1⅓ cups)
Detroit-Style Pizza
Sauce (page 36)

28 grams (1 ounce)
pecorino Romano, finely
grated (½ cup)

Red pepper flakes
(optional)

Detroit-style pizza is not traditionally sourdough, but there are two things that make this pie otherwise authentic: (1) the Wisconsin brick cheese, which melts like a dream (cheddar and mozzarella will do in a pinch), and (2) the sweet and thick Detroit-style sauce. Could you use a different sauce here? Technically, yes. But it wouldn't be a Motor City Classic.

Grease a 13 × 9-inch baking pan with the oil. Transfer the dough to the pan and stretch to fill the pan. Arrange the pan so a long side is facing you. Lightly oil your hands, then gently fold the bottom third of the dough up toward the center. Fold the top third down to cover, like you're folding a business letter. Starting at one end and using your fingertips, decisively dimple the dough from end to end, pressing firmly until you feel the bottom of the pan but not so hard that you tear through the dough, stretching the dough into the edges of the pan as you dimple. If the dough resists, cover it, let it rest for 30 minutes, and try again.

Cover the pan and let the dough rise at warm room temperature for 2 to 3 hours, until puffy. During the last hour of the rise, position a rack in the bottom third of the oven. Place a baking steel or stone on the rack and preheat the oven to 500°F.

Bake: Slide the pan onto the steel or stone and bake until the dough has set but has barely taken on any color, 10 to 12 minutes.

Remove the pan from the oven. Starting at the edges of the pan, sprinkle a thick layer of brick cheese where the dough meets the pan edge; it will sizzle on contact with the pan. Once you've made this cheese moat, spread the remaining cheese across the interior of the dough. Spoon thick stripes of sauce on the diagonal on top of the cheese layer.

Return the pizza to the oven and bake until the edges are deeply colored and crisp, 12 to 14 minutes.

Remove the pan from the oven and run a dull knife around the edge of the pan to loosen the pizza from the edge. With courage and conviction (and a large spatula to aid you), immediately slide the pizza out of the pan onto a wire rack (this will prevent it from steaming in the pan and losing its crisp crust). Let cool for a few minutes, then sprinkle with the pecorino and red pepper flakes, if using. Transfer to a cutting board and cut into squares.

Roasted Cauliflower and Gruyère

Makes one 13 × 9-inch pizza

62.5 grams (5 tablespoons) extra-virgin olive oil, divided

1 batch (807 grams) Sourdough Detroit Dough (page 219)

2 medium heads cauliflower (about 3 pounds), cut into small florets (about 8 cups)

1 teaspoon fine salt

½ teaspoon freshly ground black pepper

170 grams (6 ounces) Gruyère, shredded (1½ cups)

170 grams (6 ounces) low-moisture whole-milk mozzarella, shredded (1½ cups)

312 grams (1 cup plus 2½ tablespoons) Parmesan Béchamel (page 37)

25 grams (¼ cup) Garlicky Panko (page 53)

2 tablespoons finely chopped fresh flat-leaf parsley

Grated lemon zest, for sprinkling (optional)

Flaky salt, such as Maldon, for sprinkling

Is it worth making béchamel sauce just to put it on pizza? Yes—but only if it means the pizza is dumbfoundingly good. And this one, with all its roasted, cozy, savory notes of cauliflower gratin, is.

Grease a 13 × 9-inch baking pan with 1 tablespoon of the oil. Transfer the dough to the pan and stretch to fill the pan. Arrange the pan so a long side is facing you. Lightly oil your hands, then gently fold the bottom third of the dough up toward the center. Fold the top third down to cover, like you're folding a business letter. Starting at one end and using your fingertips, decisively dimple the dough from end to end, pressing firmly until you feel the bottom of the pan but not so hard that you tear through the dough, stretching the dough into the edges of the pan as you dimple. (If the dough resists, cover it, let it rest for 30 minutes, try again, and then proceed with the recipe.)

Cover the pan and let the dough rise at warm room temperature for 2 to 3 hours, until puffy.

Prepare the topping: Spread the cauliflower florets on a rimmed baking sheet. Add the remaining 4 tablespoons oil, the salt, and pepper and toss to coat, then spread the cauliflower in a single layer. During the last hour of the dough's rise, place the pan in the cold oven, then turn the oven to 500°F. Roast the cauliflower, stirring occasionally, until tender and well browned, 25 to 30 minutes. Set aside to cool; keep the oven on. Once cool, chop into small pieces.

In a medium bowl, combine the Gruyère and mozzarella; set aside.

Bake: Once the dough has risen, slide the pan onto the steel or stone and bake until the dough has set but has barely taken on any color, 10 to 12 minutes.

Remove the pan from the oven. Dollop the béchamel all over the dough, then use an offset spatula to spread in an even layer all over the parbaked crust, leaving a ½-inch border. Starting at the edges of the pan, sprinkle a thick layer of cheese where the dough meets the pan edge; it will sizzle on contact with the pan. Once you've made this cheese moat, spread half of the remaining cheese across the interior of the dough. Top with the cauliflower, then sprinkle with the remaining cheese.

Slide the pan back onto the steel or stone and bake until the top is deeply colored and the edges are browned and crispy, 12 to 14 minutes.

Remove the pan from the oven and run a dull knife around the edge of the pan to separate the crispy, cheesy edge of the pizza from the edge of the pan. With courage and conviction (and a large spatula to aid you), immediately slide the pizza out of the pan onto a wire rack (this will prevent the crust from steaming in the pan and losing its crisp crust). Let cool for a few minutes, then sprinkle with the panko, parsley, lemon zest (if using), and flaky salt. Transfer to a cutting board and cut into squares to serve.

Sausage and Vodka Sauce

Makes one 13 × 9-inch pizza

12.5 grams (1 tablespoon) extra-virgin olive oil

1 batch (807 grams) Sourdough Detroit Dough (page 219)

170 grams (6 ounces) sweet or hot Italian sausage, casings removed (about 2 links)

340 grams (12 ounces) brick cheese, shredded (3 cups) **or** 170 grams (6 ounces) low-moisture whole-milk mozzarella cheese (1½ cups) **plus** 170 grams (6 ounces) cheddar cheese, shredded (1½ cups)

350 grams (1¼ cups) Spicy Vodka Sauce (page 36)

28 grams (1 ounce) Parmigiano-Reggiano, finely grated (½ cup)

Red pepper flakes (optional)

Two full links of sausage and a good amount of cheese make this a seriously robust pie, which is why we use a Detroit crust for it—we know it won't buckle under all those toppings. For even more flavor, sometimes we like to sprinkle a bed of sesame seeds on the bottom of the pan before we press the dough into it; the sesame plays well with the spicy flavors of the sauce.

Grease a 13 × 9-inch baking pan with the oil. Transfer the dough to the pan and stretch to fill the pan. Arrange the pan so a long side is facing you. Lightly oil your hands, then gently fold the bottom third of the dough up toward the center. Fold the top third down to cover, like you're folding a business letter. Starting at one end and using your fingertips, decisively dimple the dough from end to end, pressing firmly until you feel the bottom of the pan but not so hard that you tear through the dough, stretching the dough into the edges of the pan as you dimple. If the dough resists, cover it, let it rest for 30 minutes, and try again.

Cover the pan and let the dough rise at warm room temperature for 2 to 3 hours, until puffy. During the last hour of the rise, arrange racks in the lower and upper thirds of the oven. Place a baking steel or stone on the lower rack and preheat the oven to 500°F.

Once the dough has risen, slide the pan onto the steel or stone and bake until the dough has set but has barely taken on any color, 10 to 12 minutes.

Meanwhile, break the sausage into small pieces, about ½ tablespoon each, and set on a rimmed baking sheet. Bake (at the same time the pizza is parbaking, but on a different rack) until just cooked through and beginning to brown, 6 to 8 minutes. Set aside.

Remove the pizza pan from the oven. Starting at the edges of the pan, sprinkle a thick layer of brick cheese where the dough meets the pan edge; it will sizzle on contact with the pan. Once you've made this cheese moat, spread the remaining cheese across the interior of the dough. Dollop spoonfuls of sauce all over the pizza, avoiding the edges, then dot with the sausage.

Return the pizza to the oven and bake until the edges are deeply colored and crisp, 12 to 14 minutes.

Remove the pan from the oven and use a dull knife to separate the crispy, cheesy edge of the pizza from the edge of the pan. With courage and conviction (and a large spatula to aid you), immediately slide the pizza out of the pan onto a wire rack (this will prevent the crust from steaming in the pan and losing its crisp crust). Let cool for a few minutes, then sprinkle with the Parmesan and red pepper flakes, if using. Transfer to a cutting board and cut into squares to serve.

Cacio e Pepe

Makes one 13 × 9-inch pizza

12.5 grams (1 tablespoon) extra-virgin olive oil

1 batch (807 grams) Sourdough Detroit Dough (page 219)

624 grams (2⅓ cups) Parmesan Béchamel (page 37)

114 grams (4 ounces) pecorino Romano, finely grated (2 cups), divided

1 teaspoon coarsely ground black pepper

On a research trip to New York a couple of us wandered into Mama's Too, a once under-the-radar, now immensely popular slice shop with locations both uptown and downtown. There we ordered a square slice of cacio e pepe pizza that had, no joke, probably two inches of feathery pecorino grated on top. The slice went straight into the oven where all that pecorino melted and melded with the layers of cheese beneath it. After tasting this slice, we had to sit on a park bench for a while and absorb the glory of what we'd just eaten. It was so good we knew we wanted to attempt our own version. This is our homage to that slice of pizza; we believe we do it justice.

Grease a 13 × 9-inch- pan with the oil. Transfer the dough to the pan and stretch to fill the pan. Arrange the pan so a long side is facing you. Lightly oil your hands, then gently fold the bottom third of the dough up toward the center. Fold the top third down to cover, like folding a business letter. Starting at one edge and using your fingertips, decisively dimple the dough from end to end, pressing firmly until you feel the bottom of the pan but not so hard that you tear through the dough, stretching the dough into the edges of the pan as you dimple. (If your dough resists, cover it, let it rest for 30 minutes, try again, and then proceed with the recipe.)

Cover the pan and let the dough rise at warm room temperature for 2 to 3 hours, until puffy. During the last hour of the rise, preheat the oven to 500°F with a baking steel or stone on the center rack.

Once the dough has risen, bake on the center rack until the dough has set but has barely taken on any color, 10 to 12 minutes.

Remove the pizza from the oven. Dollop the béchamel sauce all over the dough, then use an offset spatula to spread in an even layer all over the parbaked crust, leaving a ½-inch border. Sprinkle half of the pecorino around the edges of the pan.

Return the pizza to the oven and bake until the top has some brown spots and the edges are browned and crispy, about 12 to 14 minutes.

Remove the pan from the oven and use a dull knife to separate the crispy, cheesy edge of the pizza from the edge of the pan. With courage and conviction (and a large spatula to aid you), immediately slide the pizza out of the pan onto a wire rack (this will prevent the crust from steaming in the pan and becoming soggy). Let cool for a few minutes, then sprinkle with the pepper and remaining pecorino. Transfer to a cutting board and cut into squares.

PIZZA NIGHT SALADS

On pizza night, a big salad is nonnegotiable. You need it to balance the meal nutritionally, sure, but it's also there for the textures and aesthetics. A slice of pizza just looks better next to a pile of salad. It tastes better, too—no matter what's on the slice, no matter what's in the salad, they can usually be combined into a bite that's greater than the sum of their parts.

Still, this is pizza night, not salad night—the salad shouldn't be the star of the show. So the recipes in this chapter are decidedly not scene-stealers. They exist to add some greenery, acidity, and crunch to the meal; to that end, they rely on whatever's in season. You can think of this collection as having a spring salad, summer salad, fall salad, and winter salad. But really, they're pizza salads—the best salads of all.

Butter Lettuce Salad with Herby Buttermilk-Avocado Dressing

Serves 4 to 6

For the dressing:
113 grams (½ cup) buttermilk, well shaken, plus more as needed

28 grams (2 tablespoons) fresh lime juice

1 garlic clove, grated

1 small avocado, halved, pitted, and peeled

½ cup fresh soft herbs of your choice, such as cilantro, basil, parsley, dill, and/or chervil

1 teaspoon honey

¾ teaspoon fine salt, plus more to taste

½ teaspoon freshly ground black pepper, plus more to taste

For the salad:
2 heads butter lettuce, torn into bite-size pieces (about 10 cups)

8 radishes, sliced paper thin

1 English or 2 Persian cucumbers, sliced ¼ inch thick

1 cup shelled fresh peas

1 small avocado, halved, pitted, peeled, and diced

Fine salt and freshly ground black pepper

Here billowy butter lettuce is speckled with all the soft herbs of early spring. Slivers of radish and cucumber provide crunch, a handful of peas adds pops of sweetness, and the avocado is there for creaminess—both in the salad itself and in the tangy dressing.

Make the dressing: Combine the buttermilk, lime juice, garlic, avocado, herbs, honey, salt, and pepper in a blender and blend until creamy and emulsified. Thin as needed with additional buttermilk, 1 teaspoon at a time, if desired. Season to taste with additional salt and pepper. The dressing can be made ahead and stored in a lidded container in the fridge for up to 3 days.

For the salad: Spoon ½ cup of the dressing into the bottom of a large serving bowl. Top with the lettuce, radishes, cucumber, and peas. Toss together until evenly coated. Add the diced avocado and toss gently to combine. Season the salad with salt and pepper and serve right away, with additional dressing on the side.

Farm Stand Salad

Serves 4 to 6

For the croutons:
100 grams (3½ ounces) crusty bread, crusts trimmed and torn into ½-inch pieces (2 cups)

25 grams (2 tablespoons) extra-virgin olive oil

¼ teaspoon fine salt

¼ teaspoon freshly ground black pepper

For the vinaigrette:
¾ cup fresh soft herbs of your choice, such as basil, cilantro, parsley, and/or mint, divided

28 grams (2 tablespoons) champagne vinegar or white wine vinegar

Grated zest of 1 orange (about 1½ teaspoons)

28 grams (2 tablespoons) orange juice

28 grams (2 tablespoons) lemon juice

21 grams (1 tablespoon) honey

1 teaspoon Dijon mustard

¾ teaspoon fine salt, plus more to taste

¼ teaspoon black pepper, plus more to taste

½ teaspoon chopped fresh thyme

75 grams (6 tablespoons) extra-virgin olive oil

For the salad:
¼ small red onion, sliced paper thin

2 large handfuls arugula

1 cup fresh corn kernels (from about 1 large ear)

1 small zucchini, trimmed and shaved with a vegetable peeler into thin ribbons

1 pint cherry tomatoes, halved

1 English or 2 Persian cucumbers, peeled, halved, seeded, and sliced ¼ inch thick

Summer is arguably the easiest season in which to make a great salad; any ingredient you'd want is at its peak. This one features a summer triple threat (corn, tomatoes, zucchini) with just a few handfuls of greens tossed in and a lot of fresh herbs. Croutons add welcome crunch, but you could omit them and just pile the salad right on top of your pizza instead.

Make the croutons: Preheat the oven to 350°F. Toss the bread in a large bowl with the oil, salt, and pepper. Spread on a rimmed baking sheet in a single layer and bake, stirring occasionally, until golden brown and crispy, 12 to 15 minutes. Let cool on the pan. The croutons can be made up to 1 day ahead; once cool, transfer to an airtight container and store at room temperature (and try not to eat them all).

Make the dressing: Coarsely chop half the herbs; set the remainder aside for the salad. In a medium bowl, whisk together the vinegar, orange zest and juice, lemon juice, honey, mustard, salt, pepper, and thyme. Stir in the chopped herbs, then slowly whisk in the oil. Season to taste with additional salt and pepper and set aside until ready to use. The dressing can be made ahead and stored in a lidded container in the fridge for up to 2 days.

Make the salad: Put the onion in a small bowl and add cold water to cover. Let soak for 20 minutes (this will temper the bite of the onion). In a large serving bowl, combine the arugula, corn, zucchini ribbons, cherry tomatoes, and cucumber. Drain the onion, pat dry with paper towels, and add to the salad. Gently tear the remaining herbs into smaller pieces and add to the salad, along with the croutons. Drizzle ½ cup dressing over and toss to combine. Season to taste with additional salt and pepper. Serve immediately with additional dressing on the side.

Deep Green Salad with Cheesy No-Cheese Dressing

Serves 4 to 6

For the dressing:

100 grams (½ cup) neutral oil, such as grape-seed or canola

60 grams (¾ cup) nutritional yeast

57 grams (¼ cup) water

28 grams (2 tablespoons) apple cider vinegar

14 grams (1 tablespoon) low-sodium soy sauce or tamari

1 teaspoon maple syrup

½ teaspoon freshly ground black pepper

1 large garlic clove, finely chopped or grated

For the salad:

1 large bunch lacinato kale (about 300 grams/ 10½ ounces), coarse center stems removed and leaves cut into ribbons

Fine salt, to taste

1 large bunch Swiss or rainbow chard (about 250 grams), coarse center stems removed and leaves cut into ribbons

40 grams (⅓ cup) pistachios, toasted and finely chopped

Kale salads are now stalwarts of a certain kind of pizzeria (the kind that serves natural wine), and for good reason: The hearty greens are a great counterpoint to a cheesy slice, tricking us into thinking our pizza dinner is a balanced meal. In the long, dark months of fall and winter, kale (and chard, which plays Best Supporting Actor in this salad) are reliably available, so this is the salad we turn to when summer seems a long way off. The nutritional yeast in the dressing delivers a potent hit of umami, making us think of aged cheese (even though it's cheeseless).

Make the dressing: Combine the oil, nutritional yeast, water, vinegar, soy sauce, maple syrup, pepper, and garlic in a blender and blend until smooth and creamy. Taste and adjust the amounts of vinegar, pepper, and syrup as desired. The dressing should taste assertive—salty, acidic, and slightly sweet. The dressing can be made ahead and stored in a lidded container in the refrigerator for up to 5 days.

Make the salad: Put the kale in a large bowl and season with salt. Aggressively squeeze the kale with your hands until the pieces have softened and turned a darker shade of green, 1 to 2 minutes. Add the chard to the bowl and mix it into the kale, squeezing gently to soften.

Spoon about half of the dressing over the salad and toss with tongs or your hands to coat; the greens should be well dressed but not gloppy or sopping. Sprinkle in most of the pistachios and toss to combine. Taste the salad and season with salt. Sprinkle with the remaining pistachios and serve with additional dressing on the side.

Chicory Caesar with Parmesan Frico

Serves 4 to 6

For the frico:
56 grams (2 ounces) Parmigiano-Reggiano, finely grated (1 cup)

For the dressing:
56 grams (¼ cup) mayonnaise, preferably Hellman's

28 grams (1 ounce) Parmigiano-Reggiano, finely grated (½ cup)

4 anchovy fillets

1 tablespoon capers

1 tablespoon Dijon mustard

1 garlic clove

1 teaspoon grated lemon zest

1 teaspoon lemon juice

Dash of Worcestershire sauce

¼ teaspoon fine salt, plus more to taste

Freshly ground black pepper, to taste

100 grams (½ cup) extra-virgin olive oil

For the salad:
226 grams (8 ounces) escarole, cut into 1- to 2-inch-wide ribbons (about 8 cups)

226 grams (8 ounces) radicchio, leaves separated and torn into bite-size pieces (about 8 cups)

In this light reimagining of Caesar salad, assertively bitter chicories stand in for the romaine, an excellent foil for the punchy anchovy dressing. While traditionally Caesar salad is made with raw egg yolks, we've opted for mayonnaise instead (which is mostly egg yolks and oil, after all); it gives the dressing a rich creaminess. Can the anchovies be omitted, you ask? We don't recommend it. But if you don't have any in your pantry, a dash of fish sauce can be used instead. The bits of Parmesan frico play the role of a crouton (crunchy, irresistible); they make the salad.

Make the frico: Preheat the oven to 400°F. Line a rimmed baking sheet with parchment paper. Using a tablespoon, scoop the grated Parmesan onto the baking sheet in 1-tablespoon mounds, spacing them 4 inches apart. Gently flatten each cheese mound with the back of the spoon until you have a disk that measures about 3 inches wide. Bake for 5 to 6 minutes, or until the cheese is melted and beautifully golden brown. Remove from the oven and let cool for 10 to 15 minutes (the frico will continue to crisp as it cools). The frico can be made up to 1 day ahead; once cool, store in an airtight container at room temperature.

Make the dressing: Combine the mayonnaise, Parmesan, anchovies, capers, mustard, garlic, lemon zest and juice, Worcestershire sauce, salt, and pepper in a blender or food processor. Blend or pulse until smooth, then scrape down the sides of the bowl. With the machine running, slowly drizzle in the oil until emulsified. Season to taste with additional salt and pepper. The dressing can be made ahead and stored in a lidded container in the fridge for up to 5 days.

Make the salad: Place the escarole and radicchio in a large serving bowl. Drizzle the dressing over the top of the greens, then mix until thoroughly coated. Crumble the frico into bite-size pieces, add to the salad, and toss gently to combine. Serve immediately.

PIZZA NIGHT DESSERTS

When all that's left of the pizza is crumbs, and the salad bowl has nothing but a sheen of dressing, it's time for an intermission: You take a break, pour an amaro, sip an espresso, regain your strength.

But twenty minutes later? It's time for act two.

Pizza Night is an event—even (especially!) if it's just for you—and it deserves a strong, sweet closing. But not every dessert is a good fit. Even the lightest pizzas will leave a person pretty satiated, so we look to little bites like biscotti, or rich desserts that you can take as little, or as much of, as you like. It's probably not a coincidence that Italian (and Italian American) desserts are perfect for this.

First up: cookies, which are ideal casual endings, great for nibbling while you linger with wine. To go the extra mile, make a few of them and display a proper Italian American cookie platter. Or set out a whole cake with a knife and a set of plates. Let people serve themselves—the cakes in this chapter are built to be satisfying in even the smallest slice.

Of course, ice cream is also a perfect pizza night dessert. The no-churn method we employ in the spumoni is paradigm-shifting, and makes for dreamy, decadent slices. For a lighter option, there's always granita, and we offer an Aperol Spritz version—a dessert that ends Pizza Night strong in more ways than one.

Italian Rainbow Cookies

Makes about 32 cookies

For the cake:
195 grams (¾ cup) almond paste, homemade (recipe follows) or store-bought, cold

149 grams (¾ cup) sugar

¼ teaspoon fine salt

85 grams (6 tablespoons) unsalted butter, at room temperature

¾ teaspoon almond extract

3 large eggs (150 grams)

150 grams (1¼ cups) unbleached all-purpose flour

Red and green food coloring

For the filling:
170 grams (½ cup) apricot jam, divided

For the glaze:
170 grams (1 cup) semisweet or bittersweet chocolate wafers, divided

These layered cookies are really more like tiny slices of three-layer cake, each layer sandwiched together with apricot jam. Using a fork to make squiggles in the chocolate glaze before it sets is traditional and, in our opinion, mandatory.

Note: Chocolate chips can be used for the glaze, but we've found that wafers give a smoother finish. And while store-bought almond paste can be used in this recipe, we don't recommend it—the flavor is just wildly better when you make it yourself.

Position the oven racks in the center of the oven and preheat the oven to 350°F. Lightly grease three 8-inch square pans or line each pan with a parchment sling. If you have only one 8-inch square pan, simply bake the layers one at a time.

Make the cake: In the bowl of a stand mixer fitted with the flat beater attachment or in a large bowl if using an electric hand mixer, break the almond paste into large chunks. Add the sugar and salt and mix on low speed until sandy. The almond paste will break down into smaller pieces and become uniform in size.

Add the butter and almond extract. Beat on medium speed until the mixture is slightly fluffy and lightened in color, stopping to scrape the sides of the bowl as needed. Add the eggs, one at a time, mixing until each is fully incorporated before adding the next. Add the flour and mix until smooth.

Divide the batter into thirds. Portion approximately 235 grams (1 cup) batter each into 2 medium bowls. Leave the remaining third in the mixing bowl. To one bowl, add red coloring until the batter is vibrantly colored. To another bowl, add green coloring until the batter is vibrantly colored. Leave the batter in the mixing bowl plain.

Transfer each of the batters to one of the prepared pans and spread evenly; the layers will be thin. If you only have one pan, start by baking the plain layer first while the other batters rest at room temperature, then bake the green layer, then the red layer. There's no need to wash the pan between bakes—just be sure that the pan has cooled completely before lining with fresh parchment and baking the next layer.

Bake each layer for 9 to 11 minutes, until the cake springs back to the touch and looks dry in the center.

Remove the cake from the oven and cool in the pan for 10 minutes before turning it out to cool completely on a rack. Be sure that all the cake layers are completely cool before assembling.

Recipe continues

Assemble the rainbow cookies: Spread 85 grams (¼ cup) of the jam on top of the green layer of cake, spreading it all the way to the edges. Place the plain layer of cake on top of the jam and apply firm pressure to sandwich the two layers together.

Spread the remaining 85 grams (¼ cup) jam over the top of the plain layer, spreading it all the way to the edges. Place the red layer of cake on top and, again, apply firm pressure to sandwich all three layers together. Wrap tightly in plastic wrap.

Place the wrapped layers in a 13 × 9-inch pan (or any pan larger than an 8-inch square) and place an 8-inch square pan on top. Place 4 to 6 heavy cans (or something of comparable weight) inside the 8-inch square pan to weigh it down, compressing the cake layers below. Refrigerate the layers overnight with the heavy weights on top.

Glaze the rainbow cookies: Remove the cake layers from the refrigerator, unwrap, and place the cake, green layer down, on a cutting board. In a medium microwave-safe bowl, place 85 grams (½ cup) of the chocolate wafers and heat in 20-second increments at 50% power until melted, stirring after each burst. (Alternatively, melt the chocolate in a small saucepan over low heat, stirring frequently.) Stir the chocolate until smooth.

Spread the melted chocolate over the top of the red layer of cake, spreading it all the way to the edges. It's OK if some chocolate drips down over the edges.

Let the chocolate set either at room temperature or in the refrigerator. Before the chocolate fully sets, use the tines of a fork to create wavy lines over the chocolate. Once fully set, flip the assembled layers over. In the same microwave-safe bowl or saucepan, melt the remaining 85 grams (½ cup) chocolate wafers until smooth. Spread the melted chocolate over the top of the green layer of cake, spreading it all the way to the edges. It's OK if some chocolate drips down over the edges.

Let the chocolate set either at room temperature or in the refrigerator. Before the chocolate fully sets, use the tines of a fork to create wavy lines over the chocolate.

Once fully set, use a warm chef's knife to trim the sides of the square (baker's snack!) for a neat presentation before cutting the remainder of the rainbow cookies into pieces. (We like using an 8 × 4 pattern to make slices about 1¾ × 1 inch in size.) Serve the rainbow cookies at room temperature.

Store any leftover rainbow cookies in the refrigerator in an airtight container for up to 2 weeks. Let the pieces to come to room temperature before serving. The sandwich of assembled bars can also be frozen, well wrapped, for up to 2 months. When ready to serve, defrost in the refrigerator overnight, then glaze, cut, and serve.

ALMOND PASTE

Makes 375 grams (1½ cups)

168 grams (1¾ cups) almond flour

170 grams (1½ cups) confectioners' sugar

1 large egg white

⅛ teaspoon fine salt

1 to 1½ teaspoons almond extract, to taste

Combine the almond flour and confectioners' sugar in the bowl of a food processor or in the bowl of a stand mixer. Process or mix to blend briefly, just to combine.

Add the egg white, salt, and almond extract, processing or mixing until the mixture comes together and forms a malleable ball.

Remove the almond paste from the processor or mixer, scraping any residue from the sides of the bowl.

Shape the paste into a log. Double wrap it in plastic and refrigerate until firm, about 2 hours, before using.

Store the almond paste, tightly wrapped, for up to 1 month in the refrigerator, or up to 3 months in the freezer.

Glazed Ricotta Cookies

Makes 2 dozen cookies

For the cookies:
150 grams (1¼ cups) unbleached all-purpose flour

41 grams (¼ cup) semolina flour

1 teaspoon baking powder

¼ teaspoon baking soda

½ teaspoon fine salt

85 grams (6 tablespoons) unsalted butter, at room temperature

149 grams (¾ cup) granulated sugar

1 large egg (50 grams), at room temperature

227 grams (1 cup) ricotta, whole-milk or part-skim

1 teaspoon pure vanilla extract

Grated zest of 1 lemon or ½ orange

For the glaze:
255 grams (2¼ cups) confectioners' sugar

½ teaspoon pure vanilla extract

28 to 56 grams (2 to 4 tablespoons) milk, preferably whole

Sprinkles, nonpareils, or lemon zest, for decorating

These soft, pillowy cookies have a humble look that doesn't adequately convey how rich, moist, and delicious they are. That's why we really insist on sprinkles (white sprinkles are elegant, rainbow sprinkles are a party).

We love how the semolina in these cookies gives them a beautiful pale yellow color and a delicate crunch, but if you don't have any, you can omit the semolina and increase the amount of all-purpose flour to 180 grams (1½ cups).

Make the dough: In a medium bowl, whisk together the flours, baking powder, baking soda, and salt. Set aside.

In the bowl of a stand mixer fitted with the flat beater attachment or in a large bowl if using an electric hand mixer, combine the butter and granulated sugar. Beat on medium speed until smooth, 1 to 2 minutes. The mixture will not be lightened in color or fluffy in texture.

Add the egg and mix until fully combined. Scrape down the sides and bottom of the bowl and beat briefly. Add the ricotta, vanilla, and zest and briefly mix to fully combine.

Add the dry ingredients to the ricotta mixture all at once. Mix slowly until no dry floury streaks remain. Cover the bowl or transfer the dough to an airtight container and chill for at least 2 hours, or up to overnight.

When you're ready to bake, position the oven racks in the center of the oven and preheat the oven to 350°F. Line 2 rimmed baking sheets with parchment paper.

Scoop the chilled dough into generous tablespoon portions (a rounded tablespoon cookie scoop works well here). Place the dough balls on the prepared baking sheets, spacing them evenly apart (about 12 dough balls per baking sheet).

Bake the cookies for 15 to 17 minutes, rotating the pans from top to bottom and turning them from front to back halfway through baking, until the edges of the cookies just start to turn light brown. Remove the cookies from the oven and let them cool completely before icing.

Make the glaze: Once the cookies are completely cool, sift the confectioners' sugar into a large bowl. Using a whisk, stir in the vanilla, then mix in 28 grams (2 tablespoons) of the milk, adding additional milk by the tablespoon until the desired consistency is reached. The glaze should be thick, like cold honey.

Dollop 1 to 2 teaspoons of glaze on top of each cookie and spread it to the edges. While the glaze is still wet, top with sprinkles. The glaze starts to dry out quickly, so it is best to top 2 to 3 cookies at a time to help the sprinkles adhere before a crust forms.

Store any leftover ricotta cookies in an airtight container at room temperature for up to 3 days. For longer storage, the unglazed cookies can be frozen; let thaw, then glaze and garnish.

Pizzicati

Makes 3 dozen cookies

Grated zest of ½ lemon

50 grams (¼ cup) granulated sugar

57 grams (½ cup) confectioners' sugar, plus more for dusting

210 grams (1¾ cups) unbleached all-purpose flour

21 grams (3 tablespoons) cornstarch

½ teaspoon baking powder

¼ teaspoon fine salt

113 grams (8 tablespoons) unsalted butter, at room temperature, cut into ½-inch cubes

1 large egg (50 grams)

1 teaspoon pure vanilla extract

170 grams (½ cup) fig preserves, or jam of choice (see headnote)

Also known as pinch cookies because of their distinctive shape, pizzicati are delicate jam-filled shortbread cookies. You can use whatever jam you like (we go for fig preserves); just know that jam can vary in viscosity, so we recommend baking a test cookie before filling the entire batch. (Note: The baker always gets to eat the test cookie, even if the test goes well—it's baker's law!)

Rub the lemon zest into the granulated sugar in the bowl of a stand mixer fitted with the flat beater attachment or in a large bowl if using an electric hand mixer. Sift the confectioners' sugar, flour, cornstarch, baking powder, and salt into the mixing bowl. Mix on low speed to combine.

With the mixer still on low speed, add the butter a few cubes at a time and mix into the dry ingredients until fine, even crumbs form. Scrape down the bowl once midway through mixing to make sure everything is fully combined. Add the egg and vanilla and mix until the dough starts to form.

Turn the dough out onto a lightly greased piece of parchment paper. Loosely form the dough into a square and place a second lightly greased piece of parchment over the top. Roll the dough out into a 12-inch square, about ⅛ inch thick. If you need to, trim any scraps off where the dough spreads too much and place them wherever needed to make the 12-inch square. Remove the top piece of parchment paper and set aside.

Using a pizza wheel or sharp knife, cut the dough into a 6 × 6 pattern to create 2-inch squares. Once cut, replace the parchment on top and slide the dough onto a rimmed baking sheet. Cover the pan with plastic wrap and refrigerate for 30 minutes. Arrange racks in the upper and lower thirds of the oven and preheat the oven to 350°F. Line 2 rimmed baking sheets with parchment paper.

Remove the dough from the refrigerator and, with the help of a thin spatula, divide the dough squares evenly between the parchment-lined sheets. Place ½ teaspoon fig preserves in the center of each square of dough. To shape the cookies, pinch two opposite corners together.

Bake the cookies for 10 to 12 minutes, until the points are just starting to brown, rotating the pans from top to bottom and turning them from front to back halfway through baking.

Remove the cookies from the oven and let cool fully on the sheets. Sift a light dusting of confectioners' sugar over the cookies to finish.

Store cookies in an airtight container at room temperature for up to 3 days. Freeze for longer storage.

Piped Shortbread Cookies

Makes about 2 dozen cookies

170 grams (12 tablespoons) unsalted butter, softened

57 grams (½ cup) confectioners' sugar, sifted if lumpy

1 tablespoon vanilla bean paste or pure vanilla extract

¼ teaspoon fine salt

160 grams (1⅓ cups) unbleached all-purpose flour

28 grams (¼ cup) cornstarch

113 grams (⅓ cup) semisweet or bittersweet chocolate, melted, for dipping (optional)

Pistachios, walnuts, or pecans, toasted and finely chopped, for garnish (optional)

Rainbow sprinkles, for garnish (optional)

A stalwart of the Italian American bakery canon, these shortbread cookies are buttery and tender (thanks to the addition of cornstarch), with slightly crisp edges. Pipe them into whorled rosettes or into logs, then dip into melted chocolate and garnish with sprinkles or chopped nuts. You'll need a star tip and a pastry bag to make these cookies.

Arrange oven racks in the upper and lower thirds of the oven. Preheat the oven to 350°F. Lightly grease 2 rimmed baking sheets or line with parchment paper.

In the bowl of a stand mixer fitted with the flat beater attachment or in a large bowl if using an electric hand mixer, beat the butter on medium-high speed until the butter is very smooth and creamy, 3 to 5 minutes. Stop to scrape down the sides of the bowl as needed.

Add the confectioners' sugar, vanilla, and salt and continue beating until smooth. Add the flour and cornstarch, mixing on low speed until the mixture comes together to form a soft dough.

Transfer about half of the dough to a pastry bag fitted with an open star tip. (The larger the star tip, the easier it will be to pipe the cookie dough; Ateco tips #825 and #827 work well. Filling the pastry bag with only half the dough also makes piping more manageable; refill the bag as needed until you pipe all the dough.)

Pipe cookies onto the prepared baking sheets in the desired shapes, spacing them about 1 inch apart; a straight line about 2 inches long or rosettes that are 1½ to 2 inches in diameter are good places to start.

Bake the cookies for 10 to 14 minutes, rotating the baking sheets top to bottom and turning them from front to back halfway through, until the edges just begin to brown. Remove them from the oven and let them cool on the sheets for 10 minutes before transferring them to a rack to cool completely.

If desired, decorate the cool cookies by partially dipping them in melted chocolate and sprinkling nuts or sprinkles on the chocolate before it sets. Let stand until the chocolate has set.

Store cookies in an airtight container at room temperature for up to 3 days. Undipped cookies can be frozen for longer storage.

Biscotti

Makes 20 to 24 biscotti

142 grams (1 cup) whole raw almonds

232 grams (2 cups) 00 flour, plus more for dusting

149 grams (¾ cup) sugar

1 teaspoon baking powder

½ teaspoon fine salt

2 large eggs (100 grams)

25 grams (2 tablespoons) extra-virgin olive oil

1 teaspoon pure vanilla extract

1 teaspoon almond extract

Biscotti get a bad rap, but maybe that's because people are eating them all wrong. This version is staunchly, marvelously traditional—loaded with toasted nuts and very crunchy. It's absolutely imperative it be served with—and dipped in—espresso or a glass of vin santo.

Position a rack in the center of the oven and preheat the oven to 350°F. Line a rimmed baking sheet with parchment paper.

Spread the almonds in a single layer on the baking sheet, transfer to the oven, and bake for 8 to 10 minutes until the almonds are fragrant and just starting to darken in color. Set aside to cool slightly.

In a large bowl, whisk together the flour, sugar, baking powder, and salt, then add the almonds. In a separate bowl, whisk together the eggs, oil, vanilla, and almond extract. Add the wet ingredients to the dry ingredients and mix to combine. The dough might look a little dry, but that's normal. Transfer the mixture to a lightly floured work surface and gently knead until it comes together into a smooth dough. It should just take a few gentle folds.

Shape the dough, dusting the work surface with additional flour as necessary to prevent sticking, by rolling the dough into a log about 2 inches in diameter and 18 inches in length. Cut the log in half crosswise and place both pieces on the parchment-lined baking sheet, spacing them evenly. Lightly press each piece of dough down to gently flatten it so it's about 2½ to 3 inches wide.

Bake for 28 to 30 minutes, until light brown all over and firmly set. Remove from the oven and let cool on the baking sheet for 15 to 20 minutes. (Keep the oven on.)

Transfer the logs to a cutting board and use a serrated knife to cut each log on a slight diagonal into ½-inch-thick slices. Saw the knife back and forth instead of pressing down, to keep the biscotti from crumbling.

Stand the biscotti pieces on their bottom edge on the parchment-lined baking sheet. Spacing isn't critical, so feel free to place them close together.

Return the biscotti to the oven and bake for 18 minutes, until they are golden brown and feel slightly dry. Let the biscotti cool to room temperature on the pan or a wire rack. They will crisp up completely as they cool.

Biscotti will keep in an airtight container at room temperature for up to 3 weeks; freeze for longer storage.

Pignoli

Makes about 4 dozen cookies

375 grams (1½ cups) almond paste, homemade (page 245) or store-bought

198 grams (1 cup) granulated sugar

¼ teaspoon fine salt

48 grams (½ cup) almond flour

2 large egg whites, lightly beaten

1 teaspoon pure vanilla extract

397 grams (3 cups) raw pine nuts

These southern Italian cookies get a distinctive chewiness from almond paste—an appealing contrast to the cookies' pine nut–crusted exterior. If tucked away somewhere you have fancy, pretty pine nuts (yes, those are a thing), this is the time to use them.

Arrange oven racks in the upper and lower thirds of the oven. Preheat the oven to 325°F. Lightly grease 2 rimmed baking sheets or line with parchment paper.

In the bowl of a stand mixer fitted with the flat beater attachment or in a large bowl if using an electric hand mixer, break the almond paste into large chunks. Add the sugar, salt, and almond flour and mix on low speed until the mixture is uniformly crumbly. Add the egg whites, one at a time, mixing to make a smooth paste. Stir in the vanilla.

Place the pine nuts in a medium bowl or dish.

Scoop the dough by heaping teaspoon, one or two at a time, onto the pine nuts. Gently roll the dough around in the pine nuts to fully cover. Place the pine nut–covered dough balls on the parchment-lined baking sheets, evenly spaced.

Bake for 18 to 22 minutes, rotating the pans from top to bottom and turning them from front to back halfway through baking, until the cookies start to lightly brown around the edges. Remove the cookies from the oven and let cool completely before moving.

Store pignoli in an airtight container at room temperature for up to 10 days. Freeze for longer storage.

Chocolate-Hazelnut Skillet Cookie

Makes one 10-inch skillet cookie

213 grams (1 cup packed) dark brown sugar

50 grams (¼ cup) granulated sugar

113 grams (8 tablespoons) unsalted butter, melted and cooled

1 large egg (50 grams), at room temperature

1 large egg yolk, at room temperature

2 teaspoons pure vanilla extract

150 grams (1¼ cups) all-purpose flour

1 teaspoon fine salt

½ teaspoon baking powder

71 grams (½ cup) hazelnuts, roasted and coarsely chopped

57 grams (⅓ cup) semisweet chocolate chips

40 grams (2 tablespoons) chocolate-hazelnut spread, such as Nutella

A giant, chewy, shareable cookie is the perfect dessert for a pizza party—you can slice it into pizza-like wedges, or serve it warm and let everybody dig in with a spoon. This is an especially easy cookie that uses melted butter (no softening required!) and is mixed by hand. But thanks to the swirl of chocolate-hazelnut spread on top, it has a sophisticated edge.

Position a rack in the center of the oven and preheat the oven to 350°F.

In a large bowl, combine the brown sugar, granulated sugar, and melted butter. Add the egg, egg yolk, and vanilla and mix to combine. Scrape the sides of the bowl.

Add the flour, salt, and baking powder and stir until almost combined. A few streaks of flour are OK. Scrape the sides of the bowl.

Add the hazelnuts and chocolate chips and stir until no flour streaks remain.

Transfer the dough to a well-seasoned 10-inch cast-iron skillet and spread into an even layer. Dollop the chocolate-hazelnut spread on top of the cookie dough and use a butter knife or wooden skewer to swirl it gently, creating a marbled effect.

Bake the skillet cookie for 25 to 30 minutes, until it is evenly golden brown across the top and pulls away from the sides of the skillet slightly.

Remove the skillet from the oven and cool on a wire rack for 25 to 30 minutes in the skillet. Slice using a dull knife to prevent damaging the skillet.

Store any leftover skillet cookie in an airtight container at room temperature for up to 3 days. Reheat individual portions in the microwave, if desired.

Tiramisu

Makes one 8-inch square cake

For the cake:
3 large eggs (150 grams), separated

¼ teaspoon cream of tartar

149 grams (¾ cup) granulated sugar, divided

¼ teaspoon fine salt

28 grams (2 tablespoons) cold water

1 teaspoon pure vanilla extract

90 grams (¾ cup) unbleached all-purpose flour

1 teaspoon baking powder

For the soak:
113 grams (½ cup) boiling water

50 grams (¼ cup) granulated sugar

2 teaspoons espresso powder

76 grams (⅓ cup) Kahlúa or other coffee liqueur of your choice, or amaretto

For the filling:
340 grams (1½ cups) heavy cream

170 grams (¾ cup) mascarpone cheese

2 teaspoons pure vanilla extract

Ladyfingers are commonly the "cake" layer of choice for tiramisu, but most store-bought ladyfingers aren't the freshest, and making them from scratch can be tedious. So here we swap in a sponge cake layer for the cookies. (Don't worry: The creamy mascarpone and espresso-amaretto soak were retained.) If you want to skip the booze, substitute an additional 76 grams (⅓ cup) boiling water and an additional 1 teaspoon espresso powder.

Preheat the oven to 350°F. Lightly grease two 8-inch square pans; line them with parchment paper and grease the parchment.

Make the cake: In the bowl of a stand mixer fitted with the whisk attachment or in a large bowl if using an electric hand mixer, combine the egg whites and cream of tartar. Beat on high speed until soft peaks form. Gradually add 37 grams (3 tablespoons) of the sugar, continuing to beat until the mixture is stiff and glossy. Set aside. (If you have only one stand mixer bowl, transfer the whites to another bowl so that you can use the stand mixer bowl for the next step.) Gently tap the whisk attachment or beaters against the side of the bowl to knock off as much of the whites as possible; no need to clean them before using them to beat the yolks.

In another large bowl, beat the egg yolks on high speed until well combined. Add the remaining 112 grams (½ cup plus 1 tablespoon) sugar and the salt and beat until the mixture thickens, 3 to 5 minutes. When you stop beating, the mixture should fall in ribbons as you lift the beaters out of the bowl.

Add the cold water and vanilla to the egg yolk mixture, beating to combine, then stir in the flour and baking powder, beating just to combine.

Stir about one-third of the egg white mixture into the batter to lighten it. Then use a flexible spatula to gently fold in another third of the egg whites, this time being more careful not to deflate the whites. Once it is mostly incorporated, fold in the remaining third of the whites, using gentle folding motions to combine the batter until no streaks of white are visible.

Divide the batter evenly between the prepared pans, portioning about 205 grams (generous 1¾ cups) per pan; gently smooth the top.

Bake the cakes for 12 to 16 minutes, until a toothpick inserted in the center comes out clean. Remove from the oven and set on a rack. Loosen the edges with a spatula or dull knife and let cool.

Ingredients and recipe continue

57 grams (½ cup) confectioners' sugar

For assembling:
11 grams (2 tablespoons) cocoa powder, divided

While the cake cools, make the soak: In a small bowl or liquid measuring cup, combine the boiling water, sugar, and espresso powder. Stir until the sugar is completely dissolved, then stir in the liqueur.

Make the filling: In the bowl of a stand mixer fitted with the whisk attachment or in a large bowl if using an electric hand mixer, combine the cream, mascarpone, and vanilla and whisk on low speed until the mixture is smooth. Slowly add the confectioners' sugar, increase the speed to medium-high, and whisk until soft to medium peaks form.

Assemble the tiramisu: Turn both cake layers out of the pan; wash and dry one pan and set aside. Brush 57 grams (about ¼ cup) of the soak across the top of each cake layer (using ½ cup total). Allow the soak to fully absorb into the cake (it won't take long). Place one layer, soaked side down, into the clean 8-inch square pan.

Brush another 57 grams (about ¼ cup) of the soak onto the plain, unsoaked side of the cake layer that was just placed in the pan. Spread half of the filling (about 285 grams/1¾ cups) over the top of the soaked cake layer.

Sift half of the cocoa powder over the entire surface of the filling. Gently place the second layer of cake, soaked side down, over the cocoa powder. Brush the remaining soak (about ¼ cup) onto the unsoaked side of the cake layer that was just placed in the pan. Spread the remaining filling over the cake layer, then finish by sifting the remaining cocoa powder over the top.

Cover the assembled tiramisu and let it chill in the refrigerator for at least 2 hours, or overnight, before serving. Serve cold.

Store any leftover tiramisu, covered, in the refrigerator for up to 3 days.

Lemon Ricotta Cake

Makes one 8-inch round cake

For the cake:
174 grams (1½ cups) 00 flour **or** 180 grams (1½ cups) unbleached all-purpose flour

2 teaspoons baking powder

¼ teaspoon fine salt

113 grams (8 tablespoons) unsalted butter, at room temperature

198 grams (1 cup) granulated sugar

Grated zest of 1 large or 2 small lemons

3 large eggs (150 grams), separated

227 grams (1 cup) whole-milk ricotta

1½ teaspoons pure vanilla extract

For the glaze:
28 grams (2 tablespoons) fresh lemon juice

43 grams (3 tablespoons) coarse sparkling sugar **or** 34 grams (3 tablespoons) turbinado sugar

57 grams (½ cup) confectioners' sugar

This cake has a plush, melt-in-your-mouth texture and a tightly knit crumb. That's thanks to the moisture and richness of the ricotta, of course, but also the finely milled 00 flour, which keeps the cake super soft and light. Eat wedges with your post-pizza espresso, but save at least one to have with your morning coffee.

Position a rack in the center of the oven and preheat the oven to 400°F. Line the bottom of an 8-inch round cake pan with parchment paper and grease the parchment and sides of the pan.

Make the cake: In a medium bowl, whisk together the flour, baking powder, and salt.

In the bowl of a stand mixer fitted with the beater attachment or in a large bowl if using an electric hand mixer, beat together the butter, granulated sugar, and lemon zest on medium speed until light and fluffy, 3 to 5 minutes. Scrape down the bowl, add the egg yolks, and beat until combined, about 1 minute. Add the ricotta, vanilla, and dry ingredients and beat on low until no dry streaks remain. Set aside.

In a medium bowl, whisk the egg whites by hand until very frothy, 1 to 2 minutes (no need to reach soft peaks).

Add the egg whites to the batter and mix on medium speed, scraping down the sides of the bowl as needed, until the batter becomes smooth (it will be quite gloppy at first). Finish mixing by hand to make sure everything is incorporated.

Transfer the thick batter to the prepared pan and smooth it into an even layer.

Bake for 20 to 25 minutes, until the cake is deeply golden, then tent with aluminum foil and bake 8 to 10 minutes more. The cake is done when it's set, has pulled away from the sides of the pan slightly, and springs back when lightly pressed.

Remove the cake from the oven and let it cool in the pan on a wire rack for 10 minutes.

While the cake cools, make the glaze: In a small bowl or liquid measuring cup, whisk together the lemon juice, sparkling sugar, and confectioners' sugar until no dry confectioners' sugar remains.

Turn the cake out onto the wire rack, flip the cake so it's right side up, and set the rack atop a plate or parchment-lined baking sheet. Pour the glaze evenly over the top of the cake, all the way to the edges. Let the cake cool until the glaze is set, about 30 minutes. Serve it slightly warm or at room temperature.

Store leftover cake in an airtight container at room temperature for up to 4 days.

Chocolate-Glazed Olive Oil Cake

Makes one 8-inch round cake

For the cake:
150 grams (1¼ cups) all-purpose flour

198 grams (1 cup) sugar

½ teaspoon baking powder

½ teaspoon baking soda

Rounded ½ teaspoon fine salt

2 large eggs (100 grams)

100 grams (½ cup) extra-virgin olive oil

170 grams (¾ cup) milk, preferably whole

Grated zest of 1 orange

57 grams (¼ cup) orange juice

1 teaspoon pure vanilla extract

For the ganache:
113 grams (⅔ cup) bittersweet chocolate chips (66%)

57 grams (¼ cup) water

Small pinch of fine salt

2 teaspoons extra-virgin olive oil

This classic olive oil cake is easy (mixed by hand!), versatile, and not at all fancy—until you dress it up in a gorgeous sheath of bittersweet chocolate ganache. Choose a fruity, mild olive oil here rather than one that's assertively grassy or bitter.

Make the cake: Position a rack in the center of the oven and preheat the oven to 350°F. Lightly grease an 8-inch round cake pan and line the bottom with parchment paper.

In a medium bowl, whisk together the flour, sugar, baking powder, baking soda, and salt.

In a large bowl, vigorously whisk the eggs and oil until emulsified; the mixture should look creamy and yellow. Whisk in the milk, orange zest, orange juice, and vanilla. While whisking, gradually add the dry ingredients to the wet; continue to whisk until well combined and no lumps remain.

Pour the batter into the prepared pan and bake for 35 to 40 minutes, until the cake is golden brown on top and springs back when gently pressed.

Remove the cake from the oven and transfer it to a wire rack; run an offset spatula or dull knife around the edge of the cake, then allow it to cool in the pan for 30 minutes. Turn the cake out onto the rack to cool completely.

While the cake cools, make the ganache: In a small microwave-safe bowl, combine the chocolate chips, water, and salt. Microwave in 20-second increments, stirring between each, until the chocolate is nearly or completely melted. Stir gently to form a smooth mixture (don't panic if it looks grainy at first). Stir in the oil until completely combined. Let the ganache cool and thicken slightly at room temperature, stirring occasionally, for about 10 minutes.

Set the cake, still on its wire rack, over a parchment-lined baking sheet. Pour the ganache over the top of the cake, using a small offset spatula to encourage it to reach the edge of the cake and drip over in places.

Let the cake sit at room temperature until the ganache is set, about 2 hours. (If you're in a rush, transfer the cake to the refrigerator for 10 minutes to speed up the setting process.) When you're ready to serve, slice the cake with a hot, dry knife.

Store any leftover cake well wrapped at room temperature for up to 4 days. The cake will become moister and more flavorful as it sits.

Mocha Mousse with Espresso Whip

Makes 3½ cups (6 to 8 servings)

For the mousse:
140 grams (5 ounces) semisweet or bittersweet chocolate (60% to 66%), finely chopped

2 large egg yolks, at room temperature

50 grams (¼ cup) granulated sugar

⅛ teaspoon fine salt

284 grams (1¼ cups) heavy cream, cold, divided

¾ teaspoon pure vanilla extract

⅛ teaspoon espresso powder

For the espresso whipped cream:
227 grams (1 cup) heavy cream, cold

28 grams (¼ cup) confectioners' sugar, sifted if lumpy

1 teaspoon pure vanilla extract

¼ teaspoon espresso powder

Is mousse a perfect dessert? We ponder the thought all the way to the bottom of the bowl, one spoonful at a time. We love the combination of coffee and chocolate, so here we double down, adding espresso powder to both the mousse and the whipped cream we spoon on top. For a straight chocolate version, just omit the espresso powder.

Make the mousse: Place the chocolate in a large heatproof bowl. Position a fine-mesh sieve over the top.

In a medium saucepan off the heat, whisk the egg yolks. Add the granulated sugar and salt and whisk until well combined. Gradually add 114 grams (½ cup) of the heavy cream and whisk until fully incorporated, being sure to reach the creases of the pan. Set over medium heat and cook, whisking constantly, until the mixture reaches 160°F when measured with a digital thermometer (it will be thick enough to coat the back of a metal spoon). Pour the mixture through the sieve into the bowl of chocolate. Add the vanilla and espresso powder to the chocolate. Gently whisk the chocolate mixture until smooth, then let it cool to room temperature, stirring occasionally to promote even cooling, 20 to 30 minutes.

In the bowl of a stand mixer fitted with the whisk attachment or in a large bowl if using an electric hand mixer or beating by hand, beat the remaining 170 grams (¾ cup) of the heavy cream on high speed until you reach stiff peaks (a peak should support itself without drooping over). Whisk one-third of the whipped cream into the chocolate mixture to lighten it, then add the remaining whipped cream and gently fold until no white streaks remain.

Transfer the chocolate mousse to a large serving bowl or to individual ramekins, small glasses, or jars. Cover and chill the chocolate mousse until set, at least 6 hours.

Make the espresso whipped cream: When ready to serve, in the bowl of a stand mixer fitted with the whisk attachment or in a large bowl if using an electric hand mixer or beating by hand, combine the cream, confectioners' sugar, vanilla, and espresso powder. Beat on high speed until the cream holds soft peaks.

Serve the chocolate mousse topped with the whipped cream.

Store mousse, without any toppings, covered in the refrigerator for up to 4 days.

Spumoni Semifreddo

Makes one 9 x 4-inch spumoni

For the base:
454 grams (2 cups) heavy cream or whipping cream

397 grams (one 14-ounce can) sweetened condensed milk

1 teaspoon pure vanilla extract

¼ teaspoon fine salt

For the cherry layer:
53 grams (⅓ cup) Luxardo cherries, halved (10 to 12 whole cherries)

36 grams (2 tablespoons) Luxardo cherry liquid

For the pistachio layer:
30 grams (¼ cup) pistachios, coarsely chopped

28 grams (2 tablespoons) pistachio paste

For the chocolate layer:
57 grams (⅓ cup) semisweet chocolate wafers or chopped bar chocolate, melted and cooled

Hot fudge, for serving (optional)

There are so many reasons to make this semifreddo. Chief among them is that it requires no ice cream machine—just a little mixing, layering, and freezing. A slice is satisfying on its own, but when you serve it with hot fudge? Watch out.

Make the base: In the bowl of a stand mixer fitted with the whisk attachment or in a large bowl if using an electric hand mixer, beat the heavy cream, condensed milk, vanilla, and salt on medium speed until medium peaks form. Divide the whipped mixture evenly among 3 bowls, about 275 grams (scant 2 cups) per bowl.

To make the cherry layer: Add the cherries and cherry liquid to one bowl and use a spatula to stir until combined.

To make the pistachio layer: Add the pistachios and pistachio paste to another bowl and use a spatula to stir until combined.

To make the chocolate layer: Add the melted chocolate to the last bowl and use a spatula to stir until combined.

To assemble: Line a 9 × 4-inch loaf pan with an 8½ × 16½-inch piece of parchment paper, then line the entire loaf pan with plastic wrap. There should be an overhang of parchment on the two long sides of the pan, and an overhang of plastic wrap on all sides of the pan.

Transfer the cherry mixture to the prepared pan and use a small offset spatula or the back of a spoon to smooth into an even layer. Gently tap the loaf pan on the counter to create a surface that's as flat as possible.

Dollop the pistachio mixture on top of the cherry mixture in 4 or 5 portions. Use a small offset spatula or the back of a spoon to smooth into an even layer, then gently tap the loaf pan again on the counter.

Finally, dollop the chocolate mixture on top of the pistachio mixture in 4 or 5 portions. Use a small offset spatula or the back of a spoon to smooth into an even layer, then gently tap the loaf pan again on the counter.

Place a piece of plastic wrap directly on top of the spumoni (this helps to prevent any ice crystals from forming) and transfer to the freezer. Allow to chill until completely frozen, about 6 hours or overnight.

To serve: Remove from the freezer, uncover the loaf pan, and use the parchment paper sling to help unmold and invert the spumoni onto a cutting board or serving plate. Gently remove the plastic wrap and let the spumoni thaw at room temperature for 5 to 10 minutes before slicing. For the neatest slices, run a sharp chef's knife under hot water, dry it off, then cut the spumoni crosswise into slices.

Store any leftovers in the freezer, wrapped in plastic, for up to 1 week.

Aperol Spritz Granita

Makes 4 to 6 servings

180 grams (¾ cup) prosecco

113 grams (½ cup) Aperol

57 grams (¼ cup) lukewarm water (85° to 90°F)

30 grams (2½ tablespoons) granulated sugar

28 grams (2 tablespoons) freshly squeezed orange juice

1 orange, sliced into wedges, for garnish

If you're hosting an outdoor summer pizza party, your focus needs to be on the pies. This make-ahead, cocktail-inspired granita lets you do just that; it will keep in the freezer for up to a month, so you can make a batch in advance and bust it out on the next hot day.

In a medium bowl, combine the prosecco, Aperol, water, sugar, and orange juice. Whisk until the sugar is fully dissolved.

Strain the mixture through a fine-mesh sieve into an 8-inch square baking pan and freeze, uncovered, for at least 4 hours and up to 24 hours.

When ready to serve, use a fork to scrape the surface of the granita to create translucent, icy shards. Portion the granita into chilled glasses, garnish with orange wedges, and serve immediately.

Store leftover granita in an airtight container in the freezer for up to a month.

Raspberry-Pistachio Eton Mess

Makes 6 to 8 servings

2 large egg whites (60 to 70 grams), at room temperature

¼ teaspoon cream of tartar

Pinch of fine salt

149 grams (¾ cup) granulated sugar, divided

360 grams (3 cups) fresh raspberries, divided

Grated zest of 1 lemon

2 teaspoons lemon juice

397 grams (1¾ cups) heavy cream, cold

2 teaspoons pure vanilla extract

21 grams (3 tablespoons) confectioners' sugar

60 grams (½ cup) roasted pistachios, coarsely chopped

Like a lighter version of a trifle, this British dessert combines billowy whipped cream, crunchy meringues, fresh raspberries, and chopped pistachios into a "more than the sum of its parts" dessert. If making meringue from scratch seems like too much of a project for something that then gets crumbled and drowned in whipped cream, you can also use store-bought meringues; you'll need about 117 grams (4 cups) of vanilla-flavored meringue cookies.

Make the meringue: Position a rack in the center of the oven and preheat the oven to 200°F. Line a rimmed baking sheet with parchment paper.

In the bowl of a stand mixer fitted with the whisk attachment or in a large bowl if using an electric hand mixer, combine the egg whites, cream of tartar, and salt. Beat until white and foamy, then gradually add 113 grams (½ cup plus 1 tablespoon) of the granulated sugar, mixing all the while, until the mixture is stiff and glossy.

Transfer the meringue to the prepared baking sheet and spread into a thin, even layer about 15 × 10 inches.

Bake for 1½ hours. Turn off the oven with the meringue still inside and the door shut; leave it there until completely cool, at least 3 hours and up to overnight.

Break the meringue into roughly 1-inch shards (some smaller pieces are OK, no need to be too precise). Set aside until ready to assemble the Eton mess, or store the meringue shards in an airtight container at room temperature for up to 2 weeks in advance.

Prepare the fruit: In a medium bowl, combine half (180 grams/1½ cups) of the raspberries with the remaining 36 grams (3 tablespoons) granulated sugar, lemon zest, and lemon juice. Use a fork to crush the raspberries into a chunky consistency. Set aside while preparing the whipped cream.

Make the whipped cream: In the bowl of a stand mixer fitted with the whisk attachment or in a large bowl if using an electric hand mixer, beat the cold cream and vanilla on medium-high speed until the mixture starts to look foamy, about 20 seconds. Sift the confectioners' sugar into the cream and continue beating until the cream becomes thick and voluminous and forms medium peaks, 30 to 45 more seconds (be careful not to overwhip).

Assemble the Eton mess: Spoon about one-quarter of the whipped cream into a 3-quart trifle dish (or other clear, straight-sided serving vessel, so you can see the layers) and spread into an even layer. Spoon about one-quarter of the crushed raspberry mixture evenly on top. Scatter about one-quarter of the meringue shards and about one-quarter of the remaining whole raspberries on top of the raspberry mixture. Sprinkle about one-quarter of the pistachios evenly on top. Repeat this layering process 3 more times, until all ingredients are used.

Eton mess is best enjoyed right away but can be stored in the refrigerator, uncovered, for up to 2 hours. The meringue will soften over time.

Salty Maple Pears with Brown Butter Streusel

Makes 4 to 6 servings

For the streusel:

85 grams (6 tablespoons) unsalted butter

120 grams (1 cup) all-purpose flour

80 grams (¼ cup plus 2 tablespoons) light brown sugar

27 grams (¼ cup) pecans, coarsely chopped

½ teaspoon ground cinnamon

⅛ teaspoon fine salt

½ teaspoon vanilla extract

For the pears:

28 grams (2 tablespoons) unsalted butter

½ teaspoon fine salt

1½ pounds firm but fragrant pears, such as Bosc (3 to 4 pears), peeled, halved, and cored

48 grams (2½ tablespoons) maple syrup

1 tablespoon water

1 teaspoon lemon juice

Mascarpone, ice cream, yogurt, or the creamy dairy of your choice, for serving

Think of these fragrant, streusel-topped roasted pears as a deconstructed fruit crisp. The pears get a kick start on the stovetop, then finish cooking in the oven; for that reason, you'll need a cast-iron or stainless-steel skillet. If you use firm-ripe pears, like Bosc, the halved fruit will hold its shape beautifully when it's roasted. The sandy, buttery streusel edges toward salty (in a good way), but the sweet pears hold it in check.

Arrange racks in the center and lower third of the oven and preheat the oven to 375°F.

To make the streusel: In a 10-inch cast-iron or stainless-steel skillet, melt the butter over medium heat, then continue to cook it, watching carefully, until it releases its nutty aroma and dark golden-brown bits collect at the bottom of the pan. (If you are using a cast-iron skillet, check the butter frequently by scooping it up into a spoon to monitor the color.) Remove the pan from the heat and let the butter cool slightly.

In a medium bowl, whisk together the flour, brown sugar, pecans, cinnamon, and salt. Add the brown butter and vanilla to the dry ingredients and mix with a spatula until no dry flour remains and clumps begin to form. Transfer the streusel to a parchment-lined baking sheet and spread it into an even layer, breaking up any large clumps with your fingers.

Bake on the center rack for 9 to 12 minutes, stirring halfway through, until golden brown and toasty-smelling. Remove from the oven and let the streusel cool completely on the baking sheet. While the streusel bakes, make the pears.

To make the pears: Return the skillet to the stove over medium heat and add the butter. When the butter starts to sizzle, add the salt and swirl to dissolve.

Add the pears, cut side down in a single layer, and cook, adjusting the heat as necessary, until golden brown on the bottom, 4 to 8 minutes. Remove from the heat and add the maple syrup, water, and lemon juice, swirling the skillet to evenly distribute.

Cover the skillet (a piece of foil works well if you don't have a lid) and place on the lower rack of the oven. Bake for 15 minutes, then use a thin spatula to flip the pears over so they are cut side up, re-cover the skillet, and return to the oven for 15 to 20 minutes, until the pears are completely tender. If there's a lot of liquid in the pan (the amount of pan juices will vary depending on the type of pear), remove the lid and return the skillet to the oven for 3 to 5 minutes, until the juices in the pan have slightly reduced.

Let the pears cool slightly, then serve warm with a scoop of mascarpone, lots of streusel, and any juices from the pan.

Store leftover pears in the refrigerator, covered, for up to 3 days. Any leftover streusel can be stored in an airtight container at room temperature for up to 1 week (it's great on yogurt!) or in the freezer for up to 3 months.

Pizza Fritta

Makes 9 pieces

Neutral oil, for frying

All-purpose flour, for dusting

1 ball (275 grams) Neapolitan Dough (page 161)

Confectioners' sugar, for dusting

So it's the end of the night and everybody's had enough pizza, and in fact maybe you've already had dessert—people are lingering with their coffees and wines. But there's some extra dough in the refrigerator. Do you waste it? Of course not. You keep it for tomorrow's lunch—or you gather everybody in the kitchen to fry these little doughnuts together. Like nearly every fried thing, these are best eaten hot from the oil. Yes, you'll get confectioners' sugar everywhere, and yes, that's kind of the point.

Pour 3 inches of oil into a heavy-bottomed, high-sided pot and set over medium-high heat. Line a rimmed baking sheet with paper towels and set nearby.

Lightly flour a work surface, then transfer the dough to it. Using your hands, flatten the dough into a 6- to 7-inch square that's about ½ inch thick. With a bench knife or sharp knife, cut the dough into 9 equal pieces. Press each piece down to flatten it to ⅓ inch.

When the oil registers 350°F on a deep-fry or instant-read thermometer, carefully lower 2 or 3 pieces of dough into the oil, taking care not to crowd the pan, and fry for about 90 seconds, until golden brown on the bottom. Use a heatproof slotted spoon or spider to flip each piece of dough and fry on the second side, until golden brown and cooked through, about 90 seconds more. Use the spoon or spider to remove the fried dough from the oil and set on the paper towel–lined baking sheet to drain. Let the oil return to temperature, then fry the remaining dough pieces. When all the dough has been fried, pile them on a serving plate and sift confectioners' sugar over. Eat right away.